Stephen Chambers

THE RELIGIONS OF
THE ROMAN EMPIRE

ASPECTS OF GREEK AND ROMAN LIFE

General Editor: H. H. Scullard

THE RELIGIONS
OF THE
ROMAN EMPIRE

John Ferguson

THAMES AND HUDSON

PRINTED IN GREAT BRITAIN BY
THE CAMELOT PRESS LTD, LONDON AND SOUTHAMPTON

ISBN O 500 40014 8

FOR

ELNORA

WITH GRATITUDE FOR THE THRILL

OF EXPLORING

THE ROMAN EMPIRE

TOGETHER

CONTENTS

LIST OF ILLUSTRATIONS

FOREWORD

T. R. GLOVER's *The Conflict of Religions in the Early Roman Empire* was for me a seminal book; it is still exciting to read. But it leaned too heavily on literary evidence, and there was need for a new book which takes account of archaeological evidence, and in particular the very considerable amount of evidence which has emerged in the last fifty years. This is what I have sought to do. I cannot challenge comparison with Glover's delightful breadth; this is a less discursive age, even had I the capacity. But I hope I have inherited in myself, even if I cannot convey it as he did, something of his warm, rich humanity, and I hope that the visual illustrations which Messrs Thames and Hudson provide so generously and tastefully will compensate for the lack of verbal embellishment.

My story is set somewhat later than his. I have taken a notional date of about AD 200, which seems to me the most fascinating period, and have scrutinized with some care the century before and the century after that date. But I have not hesitated to adduce evidence from the first century AD, where it seemed to me to point forward, nor from the fourth, where it illuminated what had gone before.

The basic work behind this book lay in a graduate seminar which I conducted in the University of Minnesota as Hill Visiting Professor during the session 1966–67. I am grateful to the University and the Chairman of the Classics Department, Professor Robert Sonkowsky, for that opportunity. My debt to the members of that seminar for the stimulus of those discussions is incalculable; *quos honoris causa nomino*: Jim Baron, Susan Cole, Gabriele Erasmi, Sister Ursula Foley, John Hay, George Hoffman, Jim Hurtak, Alex Macdonald, Father Paul Mohrbacher, Tim Slade, Shirley Stewart, Dana Sutton, Warren Volckenbaum,

John Wheatley. I have cribbed shamelessly from them. While engaged on this I have been writing a brief account for E. G. Parrinder's *Encyclopedia of World Religions*, and have repeated some few phrases.

I have an idiosyncratic dislike for little numerals in the text as well as for footnotes, and have tried to provide a text which can be read coherently by those who want to trace the general picture, together with, at the end, a selective bibliography for those who want to read more widely, and references for those who want to look at the original sources. Much of the archaeological evidence I have seen for myself; ten years in Nigeria enabled us to explore much of the Roman Empire by devious routes between Lagos and London, and summers have been partly spent in chasing the Romans round Britain and France; a special debt here is due to Sheila and Murray Haggis; in addition two years in the United States have opened to us the masterpieces in museums there. The final writing was done in Britain in the (alleged) summer of 1968 where I was grateful for the sheltering hospitality of Cambridge University Library in murk and the Institute of Classical Studies in flood, and at Hampton Institute as part of my work as Old Dominion Professor of Humanities, not the least of the debts I owe to that excellent institution. My wife and mother have read the book in manuscript, but are responsible neither for errors of fact nor for individuality of English; my wife has also compiled the index. Mr Stephen Rosenquist checked a number of references for me. Mr Graham and Mr Clayton of Thames and Hudson have been most constructively helpful. Gratitude is due to them, and especially to my friend and secretary Miss Connie Moss for the alchemy whereby she has transformed leaden scrawls into golden type, and to another friend and secretary, Mrs Doreen Lewis, for her skilled proof-reading. Final thanks to Professor H. H. Scullard for all his help and encouragement.

J.F.

CHAPTER I

THE GREAT MOTHER

THE WORSHIP OF A FEMININE ARCHETYPE is deeply embedded in human nature. Analytical psychology has suggested that the primal image is that of the *ouroboros*, the snake devouring its own tail, the Great Round in which male and female, positive and negative, unconscious elements, conscious elements and elements hostile to consciousness are intertwined. From this primordial undifferentiated symbol are crystallized the images of the Great Mother and the Great Father. We all have in us the forces of masculinity and femininity (which Jung calls *animus* and *anima*). It is therefore not surprising that a male-dominated society of hunters, such as is found in the stone age, should concentrate its worship upon the female image; indeed, of some sixty statues surviving from the palaeolithic period no less than fifty-five are female, and the male figures are sketchily and casually conveyed. The elemental powers of the female are two: creative-transformative and protective-nutritive. The female thus presides over all growth in nature; there is a magnificent example in a stone-age rock-drawing from Algeria, where a hunter is about to shoot an ostrich, and he is linked by a line to a female figure in the background, genitals to genitals. The feminine power or *mana* is needed if he is to conquer the animal. The female also presides over the cave or home; the cave is one of her images or symbols, and most of our surviving statuettes come from caves.

The Great Mother is thus even at an elementary stage a complex archetype, and becomes more complex with closer examination. For power is awful and unpredictable. It may heal or it may destroy. It may work for life or it may work for death. The Great Mother thus has many manifestations, many faces as it were. We may analyse them for purposes of clarity, if we remember that they may be held together in a single synthesis. The *mysterium* is alike *tremendum* and *fascinans*. Thus the Mother may appear as the Good Mother, who brings life, like Isis or Demeter or Mary; she may appear as the Terrible Mother who is associated with death, like the Indian Kali, or the Gorgon whose gaze turned all to stone. But the Greeks succeeded in holding in one being Selene–Artemis–Hecate in whom the powers of life and death are blended, and the Roman attitude to the eastern goddess Cybele was in early times ambivalent. Similarly the Mother may appear as a power of inspiration, like the Muse, or the Jewish Sophia (the Wisdom who is hymned in *Job*, *Ecclesiasticus* and elsewhere), or as a power of madness and witchcraft, like Circe who turns men into beasts, or Medea.

When agriculture replaced hunting along the great river-valleys of India, Mesopotamia and Egypt, women achieved a social and economic importance which they had previously lacked, and society wore the robes of matriarchy. At this stage the Great Mother took on a new importance in the societies of the Near East. She was the power of nature. Her characteristic role was that of *potnia theron*, 'our Lady of the Animals', and she was so depicted. On a sealstone from Crete or in the form of a pillar at Mycenae she stands exalted, flanked by lions; as Cybele her car was drawn by lions; as Artemis at Capua she held a lion in each hand; at Hermione she trampled a lion under her feet. So Aphrodite in the Homeric hymn:

> *She reached Ida with its many springs, mother of wild animals.*
> *She crossed the mountain to go straight to the steading. Behind,*
> *fawning grey wolves and tawny lions came following,*
> *bears and lightfoot leopards ravenous for deer.*
> *She looked on them with delight, and planted desire*
> *in their hearts, and all together two by two lay down*
> *and mated in the shade of the valley.*

All the animal creation, says Neumann, is subject to our Lady of the Animals in her different guises: 'the serpent and scorpion, the fishes of river and sea, the womb-like bivalves and the ill-omened kraken, the wild beasts of wood and mountain, hunting and hunted, peaceful and voracious, the swamp birds—goose, duck, and heron—the nocturnal owl and the dove, the domesticated beasts—cow and bull, goat, pig, and sheep—the bee, and even such phantasms as griffin and sphinx.'

Thus the Great Mother retains in the agricultural phase her power over wild nature. But she is also the goddess of the grain: this is seen in Sumerian Inanna, who was mortified and humiliated in her descent into the lower world, but emerged again into the daylight. Here the goddess appears as the vegetation itself which dies and is born again. But the story is a complex one, for her consort Dumuzi (in Assyria they become Ishtar and Tammuz) is the typical vegetation-spirit, the young god who dies, and is mourned. Indeed in some versions it is to rescue him that she goes down. But on her return he refuses to pay her due homage, and she hands him over to demons. In another version her life is forfeit and he is forced to be her substitute. There are innumerable versions of his death. It is a story of great power and great persistence. Plutarch tells a yarn of a boat whose captain was named Thamous. As they were sailing close to the island of Paxi he heard a voice calling, 'Thamous'. The voice told them to announce at a later stage of their journey, 'Great Pan is dead'. They did, and the announcement was greeted with sorrow and anguish. This lamentation was typical of the annual mourning for Tammuz, and it seems that what they heard was not 'Thamous' but 'Tammuz'—'Tammuz the All-great is dead' (*pam-megas* not Pan *megas*).

The Mother was not confined to the East; there was once a great Mother-goddess among the Celts also. Strabo tells of an island near Britain where sacrifices were offered to Demeter and Kore; he is of course wrong, but there will have been a parallel Earth-Mother. We can trace her in a goddess with a cornucopiae who appeared on the monuments. Occasionally she has a name; at Autun it was Berecynthia and her statue was carried round processionally to promote the fertility of the crops. But among the Celts an unusual thing happened, though not without parallel. There was a strong tendency to think in triads, and the Mother-goddess was triplicated. Hence the group of three goddesses so often met with on monuments of the Roman Empire, and generally known by their Latin name, *Deae Matres* or Mother goddesses. They appear in a large number of appropriate guises. They are deities of fertility, they watch the prosperity of the fields, the meadows and the groves are theirs. Rivers too, which fertilize the land, are theirs, as a name like Marne (from *matrona*) may remind us. So are cross-roads, for there one may encounter the dead, and the underworld and fertility naturally go together; in the north of England they appear as the three Lamiae, or witches. They watch over women, in childbirth and at other times, and guard the homes where women do their work. They are honoured by individuals, families, households, villages, towns, tribes, a province, a nation. In short their functions are comprehensive, as we expect in the heirs of the Great Mother. They survive for a long time in an attenuated form in folklore, in Ireland as the White Women, in Wales as Y Mamau, in France as the fairies Abonde or Esterelle or Aril. (*Pl.* 8)

The Mother's names were innumerable. In Sumer she was Inanna, among the Akkadians Ishtar, in Ugarit Anat, in Syria Atargatis. At Ephesus she was Artemis–Diana, in Priene Baubo, in Cyprus Aphrodite, in Crete Rhea or Dictynna, at Eleusis Demeter, in Sparta Orthia, in Thrace Bendis, in Egypt Isis or Hathor, at Pessinus Cybele. Ma expresses most clearly her maternal power: this was a Cappadocian name. The Romans made an identification of Ma with Bellona to whom a temple was vowed as early as 296 BC; it was erected in the Campus Martius. But the *bellonarii*, as the priests were called, were Asiatics who engaged in frenzied war-dances, gashing themselves with swords and sprinkling the blood over the goddess's statue. Roman citizens were for centuries forbidden to participate, though there is evidence of secret practice; the restrictions were gradually relaxed, and by the third century AD the cult became officially recognized. But it was always overshadowed by the official Great Mother cult; the affinities were recognized and the same individual might be a priest of both divinities.

ATARGATIS

We meet her in various forms among the Nabataean Arabs. Here her usual name is Atargatis; next to that, Allat. At Khirbet

Tannur a remarkable panel in high relief shows her, larger than human, with leaves round her neck and on her forehead; she is set in a scroll of spiralling vine, with acanthus, figs, pomegranates and rosettes. Here she is characteristically a vegetation goddess. This however was only one of nine costumes in which she has been recognized in that temple alone. Another representation shows her with stalks of grain. The association with a lions' torque links her with Cybele; so at Hatra, Raha, and Dura-Europos she is shown flanked by lions. One representation depicts her with a cornucopiae; this is again natural for a vegetation-goddess; it also unites her with Tyche (Fortune). It is in association with Tyche, as we shall see, that she bears a rudder in her hand or wears the mural crown as a protector of cities. Some of her guises suggest a sky-goddess; the signs of the zodiac appear behind her head, or she carries a planetary standard. In the great relief-panel an eagle finial stood above her head, and a similar eagle is seen at Hatra. The swirling veil or scarf which surrounds her head like a nimbus is often seen as a sky-symbol, probably rightly, though this need not make a sky-goddess out of her, for the sky surrounds the earth and sea. Atargatis is assuredly not a sky-goddess; she is in origin the Earth-Mother who does not normally venture into the sky unless at night when the powers of the sky are sleeping. But her marriage to the sky-god, though she kept him in a subordinate position, enabled her to take over some of his attributes.

Her consort appears in two principal guises. The earliest was Dushara or Dusares. In some ways he appears to be simply Dumuzi or Tammuz under another name. He is subordinate to his queen, and is the king who dies and is reborn. So he is associated in tombs with the promise of continued life beyond the grave. The inscription on the Turkomaniyeh tomb at Petra speaks of the banquet benches, which existed for the cult-meals in which the dead man would expect and be expected to share, as 'the consecrated and inviolable possession of Dushara'. Further he is associated with tragic masks; the thought seems to be that the dead man in donning the mask is one with the god and secures his immortality. Masks all the world over are associated with ancestors, and ancestors, who rest in the ground, are important fertility powers. All this points to Dushara as a divine and royal ancestral spirit. But there was one peculiar feature of his cult. He had no anthropomorphic image, but was worshipped as a rectangular basalt block; such blocks appear at Petra, and the Ka'aba at Mecca is in fact one such. It is possible that there is some blurring of thought here. Meteorites are often accorded reverence; they are mysterious, different from the surrounding soil, and fall from the sky. But basalt is of volcanic origin, and comes from the depths of the earth. Such was Dushara, undifferentiated, because in the spirit-world of the ancestors, as can be seen in West African masquerades today, the individuals are undifferentiated. Finally, under Greek influence, he acquired a personality; it was that of Dionysus. Such identifications are not always reliable, but it does suggest that he was seen as a god of earth rather than sky.

The other consort was unashamedly a sky-god. This was the Semitic thunder-god Hadad, who naturally inhabited the mountain-tops and was associated with the sky. One of his titles was Ba'al-shamin, Lord of Heaven, and he was naturally identified with Zeus, especially in the form of Zeus Casius. This is clearly a second marriage, arising from the meeting of a settled agricultural people honouring the Earth-Mother with a nomadic people acknowledging a Sky-Father. Its importance here lies in the fact that such compromises, at whatever time they took their origin, were an essential part of the complex religious situation under the Roman Empire. What is more, such was the power of the Earth-Mother that Zeus–Hadad was her consort rather than the reverse. At Khirbet Tannur there appear to have been relief-panels of the two divinities side by side, but there was no representation of Zeus–Hadad to compare with the great bust of Atargatis. Of Dura-Europos Nelson Glueck writes amusingly but not unjustly:

In the famous relief of Hadad and Atargatis from Dura, the thunder god appears as the anaemic, undersized, henpecked and melancholy mate of the much bulkier, full-chinned, firm-featured, superior-appearing Atargatis. She looks as if she were accustomed to leading him by the nose. She not only dominated his person but his animal servitors. Even her attendant lions are much larger than his sickly-looking bulls, one of which has indeed been completely squeezed out of position at his left side and pokes his head out like a frightened puppy from behind the pillar.

Lucian tells us that at Hierapolis sacrifices were made to Hera–Atargatis with a noisy and ecstatic joy which contrasted with the silence accompanying the offerings to her consort, and that she had prior rights over Zeus in viewing the sacred fish.

Atargatis was also a fish-goddess, and was represented as a kind of mermaid. At Ascalon she is called by Diodorus Siculus half-fish, half-woman; Lucian describes her, in her Phoenician identification as Derceto, in similar terms. At Caesarea the statue of Artemis Ephesia bore in low relief figures resembling mermaids clutching their fishy tails; similar associations are found elsewhere. Artemis Ephesia was one of the great representations of the Mother-goddess, and her identification with Atargatis was inevitable and natural; as Nabataean trading interests spread west, they took their goddess with them, and the Atargatis–Artemis identity is found in Spain. In one story the goddess threw herself into a pool over a love-affair, and was changed to a fish. Even where the goddess is not portrayed as, or partly as, a fish, she has her sacred fish, and where possible a pool was attached to the sanctuary for them. At Hierapolis there was a sacred lake in which the image of the goddess was bathed each year; at Ascalon 'a large, deep lake filled with fish'; even at Khirbet Tannur, far inland, the excavators argue for a sacred pool in the outer court-yard. Naturally there were mythical explanations. In one she fell into the lake at Hierapolis and was saved by a fish. In another she originated from an egg which dropped from the sky into the River Euphrates; the fishes saved this and brought it to shore where it was hatched out by a dove; Zeus rewarded the fish by making them a sign in the zodiac. Of course the association is a simple one. Moisture surrounds the semen, and the Earth-Mother needs to be brought into contact with this moisture. The remarkable fecundity of fish explains the symbol's fuller development.

In many ways Atargatis' most interesting guise is a variant of this, that of the goddess of the dolphins. To find her at Khirbet Tannur, in a waterless area far from the sea and close to the desert, wearing a crown of two dolphins, was enough to arouse speculation. A dolphin relief has appeared on an altar at Abda in the Negev, a bronze dolphin in the tiny Nabataean temple by the Wadi Ramm. More important, at Hatra in Parthia two dolphins decorate the base of Atargatis' throne. At Khirbet Brak, where Atargatis was probably the chief goddess, dolphin carvings adorned one of the capitals; similar forms were found at Petra. At Petra in the baths there was a relief frieze, one section of which showed a divinity on a sea-monster. This takes us straight to the Mediterranean area, for such figures, usually with the swirling veil above their heads, are common in mosaics from bath-buildings around the Roman Empire; there is a magnificent example at Lambaesis, and another at Tebessa. They are variously identified as Aphrodite, or Galatea, or a Nereid; the identification scarcely matters; they are doublets of our goddess. She is seen in various guises at Aphrodisias in Caria. In one bust, which must represent Atargatis, she appears with the dolphins in her hair, as at Khirbet Tannur. But the great cult-statue of Aphrodite herself had dolphins and other sea-creatures associated with it. And the famous Aphrodite in the Metropolitan Museum at New York has a dolphin at her feet, and is associated with dolphins especially under her cult-title of Galenaia, or deity of calm weather.

The Syrian goddess spread over the Greek world, and her mendicant dervish priests are vividly described by Apuleius in a village of Thessaly, with shoulders bare, wielding great swords, wailing out of tune to the sound of the pipe, gesticulating, twirling with body bent till their hair stood out in the wind of their movement, lacerating their flesh with teeth or sword.

THE GREEK MOTHER

In Greece the Mother's most obvious name was Gaia or Ge, Earth. As such she had an oracle at Delphi long before Apollo. She is one of the primal couple in Hesiod's *Theogony*; she has her own hymn in the so-called Homeric hymns, where she is honoured as giving life to mortals. She was dominant before the coming of the Hellenes, so that when their great sky-god first arrived he became Posis-Das, the husband of Earth, and only a later wave established the predominance of Zeus. The Earth-Mother remained as Da-meter, the classical Demeter, who later became primarily the giver of corn; but it is her daughter Kore who is the corn-spirit. We shall meet Demeter again in the Eleusinian Mysteries; she remained a power in the land throughout.

Among the Asian Greeks however her name was Artemis, and in this guise her great centre was Ephesus. Here she was worshipped not as the virgin huntress of Greek mythology, but as the power of fertility in nature. Her statue is many-breasted, though there are those who would identify the protuberances not as breasts, but as the ripening fruit of the date-palm or the symbolical ova of the sacred bee. Her temple underwent many vicissitudes, even before, as the Byzantine bigot put it, 'by the grace of Christ and St John the Divine it became the most devastated and desolated of all'. The temple which stood in Roman times dated from the fourth century BC and ranked among the seven wonders of the world. It was about two-thirds the size of St Peter's in Rome: 425 feet long, 220 wide, 60 high, with 127 pillars of Parian marble inlaid with gold, and woodwork of cypress and cedar; it was filled with works by the great artists of the Greek world. The priestesses were called bees, and were virgin, the priests or *megabyzi* were eunuchs, drones which 'die' in fertilizing the queen-bee. The temple sustained a large staff of vergers, cleaners and attendants, *neokoroi*, and Ephesus is called on coins the *neokoros* of Artemis. On 25 May the statues of the goddess were taken up the broad processional road with music, dancing and pageantry to the theatre where they were exhibited to a congregation which might reach 30,000; in Roman times a wealthy Roman paid for a roofed portico to shield the procession from the weather. The temple had a further importance in Roman times as a sanctuary. But Ephesus was not the only place where the Mother found herself as Artemis. She was Artemis Leucophryene at Magnesia-on-the-Maeander, where she had a Panhellenic festival called the Leucophryena, and a temple which Strabo ranked above the Ephesus temple in beauty. Not in wealth, since it is recorded in one inscription that the temple revenues were not sufficient to pay for the cost of that inscription! At Antioch-near-Pisidia, which was settled from Magnesia, we naturally find the same goddess dominant. The original worship perhaps centred on a cave, where the Panagia is still honoured. Perge was another town devoted to Artemis; her temple here too was a sanctuary. The fame of Artemis Pergaea spread far; she was honoured in Pamphylia and Pisidia, Rhodes, Santorin and Egypt, and the dream-interpreter Artemidorus recommends her for worship. (*Pl. 6*)

The Aphrodite identification is of no little importance, as Lucian is at pains to assure us. Her name means 'foam-born': it has a double significance, representing the foam which surrounds the semen, and the sea from which she emerged westward to her great shrines at Paphos and Corinth. Paphos was, as an inscription of AD 198-9 puts it, 'the sacred metropolis of the cities of Cyprus'. There were other divinities, but Aphrodite was supreme. The site was subject to earthquakes, and the temple suffered. In Roman times the sanctuary was an open court with a gateway to the east, and porticos with rooms behind them on the other three sides. The main altar was bloodless, and it was said that rain never fell on it, and that no flies were to be seen round the temple. There were sacred doves, and probably sacred fish, both associated with love and fertility, and from the myth that Cinyras' daughters were driven by the goddess's anger to give themselves to strangers, we can deduce ritual prostitution. The temple had the right of sanctuary. Pilgrims were given, to take away, a phallic symbol for fertility and a lump of salt for cleansing. The sacred site lasted; Ammianus Marcellinus speaks of its fame, though by the time of Jerome it was desolate; yet one can still see young Cypriots creeping there and anointing stones or leaving their offerings.

At Corinth also the great temple high on the acropolis was Aphrodite's. Here there were more than a thousand temple-prostitutes, the 'girls of hospitality', the city's chief attraction, says Strabo. It might be an expensive business; hence the proverbial 'The voyage to Corinth is not for everyone'. Puritans were shocked; the verb 'to Corinthianize' was synonymous with sexual immorality; stories were invented of the punishment of

sexual licence; Paul wrote the indictment of contemporary
immorality in the first chapter of *Romans* after two years in
Corinth, and it is about Corinth not Rome. Yet, when the com-
mercialism is stripped away, we are only seeing the Great Mother's
power at work. Aphrodite's other great shrine was at Eryx in
Sicily where she survived into Roman times as Venus Erycina.

In Asia we find other identifications. At Pergamum, in addition
to the Great Mother herself, Athene is unnaturally prominent,
with two festivals, Panathenaea and Nicephoria; the finest copy
of Pheidias' Athene Parthenos comes from Pergamum. She is the
Mother in another guise. At Hierapolis in Phrygia with its hot
springs and alum incrustations the Earth-Mother had obvious
potency. Here she was called Leto, a local word for 'Lady' or
'Mistress', convenient as conveying to the Greeks the mother of
Apollo and Artemis, though here her divine son Lairbenus tends
to be assimilated to Dionysus. At Smyrna the most exquisite
temple was the Metroön; the Mother however is sometimes called
Sipylene, sometimes just the Goddess. At Iconium she appears
usually as the Zizimmene Mother, but also as the Boethene
Mother, the Mother from Andesia, the Mother from Quadrata.
It was at Konya in 1918 that Walter Hawley witnessed an
exhibition of dervish-dancing which stood in the direct line of
descent from the ecstatic dances of the Mother's eunuch-priests.
At Thyiateira she was called Bontene. We would only be guess-
ing at the meaning of these local names. They clearly show unity in
variety, and the hold which the Mother kept, under whatever name.

ISIS

Isis is another appearance of the Mother: indeed the representation of her with Horus became the very type of the Mother and
Child across the ages. In legend Isis was sister and consort of the
divine king Osiris. Set plotted against Osiris and sealed him up in
a coffin which floated to Byblus in Syria. Isis wandered discon-
solately, like Demeter, till she found the body. Set stole it again
and dismembered it. She recovered all the pieces except the
genitals, which she replaced by a gold image which was carried in
procession. So Plutarch. Egyptian sources add the lament over

Osiris, closely parallel to the lament over Tammuz; the impregnation of Isis by the dead Osiris, to bear Horus, and Horus' battle with Set, Isis' intervention to prevent her son killing her wicked brother, and her subsequent suffering; and the resurrection of Osiris as king of the dead, a pledge of future resurrection available for all. We are plainly dealing with fertility deities. Set is the power of the drought, Osiris the rising waters of the Nile, Isis the land awaiting the flooding of the waters. Isis was in fact called 'the betrothed of the Nile', and was represented by a conical pillar with ears of wheat on top, which was symbolically fertilized as the river broke through its dams; so the land received the fertilizing touch of the waters. But Osiris was also the corn, and effigies made of vegetable mould and stuffed with corn were buried in the graves in Egypt or found between the legs of mummies, and in a representation at Philae we see the dead body of Osiris with stalks of corn springing from it. A priest is watering the stalks from a pitcher. The picture is accompanied by an inscription, 'This is the form of him whom one may not name, Osiris of the mysteries, who springs from the returning waters.' This evidence, Plutarch apart, dates from centuries before our era, but the practices persisted. Lactantius about the year AD 300 tells that the priests beat their breasts and lamented, imitating the search of Isis for her lost son Osiris; their sorrow is turned to joy when the jackal-headed god Anubis produces a small boy, the living representative of the lost and found god. At first sight there is confusion between Osiris and Horus; but is there? The father is recreated in the son. Osiris comes in the fertilizing flood, and is revealed in the corn. What has happened in the meantime has happened outside Egypt. Isis has become a universal goddess, the chief representative of divine femininity in the ancient world. (*Pls.* 9, 55)

During this period the cult of Isis began to spread far from its original home at Philae in the south of Egypt. Her establishment at Alexandria, and consequent association with the sailors and traders of the cosmopolitan port, were a principal factor in the dissemination, and during the Hellenistic and Roman periods the cult is found in the port of Athens, at Tithorea near Delphi (the holiest of all her Greek sanctuaries, where only those called by

dreams at two festivals were admitted), in many other Greek
centres, around the islands and Asia Minor, along North Africa, in
Sardinia, in Spain (where a woman dedicates a bejewelled silver
statue for her daughter), at Pompeii, in Rome itself, and permeating through to Switzerland and Germany. It was most effective in
the imperial period where there was direct contact with Egypt;
otherwise it was spread by soldiers, traders and travellers, and
Rome itself played a part in the dissemination. The inscriptions
are mostly from the hands of either officials or slaves (or former
slaves), the latter often easterners. At first at Rome politics and
scandal bedevilled the cult, but it was widely popular, not least
with the *demi-monde*. Not only with them. When in 50 BC Aemil-
ius Paulus demanded the destruction of the temple of Isis, no work-
man would put his hand to the job. Caligula's erection of a temple
in the Campus Martius was one of his few unchallenged acts. By
the time of Caracalla the worship could be safely and enthusiastic-
ally admitted within the religious boundaries of the city. Meantime statues and monuments of the Isis cult were to be found all
over the Empire, and her symbols appear on gems and pins,
brooches and rings. Excellent evidence of the popularity of Isis is
available in a novel by Xenophon of Ephesus written about AD
200. It deals with the trials of the lovers Habrocomes and Antheia.
Apollo predicts their adventures, and that Isis will see them
through. She is as good as his word. Antheia evades unwelcome
attentions by pretending to be a priestess of Isis; at Memphis she
appeals to Isis to protect and restore her; when Polyidus tries to
rape her she escapes to the temple of Isis; near the temple the
lovers are reunited; in the temple they give thanks. We shall look
again at the process of initiation, but it was not just the secret cult
of a closed corporation. She has the universality of the Mother.

   The Earth-Mother was found within the Roman pantheon as
Tellus or Terra Mater; she may be seen gentle and beneficent on
the Ara Pacis. But she was not always kindly; an enemy army
would be consigned to her in a formal curse. She and Ceres
received the sacrifice for the dead. Ceres, the power of growth
(*creare*), is thus seen to transcend her position as power of the
harvest and appear as another aspect of the Mother. Flora too,

seen in the blossoming of the flowers, had her connection with the dead in the festival of the Floralia. All these are aspects of the Mother's power. So, in their different ways, are Juno, the power of fertility in woman, who was identified with Hera, Diana, a spirit of the wildwood, equated with Artemis, and the garden-spirit Venus, whose neuter form provided a curious equivalence for Aphrodite. (*Pls.* 4, 7, 29, 32)

CYBELE

The most familiar name of the Asiatic mother in the Roman world was Cybele, and to her the myths are attached. At Pessinus the story was told how the Great Mother was sleeping in the form of a rock. Zeus tried to rape her, but spilled his seed on the ground. Still she, who is the ground, bore a child against her will, a bisexual monster named Agdistis. Dionysus set himself to tame this creature, drugging him with wine, and tying his male sex-organs to a tree so that on awakening he castrated himself. From the blood sprang an almond (or in some versions pomegranate) tree. The daughter of the river-god Sangarius plucked fruit from this and placed it in her lap, from where it impregnated her. Her father tried to kill her, and to expose the baby on birth, but each time Cybele intervened, and the child grew into the handsome boy Attis. Cybele fell in love with the lad; we often see him standing by her throne on coins and medallions of the second or third century AD, or on a fine bronze plate now in Berlin, or riding with her in her lion-drawn chariot, again on coins or on the superb dish (patera) from Parabiago in Milan, where they are surrounded by sun, moon, earth and sea, time and the seasons. Their love was doomed. The goddess caught Attis in infidelity and drove him mad, so that he castrated himself under a pine-tree and bled to death. But this is not the end; in the Roman ceremonies the festival of mourning (*tristia*) was followed by a festival of joy (*hilaria*). The old year is dead, but the new year lives and Attis rises again. One thinks of the old Russian Eastertide festival over the dying and reviving vegetation-god, where the chorus sang

> *Dead, dead is our Kostrubonko!*
> *Dead, dead is our dear one!*

changing suddenly to

> *Come to life, come to life has our Kostrubonko!*
> *Come to life, come to life has our dear one!*

The priests of Cybele were eunuchs; self-castration in ecstasy was part of the process of initiation to the service of the goddess. The function of the castration is controversial. To Frazer it was obvious: they were giving their fertility to the goddess as a permanent offering. But Onians has argued that in early times the seed is believed to reside in the head, and the testes are not the source of the seed but the channel through which it is emitted. Castration thus preserves the seed, which is the principle of life, in the body of those who are dedicated to the Mother. This may be right, but it must be said that Onians has not succeeded in making a logical whole of all the evidence. (*Pls.* 1, 3)

Cybele came to Rome as the culmination of a series of senatorial decisions in time of crisis, spanning two centuries and more. The principal instrument of senatorial policy was the so-called Sibylline books; its object the distraction of the commons; its procedure the introduction of deities and practices from Greece and the East. It was in accordance with this policy that in 205 BC, when the tide of Hannibal's war had now turned, the senate discovered a convenient prophecy that an alien invader would be driven from Italy if the Great Mother from Ida were brought to Rome. An embassy of five was sent to Pessinus (or possibly Pergamum) to bring back the black betyl of irregular shape which was identified with the goddess. She was received by P. Scipio Nasica and established within the city boundaries in the temple of Victory. There were general junketings, and games called *Megalensia* were inaugurated. The year was 204 BC; thirteen years later, in 191 BC, she was given an independent temple not far away on the Palatine, and we may reasonably assume that this was the occasion when the festival was extended from one day to seven (4–10 April); it was at this festival that several of the best-known Roman comedies were presented. But the senate's intelligence service had failed them; the ritual of emasculation came as an appalling shock, and Roman citizens were forbidden to participate, and had to content themselves with membership of supporting Brotherhoods (*sodalitates*); M. Porcius Cato belonged to one such. Catullus' remarkable *tour-de-force*, the poem *Attis*, written no doubt from experience in Asia Minor rather than in Rome, combines a Greek horror of marring the human body's beauty with a Roman repulsion from the loss of masculinity and power. None the less, despite the law, and despite the banishment of a slave in 102 BC for emasculating himself in the goddess's service, in the year 101 a Roman named Genucius became the first citizen to be consecrated as an eunuch priest. In general the priests were Phrygian; we have vivid pictures of them in brilliantly coloured robes, and of the general procession of the goddess, accompanied by exotic instruments, flute, tambourine, cymbals and horn; of the ritual of washing the goddess in river or sea; of the mendicancy of the priests. (*Pls.* 1, 5)

The reign of Claudius saw considerable changes; these were no doubt part of a more liberal attitude to non-Romans and their practices. Restrictions on participation were now removed. The Committee of Fifteen, who exercised general control over alien cults, took part in the procession. From this period on we find the *galli*, the eunuch priests, and even the *archigallus* bearing Roman names. He is termed *Attis populi Romani* or *Atus publicus populi Romani Quiritium*, 'the public Attis of the citizens, the people of Rome'. An *archigallus* may be seen on a relief in the Capitoline Museum; his dress, hair and features are effeminate; he wears medallions on his head and an ikon as pendant to a necklace; a scourge lies on his left shoulder, and he is carrying various cult-emblems. Furthermore, though the *Megalensia* were left at their original date, a new cycle of ritual was established during the period 15–27 March, apparently introducing Attis into the Roman cult for the first time. The festival started on the Ides of March with 'The Entry of the Reed'. There was a ceremonial procession by the College of Reed-bearers, leading to the sacrifice of a bull for the fertility of the mountain fields; it seems to be a celebration of the birth of Attis, who, like Moses, was exposed among the reeds. March 22nd was 'The Entry of the Tree'. The College of Tree-bearers carried the sacred pine, decorated with violets and with wool, to the Palatine temple. This is an anticipation of the death of Attis; we might compare it to a Palm Sunday or Maundy Thursday service. March 24th, 'The Day of Blood', corresponded to Good Friday; it was a day of fasting and mourning, of the laceration of the flesh, and traditionally (though this is not attested for Rome) of the self-emasculation of the new priests. The very next day, 'The Festival of Joy', corresponded to Easter; it became one of the great festivals of Rome in the third century AD, a day of sacrifices and spectacles. It was, Macrobius tells us, a commemoration of the triumph of day over night after the spring equinox. There followed a kind of Sabbath or 'Day of Rest', and the festival concluded on 27 March with 'The Ceremony of Washing'; nothing was spared which money or art could supply, says Herodian; the cult-image, set in silver, was carried in a car in gorgeous procession to the River Almo and there ceremoniously bathed; this is the soaking of the earth in the rain which brings fertility. (*Pl. 5*)

Cybele had her Mysteries, as did Isis: we shall meet them later. The central rite was the *taurobolium*, first recorded in Pergamum in about AD 105, then at Puteoli in AD 134 (we may deduce an observance in the year 114), though there is evidence from Stephanus of Byzantium that the bull was long associated with the Asiatic cult of Ma. The name implies not a sacrifice or baptism, but something more akin to a rodeo, and the lassoing of a wild buffalo, or something of the kind. Later it changed its character and became more intimate. But the date is important; it *was* later, and we are not to think of the Asiatic Mother, any more than Isis, as the divinity of a closed cult. The demand for a divine Mother was far wider than the demand for individual devotion.

The cult spread with the Empire. In Asia it had always been important; still the prominence of coins with the Mother's image during the period from Hadrian to Gallienus is noteworthy. In Greece Rhea, Artemis and Aphrodite had been early assimilated. Pausanias records sanctuaries of the Mother at Piraeus (the port of Athens), Dyme, Patrae, Thebes and Acriae. Attis was never assimilated, and only two instances of the *taurobolium*, both in Athens, are known. The Mother's image appears on coins, but in general Greece was resistant to the great extension of the cult during this period. The north, Macedonia, Thrace and Moesia, were more welcoming. Across the Mediterranean Caesarea in Mauretania was a cult-centre, and at Carthage Augustine saw the festivals as a young man. In Spain we know of *taurobolia* at Emerita and Corduba, and dedications at Olisipo and Capera. In Gaul we know of cults at Lugdunum, Augustodunum, Tournacum, Narbo, Forum Iulii, Vasio, Dea Augusta Vocontiorum, Valentia and Tegna. In Italy there were centres at Ostia, Portus, Praeneste, Tibur, Cumae, Puteoli, Teate, Corfinium, Venafrum, Saepinum, Beneventum, Venusia, Brundisium, Falerii, Faesulae, Interamnia, Augusta Taurinorum, Mediolanum, Brixia, Verona, Aquileia, Tergeste and Capodistria. In Britain the evidence is scantier but real. No shrine has been found, except possibly one at St Albans and one at Chester, both by no means certain in their attribution. There were altars at Corbridge and Carrawburgh. Statues of both Cybele and Attis were found in London, but most other alleged statues are doubtfully identified. Attis in mourning as a tomb-figure may be no more than conventional. The celebrated bronze forceps found in the Thames may well be connected with the cult, but its purpose is obscure, and it can hardly have had place in an act of castration inflicted in frenzy with stone or sword. The evidence is that the West had come to feel a deep sense of need which the Mother had long satisfied in the East.

There is a remarkable monument to the cult in Egypt in the textile panel now in the Metropolitan Museum in New York, and tentatively attributed to the fourth century AD; there is a parallel piece in the Hermitage at Leningrad. The central figure shows Cybele in her lion-drawn chariot, brandishing the sacred stone, wearing a mural crown, with one breast bare. She is attended by a woman in ecstasy who is drawing away a figure who can only be Attis; on the other side covering her face stands the girl with whom Attis has offended, still carrying the love-gift of an apple. In the extreme corner Pan is leaving the scene in fear, with a backward look. Another monument is a charming alabaster Attis from a domestic shrine. The god sits; his features show a feminine refinement; he is holding a scourge of knucklebones such as the priests used for self-flagellation; he is nursing a sheep. On his back is the sacred pine-tree; below, a bull's head and three drops of blood are a reminder of the *taurobolium*. The inscription declares him 'King Atis newly wed'; in some versions of the myth his self-castration followed his marriage. There was evidently an accompanying figure of Cybele. (*Pl. 2*)

And, even in the West, the cult proved astonishingly persistent. It was the theme of one of the last confrontations of paganism and Christianity in the western capital. In the early 390s Valentinian II banned sacrifice and attendance at pagan temples. He died in the year 392, and under his more tolerant successor Eugenius the pagans made their last thrust. There was a ritual cleansing of the city, and a restoration of pagan rites, initiated by the consul Virius Nicomachus Flavianus. Some verses survive in a Paris manuscript describing the restoration of the rites of the Mother. Flavianus performed the *taurobolium* in person; the sacred pine-tree was carried in procession; the *Megalensia* were revived; and the Mother herself with silver lions before her appeared again to the people of Rome.

Then came Theodosius, and the Mother and her worship vanished. Or not quite. For Bossuet argued that Gnosticism was really the cult of the Great Mother under another name, and in many of the sects, the Collyridians, Montanists, Naassenes and Nicolaitans, the Holy Ghost was seen as the Female Principle. Not only so. The hunger for adoration of the power of woman was not quenched within orthodox Christianity. In parts of Italy today the statue of Mary is ceremoniously washed, and the Mother of Christ has attracted the devotion which once attached to the Great Mother of the gods.

CHAPTER II

THE SKY-FATHER

'THE SKY-GOD HAS REIGNED everywhere, his kingdom still covers the whole of the uncivilized world.' So Foucart in 1920. The dictum was, as we have already seen, overstated, but not by much. The brilliance of the over-arching sky, its changeableness, its power manifested in thunder and lightning, its contribution to life in the form of rain, all combine to associate the sky with potent divinity. 'There, where the sky is,' says an African, 'God is too.' Such a divinity is naturally feared in the storm; he is naturally honoured on mountain-tops. Sometimes he seems an aloof or withdrawn god, for the sky is withdrawn and we cannot reach it; devotion is offered to more accessible powers with clearly defined spheres of action. In the background is the Sky-Father, 'the father of gods and men', as the Greeks called Zeus, our father 'who art in heaven'. Yahweh, the god of the Hebrews, is in origin such an one, adopted from the Kenites, honoured on Sinai and Sion, the thunder his voice, the lightning his arrows, the rainbow reaching from sky to earth the symbol of his mercy. Ahura-Mazda in Iran has for his robes the unshakable vault of the sky; he, like Yahweh, survives through into the Roman Empire.

In the world of Greece and Rome the sky-god appears mostly through peoples of Indo-European language. In Egypt the sky was feminine, Nut, the matrix of creation, fecundated by the earth-god Geb. The Graeco-Roman god is named from a root associated with shining or brightness. He came to Greece with the Hellenic invaders, perhaps first as Posis-Das, earth-husband, who later was treated as Zeus' brother and pushed out into the sea as Poseidon, but who betrays his origin in the storm-god's trident. His more familiar guise is Zeus. As such his consort was Dione who shows the same root, but who was ousted by the Earth-Mother in the various forms in which Zeus encountered her in his mythological amours, and particularly under the title Hera, 'our Lady'. Before the Homeric minstrels sang of him, Zeus was supreme, a monarch with his barons as the earthly monarchs had their barons, and Mount Olympus was his palace.

A sky-god was naturally worshipped on the mountains, and at all periods from the earliest to the latest we find him so honoured. The mountain is his throne. We may reflect on the great altar of Zeus at Pergamum, high above the city, one of the wonders of the world, whose high altar within the whole altar was crowned with a curved baldachin which appears on a coin of Septimius Severus. At Argos on the acropolis there stood a temple of Zeus Larisaeus, decrepit by Pausanias' day. Outside Ephesus stands Mount Coressus; here high on a cliff is a rock-cut throne: a coin of Antoninus Pius shows Zeus enthroned on the mountain, and this must be his throne. At Antioch-on-the-Orontes there were sanctuaries of Zeus on both the local mountains, Casion and Silpion. In Samaria Yahweh's temple on Mount Gerizim was rededicated to Zeus. The sacred mountain thus becomes the meeting-point of heaven and earth. The ziggurat of Mesopotamia was such a mountain; so in different ways were Mount Sion, the acropolis at Athens, and the Capitol at Rome. (*Pls.* 10, 12)

JUPITER

At Rome, Jupiter is the same god under a closely similar guise. He is Dyaus Pitar, Dies-piter, Father Zeus, with the bright sky of day in his name. His temple was on the Capitoline Hill; his titles included Tonans (Thunderer), Fulgur (Lightning), Fulgurator (Sender of Lightning). Macrobius explains that Jupiter is the giver of light, Lucetius, and the father of day. In the temple of Jupiter Feretrius (perhaps 'Striker'), which Augustus restored, was no image, but a crude stone, no doubt believed to be a thunderbolt fallen from the sky. This stone gave rise to another title, Jupiter Lapis, whom the authorities invoked to confirm treaties with other nations. Sky-gods see all things, and naturally observe the keeping and breaking of oaths: hence the familiar Roman oath *mediusfidius* where Dius Fidius is another of Jupiter's titles. Jupiter was perhaps originally worshipped at Alba Longa, and when introduced to Rome formed a triad with Mars, perhaps a storm-god of war and agriculture, and the misty Quirinus, who presided over the Romans in assembly as Mars presided over them in the field. Later the new triad of Jupiter, Juno, Minerva (Zeus, Dione, Pallas) took control: the three shared the Capitoline temple, each, so to say, with his own apartment (*cella*). This Capitoline triad became something of a symbol of Rome, and, in the great imperial foundations in Africa of the second and third centuries AD, their temples dominate the scene, as at Thugga (where the temple dates from AD 166–67, built of the local limestone, with a fine Corinthian porch), or Thuburbo Maius (where in AD 168 the indigenes and Romans combined for the foundation) or Timgad, or Lambaesis. Jupiter was supreme, and his most familiar title was Jupiter Optimus Maximus, the Best and Greatest: so familiar that at all times it needed only the initial letters IOM. Later, especially after contact with the East, he appears as Summus Exsuperantissimus, Highest and Supremest (the Latin is an equivalent neologism). In Spain, Dacia and Pannonia Jupiter is honoured above all others; he is Highest and Most Excellent, Highest and Supremest, director of the lives of gods and men, the arbiter of destiny; a common formula is 'to Jupiter the Best and Greatest and the other immortal gods.' (*Pl.* 14)

As the culture of Greece spread in the Hellenistic age it was natural to find Zeus identified with numbers of supreme local gods. These might not always be sky-gods; they were often sun-gods; the sun is closer to man than the sky, and this contributes to the 'solarization' of the sky-god. Thus already Herodotus can identify Zeus with the Egyptian Amen-Ra. In Syria Zeus was one with the local Ba'al; at Baalbek with Hadad, the consort of Atargatis; at Doliche with the old supreme god of the Hittites who had survived in that obscure corner. Here we have two of his most widespread guises under the Roman Empire. Jupiter Heliopolitanus is found in Athens, Pannonia, Venetia, Puteoli, Rome, Gaul and Britain, and Jupiter Dolichenus travelled even more extensively. Philo of Byblus makes explicit the identification with Ba'al-shamin, the Lord of Heaven found throughout Phoenicia and Syria. At Baalbek the six standing columns of Zeus' temple remain singularly impressive; originally there were nineteen down the sides and ten at each end; they stand about 65 feet high, and the platform on which they rest, itself approached by a broad flight of steps, measured about 170 by 302 feet. Literary evidence dates the building to the reign of Antoninus Pius, but it was probably earlier; it may be seen *in toto* on third-century AD coins. From the next century Macrobius has left an account of its renown. The statue was golden, beardless, with a whip in one hand, and a thunderbolt and ears of corn in the other: an interesting blend of religious strands. As for Jupiter Dolichenus, he had two sanctuaries in Rome, one on the Esquiline, which was enlarged in the reign of Commodus by D. Junius Pacatus, and decorated and enlarged again by a group of soldiers on 1 August AD 191, the other on the Aventine, which survived well into the fourth century. There is an important inscription surviving in connection with this last. The god is described as 'Jupiter, the Best and Greatest, Dolichenus, the Eternal' and he orders a dedication to 'the preserver of the whole sky, pre-eminent godhead, unconquered provider'. There is a kind of split personality, but there is association with sky and sun. In some places Dolichenus and Heliopolitanus are found together or even identified. (*Pls.*11, 13)

Jupiter Dolichenus spread with the soldiers. It is surprising that more shrines have not been identified. There was undoubtedly an important shrine at Corbridge, where the remains of a pediment, frieze and metopes as well as a statue and altar point to a sanctuary of some elaboration. Most of the monuments in Britain come from the area of Hadrian's Wall; but we may add evidence which suggests a shrine at Ribchester, an inscription (now lost) was found at Caerleon, there is an excellent bronze head at Cirencester, and some fragments pertaining to the cult appeared on the Antonine Wall. Most of these remains can be confidently dated to the first part of the third century AD, when the cult was at its most popular. Elsewhere the most interesting cult-objects are bronze plates in the form of a triangle; one suspects that they were found in groups of three fitting together into a pyramid, which would itself symbolize the mountain; they are covered with relief-figures. One curious emblem which arises from these plates is the lily; it was also associated with Zeus by Byzantine scholars, and must be a fertility symbol connected with the sky-god's impregnation of earth. The god's normal likeness, whether on the plates or in statuettes, is squat, muscular, bearded, with double-axe in one hand and thunderbolt in the other.

SARAPIS

Another important example of the solarization of Zeus–Jupiter is seen in the cult of Sarapis or Serapis. Sarapis is a curious example of an artificially produced god. He originated at Memphis in Egypt in the sanctuary where the dead Apis bulls were entombed. The spirit which animated them was fused with Osiris to produce Osorapis. Ptolemy I, seeking a new religious concept to go with his own power, created out of this the figure of Sarapis, and imported from Sinope on the Euxine a colossal statue: it may have represented a local sun-god or sky-god. The cult caught on and became immensely popular in the Greek world. Sarapis was represented with the bearded serenity of Zeus, and honoured as Zeus Sarapis or Zeus Helios Sarapis. He acquired other characteristics; like Asclepius (and in some connections, Zeus) he was a god of healing; like Osiris or Hades, a god of the dead. For his followers he tended to oust other gods, and their triumph-shout 'One Zeus Sarapis' has come down to us in numerous inscriptions. There were seats in the temple where worshippers could sit and contemplate the cult statue in adoring meditation. Where the Alexandrian divinities were worshipped as a group, Sarapis was supreme, though in the Roman world the personal popularity of Isis tended to push him into the background.

Political suspicion of Egypt at the end of the Republic and during the early Empire checked for a while the onset of the Egyptian gods at Rome itself. It is possible that this very fact encouraged the cult's dissemination elsewhere—through the great ports and emporia, from Aquileia into the land of the Danube, from Carthage into Africa, from the French coast up the Rhône into Provence and ultimately to north-west Europe and Britain. Witness, to take two examples, the temple at York to the holy god Serapis dedicated by Claudius Hieronymianus of the Sixth

Legion, and the fine head of the god from the Walbrook
Mithraeum. At Rome itself Caligula reversed the policy of his
predecessors, and the Flavian, Antonine and Severan dynasties
alike were warm in their support of the cult; the Christian
apologist Minucius Felix, writing in the second or third century,
comments that the Egyptian cult has been completely adopted by
the Romans. We receive occasional glimpses of its power. For
example, Aelius Aristides tells us that under the Antonines there
were forty-two temples of Sarapis in Egypt. Diogenes Laertius
records that the hymn to Sarapis written by Demetrius of Phaler-
um was still sung in his own day; Diogenes no doubt took these
last words from his source, Didymus, but he thought that they
were still true. Again, Julian cites with approval the total identification Zeus Helios Sarapis, and looks on Sarapis as a kindly and
gentle god, who sets souls free from 'becoming' and does not
punish them. The cult in fact survived to the very end of the fourth
century AD. Then Theophilus, the Christian patriarch of Alexandria, took an axe to the cult-statue and directed the conflagra-
tion of the god's temple; we see him in a manuscript illustration
trampling on the shrine, and Rufinus declared that he had cut off
'the very head of idolatry'. The phrase shows the persistent power
of the Sky-Father in his manifestation as Sarapis. (*Pl.* 79)

THE CITIES OF ASIA

A glance at one or two of the cities of Asia will show how Zeus–
Jupiter held his predominant position. Laodicea, for instance, was
actually called Diospolis, city of Zeus: the city was said to have
been founded 'by revelation from Zeus given through Hermes'.
One of his cult-titles was the Syrian Aseis, 'almighty'. We see him
on coins as a father-god, or in the temple-statue, standing with a
sceptre in his left hand and an eagle perched on his right hand. At
Colossae, Zeus of Laodicea was the most prominent god. At
Magnesia-on-the-Maeander, where the Earth-Mother was dominant under the name of Artemis, the precinct of Zeus Sosipolis
adjoined her temple; he had his own festival, and the priestess of
Artemis shared in it. At Tarsus the great god was Ba'al-Tarz; to
the Persians he was Ahura-Mazda, to the Greeks Zeus, to the

Romans Jupiter. We see him sitting or standing, with sceptre in one hand and corn and grapes the other. At the cosmopolitan city of Antioch-on-the-Orontes, where Apollo had one of his most celebrated shrines, Zeus was in some ways more prominent. There was a famous statue of Zeus of the Thunderbolt; a temple which Tiberius restored (here the god appeared as Jupiter Capitolinus, a guise in which he had games even in Apollo's centre at Daphne); and sanctuaries (as we have noticed) on the local mountains, Casion and Silpion, a sure sign of the sky-god. After the earthquake of AD 115, Poseidon, the god of earthquakes, was ignored, and a temple built to Zeus the Saviour. A temple of Zeus Olympius belongs to the late-second century AD, and as late as the third century a new cult of Zeus Philius, god of friendship, was established by a Christian apostate named Theotecnus. Tralles had Zeus for its great god; the city was at one time called Dia. Official decrees were put up in his sanctuary. His main cult-title was Larasius, presumably the local name of the sky-god. There was a festival, the Olympia. Tralles was one of the cities which claimed the birth of Zeus; here too the sky descended in fertilizing rain on the earth, and coins bear the legend 'Io's marriage'. There was temple-prostitution, and we have two dedications from women who experienced mystical union with Zeus, one with the Latin name Aurelia Aemilia. The cult was in part Romanized; the common inscription 'to the god Zeus' is unnatural Greek but natural Latin. We have already recalled the great altar which dominated Pergamum. At Damascus the temple of Jupiter Damascenus was the most impressive of all the temples of Syria, being little short of 1,000 feet in length; the sanctuary had a varied career, being incorporated later into a Christian church, and again into one of the oldest and most beautiful mosques in the world. At Samaria-Sebaste the only divinities we know to have been worshipped by the Romans were the emperor, Jupiter Capitolinus and Kore. At Ptolemais the great temple was a Greek temple to Zeus; at Tyre the central legend was that of Zeus and Europa. Needless to continue the catalogue: the evidence is clear.

One of the great monuments of the power of the Sky-Father

is the address given at the Olympic Games by Dio of Prusa, 'the golden-mouthed', in AD 97. In the presence of Pheidias' statue of Zeus (which Quintilian thought added something to traditional religion), Dio elects to discourse on the divine nature. After a lengthy prologue of organized rambling he cites Hesiod in invocation of the Muses to sing of Zeus, and he turns to the gods, and especially the ruler of the universe. Knowledge of God is innate in all rational beings, and its potency arises from its truth. In addition there is the force of tradition, alike in literature and law. The result is a filial attitude towards the first, immortal parent of the human race, whom the Greeks call 'Zeus of the Ancestors'. But to the poets and lawgivers must be added the interpretative power of artists and philosophers. Dio now suggests a complimentary address to Pheidias which ends on a question whether God is adequately portrayed in human shape, and allows Pheidias a full and eloquent reply. The sculptor admits his inability to portray intelligence; he thus has to fall back on the human body as a vessel and symbol of intelligence within; we are like children crying in the night, and with no language but a cry; in any case the anthropomorphism comes from Homer and is hallowed by tradition. He then takes some of the cult-titles of Zeus, Father and King, Protector of Cities, God of Friendship, God of Comradeship, God of Suppliants, God of Hospitality, Giver of Increase, and others, and claims that he has represented them as far as is humanly possible. Yet the great lord of nature who sends rain, hail and snow, the rainbow and the meteorites, who directs the fortunes of war, and weighs the fate of men in the balance, who shakes the universe by a movement of his brow, he cannot be portrayed by art. Dio leaves some things unsaid, deliberately. We may single out four points in his analysis. First, everything is based on our innate knowledge of God; to that all else is secondary. Second, Dio believes clearly in one supreme god, whom he calls Zeus, while acknowledging that he may go by other names elsewhere. Third, he accepts the force of tradition and fuses it together in his picture of the supreme god. Finally he implies that though art may lead us towards God, it is only philosophy that can know God.

THE LATER EMPIRE

The Stoics helped to foster the exalted position of Zeus–Jupiter, for this was one, and probably the commonest, of their names for God, and from Cleanthes' great hymn onwards this was the name which struck a chord in the hearts of the faithful. Tertullian recognized that to the Stoic the very Logos, the Reason at the root of things, was the mind of Jupiter. Plutarch, too, critical as he is of Stoic theology in some ways, does not doubt their exclusive—in his views wrongly exclusive—devotion to Zeus. Seneca lists the names that the Stoic might give to God—Fate, Providence, Nature, Universe—but he starts from Jupiter. The name of Zeus is continually on the lips of Epictetus, the most deeply religious of the Stoics. Marcus Aurelius can even speak of the health of the universe as the well-being of Zeus; at another time the universe is the city of Zeus. He uses the name of Zeus less freely than Epictetus, but will speak of reason in man as a portion of Zeus, and human society as the gift of Zeus. In general it is just to say that the Stoics played a significant part in maintaining the dominant position of Zeus–Jupiter in the Graeco-Roman world.

A glance at the policy of the second-century AD emperors will show the continuing power of Jupiter. To start with Trajan. In the great Arch at Beneventum, erected in AD 115 to commemorate the emperor's achievement, Jupiter, with Juno and Minerva on either side and the other Olympian gods in attendance, welcomes Trajan, and hands the thunderbolt of power over to him. Our point here is not the exaltation of the emperor's person, so much as the fact that Jupiter and Jupiter alone can empower him. Throughout the reign there is emphasis on Jupiter; the emperor is Jupiter's representative, under Jupiter's personal protection; he takes the titles Optimus and Maximus; in the East he is identified with Zeus. A poem in the Anthology bears Trajan's name; it is a dedication to Zeus, from the sovereign of mortals to the sovereign of the immortals. Now for the first time for two centuries the Capitoline triad are seen on the coinage. Under Hadrian Zeus is of peculiar and outstanding importance. At Athens there was the great temple of Zeus Olympius, and another shrine of Zeus Pan-hellenius, and there were other shrines of Zeus Olympius at

Delos, Ephesus and Pergamum. Hadrian himself was sometimes honoured in association with Zeus, as at Athens, where the statues seem to have been statues of the emperor; sometimes, as at Prusias and elsewhere, he was identified with the god. When he was planning his world journey in the 120s he issued a coin showing Jupiter as lord of the world placing it in the emperor's care. At the end of his life coins were issued honouring Jupiter under the titles of Victor, Protector and Guardian. A dedication to Jupiter Best and Greatest appears to honour the emperor himself, identified with the god, after his death.

Antoninus Pius, as would be expected, carried on the traditional devotion to Jupiter, especially under the title of Supporter (Stator). The god appears standing with sceptre and thunderbolt; or, in a puzzling coin-type, seated on a globe holding objects which are difficult to distinguish but which look like a ship's prow and a reed. Under Marcus Aurelius we see the god seated with sceptre and Victory. A medallion of Marcus Aurelius shows the great figure of Jupiter overshadowing him and defending him. Already Syrian imagery was beginning to take firm root, and it was in this reign, in AD 176, that an impressive temple to Jupiter Heliopolitanus was erected on the Janiculum; it was destroyed in AD 341. Commodus, in his frantic career, identified himself with Hercules, who was, it must be remembered, the divine son of Jupiter. Not content with this he has a curious coin-type with the inscription IOVI IVVENI, 'to Jupiter the Youth', and has had the image of the god made in his own likeness. His earlier coinage is full of the patronage of Jupiter: the god stands with his hand on the shoulder of the young emperor, who is holding the orb or globe. Nor was the great god forgotten in the chaotic period following Commodus' assassination. Pescennius Niger has a type inscribed IOVI PRAE. ORBIS, honouring Jupiter as the ruler of the world, and Albinus dedicates to Jupiter Victor a coin inscribed VICTORIAE IOVIS, to the victory which comes from Jupiter. (*Pl.* 16)

Even when the Sun is beginning to conquer the Roman world we do well to remember that Jupiter remains for many the great god of Rome. We see him on an *aureus* of Septimius Severus, naked save for a cloth over his left shoulder, with a sceptre in his left hand, clasping the hand of the emperor, in military uniform, with his right. On another he is seated, holding out a Victory on a globe in his right hand, with an eagle before him; the inscription is to Jupiter the Protector, IOVI CONSER. Elsewhere he is called Jupiter Victor, or Unconquerable (INVICTVS), bearing the epithet which became the peculiar prerogative of the Sun. Under Caracalla we see him advancing with thunderbolt at the ready; here he is Jupiter the Defender, IOVI PROPVGNATORI. Macrinus honours Jupiter the Protector, whom we see sheltering him as he stands at the god's feet. Even Elagabalus does not wholly oust Jupiter from the coins; the god appears seated, with his eagle, holding out Victory. Jupiter, Mars and Sol are the three most prominent deities in the coinage of Severus Alexander; Jupiter appears as Conservator (Protector), Propugnator (Defender), Stator (Supporter) and Ultor (Avenger); this last is an unusual dedication, and of some importance, since it was evidently associated with the dedication or restoration of a temple to the god under that cult-title. When Maximus and Balbinus entered on their ninety-nine days of glory they were careful to put themselves under the protection of Jupiter by offering sacrifices in the Capitol, and their coinage naturally gives prominence to Jupiter Conservator. In the sad days of the mid-third century AD this is the favoured title, though Stator is also found. Jupiter protects and preserves the emperor, while Mars is declared the bringer of peace; we see Jupiter standing guard with his thunderbolt over Aemilian, the third Gordian, Gallienus. With Valerian new types appear: Jupiter is shown as a baby with the legend IOVI CRESCENTI, 'to Jupiter as he grows'. It is suited to herald a new era, as its variant IOVI EXORIENTI, 'to Jupiter as he rises', shows. For Gallienus he appears in various guises. We may note Jupiter the Victorious, with Victory and sceptre, or Jupiter the Protector with globe and sceptre. Even more important, Jupiter is the central figure in the early coinage of Aurelian; he presents the emperor with a globe or wreath, or stands holding thunderbolt or spear or sceptre. It is evident that Aurelian, whose far-seeing genius had already envisaged the need of a religious tie to unify the Empire, was seeking it in Jupiter, and it was only after his experiences in other parts of empire that he came to see the sun-god as a more nearly universal tie even than the sky-god. (*Pls.* 15–20)

Even so, Jupiter was not lost. The emperor Tacitus, who carried on Aurelian's defence of empire, prefers to exalt divine abtractions in the captions to his coins, but it is significant that it is Jupiter whom he shows presenting him with the globe, and the Sun does not appear. Above all, to Diocletian it is Jupiter who restores the world, or who protects the emperors. In his reorganization of the Empire into a tetrarchy, the senior emperors were placed under the protection of Jupiter, the junior under the protection of Hercules. The panegyrists make clear the distinction. Jupiter governs the heavens; Hercules brings peace on earth. Jupiter initiates policy; Hercules executes it. Jupiter plans; Hercules acts. The new pattern is amply represented on the coins with types of the protecting deities. Other deities appear, Mars, Minerva, Sol; Jupiter and his heroic son stand supreme. It is Jupiter who hands Diocletian the globe which he passes on to Maximian. The mood continued: while Constantine was setting the Unconquered Sun on his coins, Licinius was still honouring Jupiter the Protector. Diocletian's choice, like all the acts of that able man, was skilful and subtle. The Dalmatia from which he came paid particular homage to Jupiter and Hercules in association; the great sun-gods of Syria might be suitably identified with Sol, but they had fitted into the Olympian pantheon by identification with Zeus–Jupiter rather than with Apollo; the emphasis on the divine son of Jupiter recalled the pattern of the early Empire, as Diocletian was glad to do, while at the same time the epithet Jovius and the special protection of Jupiter gave to the imperial ruler a divine nimbus appropriate to the more exalted status developed by the Byzantines but inaugurated by Diocletian. But above all, Jupiter spoke of the eternity of Rome. 'It was,' wrote Jullian, 'the arising in the Roman world of this double cult of Jupiter, lord of the Capitol, and Hercules, hero of the Palatine, which from the first had produced the glory and sanctity of the Eternal City.' (*Pl.* 18)

CHAPTER III

THE SUN-GOD

THE SUN GIVES LIGHT AND LIFE. But it is the sky-god, not the
sun-god, who predominates in early religion. Sun-worship is a
maturer, more sophisticated experience, often associated with
monarchy as a political institution; thus in the Americas only
Peru and Mexico developed a dominant sun-cult. Often, as we
have said, we can discern the historical process of the 'solarization'
of the supreme deity, as among the ancient Hittites, in Bengal, in
Indonesia, and various parts of Africa. In the Mediterranean world
the most intense sun-worship was found in Egypt, buttressed by a
powerful priesthood and closely associated with the position of
the Pharaoh. The position was fully established by the fifth
dynasty. Ra began to absorb other gods; with Osiris he remained
in conflict. Even the revolution of Akhenaton was a change of
emphasis not essence, for the Aton honoured at Tell-el-Amarna
was the Sun's life-giving disc. In Mesopotamia Marduk, the great
god of Babylon, was originally a sun-god, and Shamash, the more
familiar sun-god, came to a prominence which he had not originally held, as astrology developed. In Babylonia the Moon-god
Sin, conceived as male, tended to have primacy, and this remained
true in Carrhae and over much of Anatolia in Roman times, but
astrology and politics combined to exalt Shamash: the sun was the
king's star. In Persia the great god was Ahura-Mazda. He is no
doubt a god of the bright sky, and in the battle of light against
darkness the Sun appears among his highest-ranking staff-officers.
In Syria the very name by which the Greeks knew Baalbek,
Heliopolis or the City of the Sun, reminds us that the Ba'al in
question was a sun-god. In Illyria there was an ancient tradition of
sun-worship, as the astral symbolism upon tombs shows.

In Greece Helios, the Sun-god proper, receives surprisingly
little attention in his own right during the classical period. True

that the sun, moon and stars were called 'deities in epiphany', and
the philosophers as well as the non-intellectuals make something
of this. True that poets and other writers single him out for their
praise. True that he is invoked in oaths, for like the sky-god he
sees all things in his over-arching course. But, on the whole,
worship of the heavenly bodies was regarded as a foreign and
undesirable practice, and only in Rhodes was there a really
prominent cult, and there it seems to have infiltrated from abroad.
Apollo, a god of uncertain but probably complex origin, usurped
something of the honour which might have been accorded to
Helios; the matter is a controversial one, but his name of Phoebus,
Shining, makes the relation almost certain. Pindar begins a paean
to Apollo with an invocation to the Sun's beam. In any event, by
the time the Greek world came into contact with Rome the situation was changed. The Hellenistic monarch affected the rayed
crown appropriate to the sun, and through the Hellenistic age the
sun is associated with justice and Utopian visions of a better world.

In Rome there are traces of an ancient cult; Julian suggested that
it went back to the days of King Numa. In the republican
calendar Sol had his festival on 9 August. He is called Sol Indiges;
the interpretation is controversial, but it may suggest a genuinely
indigenous cult on the Quirinal. There was a *pulvinar*, a couch-
throne, near the temple of Quirinus, and the gens Aurelia were
responsible for the cult. Coins from southern Italy dating back to
the end of the third century BC show the godhead radiate, and
the image appears too on Roman coins in the republican period.
With Augustus' achievement of power the Sun came to fresh
prominence. Augustus was consummate at using religion as a
means to subserve political ends. Apollo, who had a shrine at
Actium, had presided over that decisive victory. He was a peculiarly appropriate symbol for the new age, whose dawning Vergil
was already anticipating in the marriage of Octavia with Antony
—*tuus iam regnat Apollo*, 'your Apollo is king at last'. He could heal
the wounds of war; he could prosper the new art and the new
literature; above all he represented the breaking of new light over
the world. So on the breastplate of the emperor's statue at Prima
Porta the goddess Dawn is portrayed alongside the god of the Sun.

So on the Palatine arose the glorious temple of Apollo, fellow to the temple of Jupiter on the Capitol, and on its roof Sol–Apollo driving his golden chariot above the world of Rome.

It was natural that subsequent emperors should echo the practice, in seeking the flair, of the founder of empire. Caligula and Nero alike, full of youthful promise at the dawn of their reigns, were greeted as the new Sun. The Einsiedeln eclogue repeats, of Nero, Vergil's phrase *tuus iam regnat Apollo*, 'your Apollo is king at last'. The author of the skit on the death of Claudius, which has come down to us under Seneca's name, pushed into the mouth of Phoebus flattery of the new emperor:

> *Like the Morning-star scattering the stars in flight,*
> *like the Evening-star rising as the stars return,*
> *like the Sun, when dawn first relaxes the shadows*
> *and roseate escorts in the day, as he looks on the world*
> *in his brilliance, drives his car from its shelter,*
> *like these Caesar appears, like these Rome will now*
> *look upon Nero.*

Calpurnius Siculus plays on the same theme, identifying Nero with Phoebus. Nero followed the precedent of Hellenistic monarchs from the Greek world which he honoured and which honoured him, in placing his own portrait on coins with the radiate crown of the Sun. He was actually honoured in one place as 'the new Sun-god shining on the Greeks', and his statue placed in the temples of Zeus Eleutherios and Apollo Ptoos. In Rome, if this is the right interpretation of a disputed passage, he erected a gigantic statue of himself under the guise of the Sun. The Golden House was his appropriate abode, and frescoes told the story of Helios and Phaethon. Furthermore his reception of Tiridates of Armenia is full of solar symbolism, and Tiridates is recorded as saying, 'I have come to you as my god, to worship you like Mithras.' But it was in the Civil Wars into which Nero's reign finally exploded that the most significant event of this period took place. This is recorded by Tacitus: at Beneventum some soldiers of the Third Legion saluted the rising sun, 'since that is the custom in Syria'. This has been wrongly linked by some with Mithraic religion, but Mithras is not Syrian, and Syria has enough sun-gods without Mithras. None the less it is significant of the fusion of eastern and western religion which is beginning to take place. (*Pl.* 21)

MITHRAS

Mithras is indeed important. He came from India via Persia. In the Vedas he is a divinity of light subordinate to Ahura or Varuna, in the Avesta a spirit of light or fertilizing warmth, also associated with truth and the oath. He is not the sky-god. Nor is he the Sun, which is described as the eye of Mithra and Varuna; the assimilation to the Sun (Persian *mihr*) comes later. He is probably the firmament, god of the upper air which the Greeks called *aether*, mediating between heaven and earth; in Assyrian *metru* means rain. A god of the upper air, like sun and sky, sees all things, and is naturally the enforcer of oaths and compacts: in Sanskrit *mithras* means friend. The association with light and truth fitted him well into the Zoroastrian pattern of a world dualism between the forces of light and darkness, but as subordinate, a celestial soldier at Ahura's side. In Zoroaster's monotheism of light he was kept down, and appears chiefly as the power of truth. But somehow, somewhere, he became the central deity in an almost new religion.

Associated with this new religion is a myth. Mithras was born from a rock; the representations of this suggest the sun rising behind mountains; Mithras and the Sun are separate in the myth, yet their figures tend to merge and blend. The Sun was Ahura-Mazda's chief representative in the battle of light against darkness. Mithras both shares the struggle with him and ousts him from his supremacy. Ahura-Mazda's first creation had been a wild bull; Mithras seized it by the horns and held out till the bull was worn with weariness, then slung it on his shoulder and dragged it to a cave; we have here an aetiological myth explaining some kind of rodeo-rite, and the fact that Mithraic chapels were underground. The bull escaped, and the Sun sent his messenger, the Raven, to track it. In accordance with Ahura-Mazda's will Mithras with his faithful hound set off in pursuit, found the bull, pulled back its head, grasped its nostrils with his left hand and with his right plunged a dagger into its throat. From the blood of the dead bull sprang corn and other life. Ahriman, the power of darkness, sent his servants, the scorpion, ant and snake, to lap up the life-giving stream, but in vain; it spread over the earth. Through this act the Sun yielded supremacy to his ally, knelt before Mithras, was invested by him with a crown, arose and made a covenant with him. In other stories Ahriman tried to destroy the world by a flood, from which Mithras rescued mankind, or by drought, but Mithras shot an arrow into a rock and unleashed a spring; parallels with Hebrew legend are obvious. Finally he took leave of his ally the Sun in a ceremonial banquet, which was commemorated in a sacramental meal. (*Pls.* 26, 27)

It has been strongly and rightly argued that the god of Mithraism was always Ahura-Mazda. He is not mentioned in Mithraic inscriptions. But the identification of the lion-headed divinity surrounded with zodiacal signs, not with Aion but with Ahriman, conceived as god of this world (there is actually a dedication to him at York by Volusius Irenaeus; others are known; nothing like backing both horses!), makes it virtually certain that the dualism will have appeared in its totality, and the great god of light must be there in the background to counter the power of darkness. This is now confirmed in the Mithraeum at S. Prisca in Rome: in the central niche there was a reclining figure who could hardly be other than Ahura-Mazda conceived as a sky-god. Mithras is the Mediator; he stands between god and man, heaven and earth. Hence the tendency to assimilate him to the Sun, an obvious mediator. In any case the Sun could not fail to be important in a religion of light, and the spread of Mithraism in the Roman Empire reinforced and was reinforced by the general movement to sun-worship. (*Pl.* 28)

There were Mithraists in the Fifteenth Legion at Carnuntum in AD 71, and under the Flavians the cult spread. Its principal impact was in the East; in the West it is found mainly in the military frontier-provinces, or in ports and emporia. The army was the chief instrument of dissemination, treasury officials (rather oddly, since civil servants are not prone to religions of salvation) another. Commodus' acknowledgment of the affinity between solar monolatry and autocracy led to the first great period of the cult.

He must have been an initiate himself, for the scandal to spread
that he polluted the cult by murder. Diocletian heralded the
second; in AD 307 a sanctuary on the Danube was dedicated to
Mithras as the sustainer of imperial power. There was a brief
revival under Julian, before Gratian ordered the closing of the
temples in AD 377. But Mithraism scarcely touched the civil
population; it was gross exaggeration by Renan to suggest in his
celebrated epigram that if some mortal malady had afflicted the
Christian Church the world would have been Mithraist. Mithraic
sanctuaries were always small. What the religion meant to its
initiates we shall examine later. But it is a grave mistake to treat
all sun-worship as Mithraic. Mithraism played its part, but it was
a minor part.

THE RISING SUN

The image of the rising sun was important in imperial propaganda. Here is Statius licking Domitian's boots:

In glory the emperor's robe of office joins the sixteen terms
accomplished; the conqueror of Germany sheds splendour on the year
*   he opens;*
he rises with the rising sun, with the mighty constellations,
shining with great brilliance, more powerful than the star of early
*   morning.*

Beneath the nauseating flattery stands a significant image. ORIENS
becomes a catchword, a symbol that dawn will always break, and
this in effect means that the emperor will be there to bring new
light. This is particularly clear with Hadrian, who portrayed
Oriens, the sunrise, with the Sun's radiate crown. At his accession
there was a dramatic performance at Heptacomia in Egypt. The
language is high-flown, the metre—if it is verse—uncertain.
Phoebus appeared in person and spoke:

I have just risen on high with Trajan in my white-horsed chariot,
I come to you, People—you know me—Phoebus, god,
to proclaim Hadrian as the new ruler
whom all things serve for his ability
and the genius of his divine father, gladly.

In the same way, a relief from Ephesus, now in Vienna, shows Trajan, deified, ascending in glory in the chariot of the Sun. So when Hadrian climbed Etna to see the sunrise we must see the act as going beyond scientific curiosity and almost as a religious sacrament. So also he removed the colossal statue which Nero had made of himself as the Sun, eliminated Nero's features and had it rededicated to the Sun. Antoninus Pius pays honour on his coins to Apollo Augustus; he also has a medallion with Earth reclining with a baby at her breast and a cornucopiae in her hand while Sol, guided by the same morning-star whom Domitian outshone, drives his chariot upwards over a bank of clouds. The type is repeated by Commodus. Here the association is more explicit; after all, the priesthood of the cult has been in the hands of the gens Aurelia. So we find Marcus Aurelius on his death-bed, asked for the password for the day by an officer, saying, 'Go to the rising Sun; I am setting.'

Already Antoninus had begun to show particular favour to the sun-cult. Malalas actually says that he founded the great temple at Baalbek. Archaeology refutes this, but the gigantic courtyard dates from his reign. The Sun appears on his coins. At Corinth the type of Helios and the quadriga had not been seen since Nero's reign, at Prusias and Nicaea Helios also appears; at Emesa it is the local sun-god Elagabal, destined for a brief notoriety in the following century. More important, at Alexandria in AD 141-42 the emperor and Faustina are portrayed as Sun and Moon, and at Rome in AD 145-46 a coin with the legend PAX AVG shows the emperor with the Sun-god's nimbus; Fronto writing to Marcus Aurelius speaks of Antoninus as the Sun.

With the accession of the Severan dynasty sun-worship became dominant at Rome. There were four reasons for this progress. First, it had become increasingly clear that the Sun was a superb symbol and rallying-point for empire; all the motives which led Augustus to adopt it were still valid; but in addition there was the bankruptcy of the traditional religion, as Marcus' attempt at revival had sadly shown. Secondly, there was the fact that in this bankruptcy people were spontaneously turning to religions from the East, encouraged by the mobility which the great peace of the second century AD had made possible. Under the Republic, the government had introduced eastern cults to keep the people quiet, but the worship of Mithras and Jupiter Dolichenus spread spontaneously, and both were associated with the Sun. Thirdly, the power of Parthia was strong on the eastern frontiers; Persian religion told of the struggle of light against darkness and sanctified the Sun; in any event it was well to honour the power who rose from the lands of the East and came from them to burn in anger, or to warm in grace, the people of Rome. Finally, the cultural aura of the new age was diffused not by the emperor, who came from Africa, but by his consort who came from Syria.

Julia Domna was among the most remarkable women of this or any age, and she and her sister Julia Maesa were daughters of the high-priest of the Sun at Emesa. It was she who encouraged Philostratus to put together a life of Apollonius of Tyana as a counterblast to Jesus; we shall be meeting this curious semi-fictitious character again. Here we are concerned with the sun-worship which the document inculcates. In the sage's travels in India he comes to admire the temple of the Sun at Taxila, and the Brahmans for their prayers to the Sun and their levitation which draws them nearer to the Sun. So we find him with the regular practice of worshipping the Sun in the middle of the day; he proclaims that the air is the Sun's throne, and that those who would sing his praise appropriately must rise from earth and soar with the god; and he bears a name devoted to Apollo. But the new emphasis on the Sun was more than literary. Septimius built an elaborate three-storied façade to the imperial palace, called the Septizonium or Septizodium (our sources vary). It is hard to identify the precise function of this building; all that we know for certain is that it was decorated with fountains; but whatever its title it had a plainly astrological significance. Further, the coinage shows the new mood. The Sun-god is actually portrayed with the emperor's characteristic beard; the emperor himself has the title INVICTVS (unconquerable), which is the peculiar province of the Sun; the ill-fated Geta is shown radiate with his hand raised in a gesture of blessing long familiar and linked with the Sun (as on coins of Trajan); and Caracalla too appears radiate, and was even heard to claim that in driving his chariot he was emulating the Sun; the two princes are called the New Suns.

ELAGABALUS

So came Elagabalus. He was the grandson of Julia Maesa, and his Roman name was Varius Avitus, but since he had entered upon the hereditary priesthood of the Sun-god at Emesa he was known by the divine name of Elagabalus: the variant Heliogabalus, found in antiquity, is an assimilation of the Syrian Sun-god to the Greek. The new emperor made slow progress towards Rome. When he arrived he behaved with all the parochialism of a small-town mayor. His priesthood had to be recognized by the senate; the black betyl which enshrined the power of the Sun in his native Emesa had to be brought to Rome. In the suburbs he established a large, elaborate temple to which each year at midsummer he transported the god. He put on variety shows, and built race-courses and theatres, thinking that the commons would enjoy chariot-racing and theatrical spectacles in large numbers, with celebrations going on all night. (*Pl. 22*)

He set the god in a chariot which was decorated with gold and precious stones, and drove him from the city to the suburbs. The chariot he drove had six horses, the steeds white, large in size, spotless; they were decked with plenty of gold and ornamental trappings. No one held the reins; no human was allowed to mount the chariot; they escorted it as if the god were in fact driving. Antoninus [i.e. Elagabalus] ran back-wards in front of the chariots, his eyes fixed on the god, checking the horses' bridles; he made the whole journey run-ning backwards with eyes fixed on the god's front. To stop him stumbling or slipping, as he could not see where he was treading, gold dust was strewn in large quantities. On each side bodyguards supported him, anticipating the dangers of running in this way. The commons ran along the sidewalk, waving various kinds of torch and throwing flowers and garlands. The cavalry with the rest of the army carried in procession images of all the gods, particularly valuable or expensive offerings, imperial ornaments and expensive treasures, in the god's honour.

Amongst the gifts which this extravagant voluptuary liked to bestow were four-horse chariots. He married his god to Dea Caelestis, the Moon-goddess of Carthage; he himself united with one of the Vestal Virgins, the representatives of the heavenly and earthly fire consummating a cosmic union. But Elagabalus was no Aurelian. Miller wrote well:

> The offence was aggravated by Elagabalus' claim of supremacy for the provincial cult of which he was priest, and his placing in the shrine of his god, as tokens of sovereignty, the symbols of other deities. The acceptance of the sovereignty of the god would have given a powerful religious sanction to his own rule, but to attribute to him a policy of strengthening the imperial authority by attaching it to a solar monotheism would be to magnify and indeed invert the significance of his action, which was little more than an exhibition of childish egotism and of the contentiousness of Syrian Ba'al-worship. Nor was the tendency for the solar cults to become unified directing itself to a true monotheism, but rather, through syncretism, towards an abstraction or a pantheism; and it was an intellectual movement. Among the mass of solar devotees the recognition of an affinity between their cults did not diminish mutual jealousy or local exclusiveness. Not even a priest who was also Roman emperor could identify the solar religion with one of its local forms. Still less could he make his Ba'al ruler of the Roman pantheon.

Elagabalus was murdered for his excesses. He did not establish the sun-cult in a dominant position. But he did not destroy it either. His successor, Severus Alexander, shows the Sun on his coins, but eliminates the betyl, and restores him to his classical form. Rome entered upon what Renan called 'that hell of a half-century'. In the middle of it the cultured and philosophic Gallienus put forward a curious proposal. In the words of his ancient biographer, 'he gave instructions for a statue to be made, larger than Nero's Colossus, of himself in the guise of the Sun; it was left unfinished and destroyed. Its construction had actually begun on such a scale that it seemed to be twice as large as the Colossus. Furthermore he had intended to place it on the summit of the Esquiline, with a spear in its hand so that a child could climb to the top inside the shaft.' It was a curious megalomaniac scheme, as his later successors Claudius Gothicus and Aurelian agreed. Yet they owed honour to the same deity.

AURELIAN TO CONSTANTINE

It was in fact Aurelian who established the Sun as the supreme deity of Rome. He came from Illyria, a region where sun-worship was well established, and where his mother was priestess of the Sun, and the dominant part of his army came from the same area. Others of the army came from Syria, and Aurelian was deeply involved in the politics of that region. This was the period of Palmyra's ambiguous grandeur, standing, as it did, as a bastion against Parthian inroads to the Roman Empire, and as an independent state defying Rome. Palmyrene worship centred on the Sun-god, and Odenathus was even styled Palmyra's Sun-given priest. In his campaigns in the East, Aurelian visited Emesa and Palmyra; he restored the temple of the Sun at Palmyra, and incorporated statues of Bel into his own foundation at Rome. But Aurelian was restorer of the West as well as of the East, and there he found Celtic and Germanic gods of light and healing identified with Apollo. Aurelian was thus no Elagabalus, introducing a petty provincial cult. He was seeking a new divine power which would sanction his own authority, and unite the Empire East and West, as the old gods and the divinity of the emperor had alike failed to do. In AD 274 he built in Rome a magnificent temple to *deus Sol*, the only god who could do this, and established a college of senators as *pontifices dei Solis*, priests of the new cult, precisely on the lines of the ancient colleges. The god's birthday was naturally the winter solstice, identified as 25 December, a date which has nothing to do with the birth of Christ (its date is unknown), but which the Christians arrogated to themselves as a counterblast to its popularity. Coins show the change which Aurelian brought.

Jupiter Conservator gives place to SOLI INVICTO and ORIENS AVG. This last is important: the emperor rises over the world like the Sun whose vice-regent he is. The mint at Serdica produces the legend SOL DOMINVS IMPERI ROMANI, suggesting that the Sun is the true ruler of Rome; at Cyzicus we find SOLI CONSERVATORI, showing that the Sun has taken over Jupiter's role as protector. Another coin shows Fides, Loyalty, holding two ensigns, while Sol presents to the emperor a globe crowned with victory. Aurelian was a very great man, one of the greatest of the Romans, and his greatness extended far beyond the limits of military success. Ruthless with those who betrayed his trust, he preferred the path of mercy and protected civilians against exploitation by the military. Like the sun, he shone beneficently, though his rays had the power to blast. His genius is nowhere more clearly seen than in his vision of a divine unifying power for the Empire. His end was tragically wasteful; he was murdered by a secretary, who was afraid of having his petty peccadilloes uncovered. (*Pl.* 23)

The vision lived on. Constantius Chlorus also came from the Balkans, and he and his family gave their devotion to the Unconquered Sun. When he returned to Britain after the usurpation of Allectus, the great medallion which he struck proclaimed him REDDITOR LVCIS AETERNAE, the restorer of the eternal light; this is the emperor's sunrise in other language. Constantine inherited this. He linked his fortunes with the memory of Claudius Gothicus. A panegyrist of AD 310 tells how Constantine had a vision of 'his own Apollo' appearing with Victory to offer him wreaths of laurel. 'You are, like him, young, prosperity is yours, you offer salvation, you are handsome, you have authority.' So the panegyrist describes the emperor as 'our Apollo' and 'a very present god'. This is the time of the great series of coins which honour the Sun under the title SOLI INVICTO COMITI, describing the Unconquered Sun as his comrade or ally. There are here Mithraic overtones; we remember how Mithras and the Sun pledged allegiance to one another. Then in AD 312 as he marched to the Milvian Bridge he had a vision, a rare but well-attested version of the halo-phenomenon, a cross superimposed on the sun, and the words came to him, somehow, in some language,

'Triumph in this.' He put the emblem on his soldiers' shields, and triumphed. (Pl. 24)

The cross was a symbol used by Christians and pagans; the chi-rho monogram formed the initial letters of the name of Christ in Greek, but their use as a monogram before Constantine is non-Christian for the most part; the total emblem was not unfamiliar, reminiscent of the *ankh* of Egypt, a symbol of immortality, on one side, and a sun-symbol, perhaps associated with Mithraism, on another. The symbol was in fact ambiguous, and it came from Constantine's great deity the Sun. To speak of his 'conversion' is misleading. That in his reign he moves steadily towards his deathbed baptism is clear, and with that there is a corresponding movement away from the old pagan deities. But they are not lost. Through the 310s the Sun continues to appear on the coins, over the whole Empire, and in all the mints. In AD 317 Licinius put on his coin Jupiter the Protector, Constantine put the Unconquered Sun. But on one coin of his young Caesar, Sol is accompanied by the legend CLARITAS REIPVBLICAE, 'the glory of the state'. This, as Usener saw years ago, is the deliberate ambiguity of a political religion. On the great arch which still stands in Rome, most of the pagan deities have been eliminated, but the Sun and Moon remain, and the inscription ascribes Constantine's triumph non-committally to 'divine' inspiration. Even later, when the Sun disappears from the coinage, and the characteristic epithet INVICTVS, unconquerable, is replaced by VICTOR, victorious, the residual devotion is clear, and in AD 321 the proclamation of Sunday as a day of rest was made precisely because it was Sun-day. Even in the new Christian capital of Constantinople the emperor's statue stood as Apollo–Helios with a radiate crown, formed, as he believed, of nails of the true Cross; the inscription ran, 'To Constantine who shines like the Sun.' Constantine's god was a fusion of the Unconquered Sun and Christ the Victorious, but he remained a god of power, not of love. (Pl. 25)

And the Christians retained the image they had begun to hold, of Christ as Sun of Truth, Sun of Resurrection and Sun of Salvation. (Pl. 86)

1, 2 Cybele, one of the most familiar forms of the Great Mother-goddess (pp. 26–29), is seen in this Roman bronze riding in a car drawn by lions, and carrying the musical instruments used in her worship. In the Coptic textile (*below*) she dismisses an unfaithful attendant (p. 30). Both Metropolitan Museum of Art, New York.

3–5 *Above, left,* a bronze medallion of Lucilla depicting Cybele, with her turreted crown and an ornamental tympanum, riding side-saddle on a lion. Closely similar is the Antoninus Pius medallion, *right,* of Diana Lucifera riding side-saddle on a winged, horned panther. Both specimens in the British Museum. *Below,* a relief of an *archigallus,* high priest of Cybele, in the Capitoline Museum, Rome. He wears his robes and is flanked by the implements of his profession.

6–9 Four guises of the Great Mother: *left*, from the Louvre, the many-breasted Artemis of Ephesus (for other interpretations, cf. p. 21); *above*, Venus Victrix with globe and palm branch, on a gold aureus of Julia Domna; *below*, *left*, an altar to the Celtic Mother-goddesses (p. 16), in Bonn; *below*, *right*, Isis with jar and *sistrum*, in the Capitoline Museum, Rome.

MATRONIS
AVFANIABVS
QVETTIVS SEVERVS
QVAESTOR C.C.A.A
VOTVM SOLVIT L·M

10–12 Three Greek Imperial coins from eastern Mediterranean mints. The first was struck at Ephesus during the reign of Antoninus Pius. Zeus as sky-god is enthroned on Mt Coressus. He holds a thunderbolt and is showering rain upon the recumbent god of the other mountain, Pion. The design is evidently copied from a sacral-idyllic painting (pp. 33, 67); in the background a tree and shrine can be discerned. *Centre*, the great temple at Baalbek, on a coin of Septimius Severus (p. 35). *Below*, from the same reign, the altar of Zeus at Pergamum with its steps and baldachin (p. 33).

13, 14 *Left*, Jupiter Dolichenus wearing a Phrygian cap and accompanied by his bull and eagle (p. 35), in a characteristic group from the Capitoline Museum, Rome. *Opposite*, a bronze benevolent representation of Jupiter Optimus Maximus with cloak and thunderbolt, in Florence (p. 34).

15–18 Four medallions in the British Museum showing Jupiter: in a chariot (Antoninus Pius); protecting Marcus Aurelius and Lucius Verus; with the Seasons (Commodus); and with globe and Victory (Diocletian) (pp. 41–43).

19, 20 Jupiter with the emperor: *left*, on a gold aureus of Septimius Severus and, *right*, on a bronze antoninianus of Aurelian. Even with the predominance of the sun Jupiter was not forgotten (pp. 41–43).

24, 25 The great gold Arras medallion (*above*, from an electrotype in the British Museum) shows Constantius Chlorus returning to London as Restorer of the Eternal Light. In the fourth century, Constantine still has SOLI INVICTO COMITI on his coins (*below* – cf. pp. 45, 52, 55).

21–23 The increasing prominence of the Sun under the Empire. *Top*, from the first century AD, Nero with the rayed crown of the Sun-god on a bronze dupondius. From the third century, period of the Sun's triumph: *centre*, the sacred betyl carried in triumph, on a gold aureus of Elagabalus with the legend SANCT DEO SOLI ELAGABAL; *below*, the god, named SOL, noble and Apolline, on a bronze antoninianus of Aurelian, who made him supreme.

26, 27 Two Mithraic reliefs with scenes of the myth. In the upper, from the Louvre, Mithras and the Sun recline in fellowship on the hide of the bull, laid out to give the appearance of a cave. Two torch-bearers may be seen, one passing up a drinking horn, the other holding back Ahriman's power with a *caduceus*. The moon turns away. *Below*, the bull-slaying, in the Antiquario Communale, Rome. The bull's tail sprouts in a corn-ear and Ahriman's snake and scorpion can be clearly seen, as well as Mithras's hound and raven. To the left is a small representation of Mithras dragging the bull into the cave (p. 47).

28 Mithraism is closely involved with astrology. On some monuments Ahriman, the opponent of Ahura-Mazda, is portrayed with lion's head, and snake spiralling round his body; sometimes the signs of the zodiac are seen. A power of light, perhaps Mithras himself, has replaced Ahriman on this relief in Modena, and offers hope for the journey through the heavenly spheres. There is some evidence that it may have been originally an Orphic relief of the power Phanes, re-used by followers of Mithras (pp. 48, 102, 153).

CHAPTER IV

THE DIVINE
FUNCTIONARIES

IN THEIR DIFFERENT WAYS the Mother, the sky-god and the sun-god
all tend to be part of an emergent monotheism. But that monotheism is in continual tension with a functional, natural, personal,
local diversity of gods.

Henri Bergson in his remarkable work *The Two Sources of
Morality and Religion* argued that in what he called the Closed
Society the prime function of religion is the preservation of the
social order. Religion provides the supernatural sanctions and
tabus which stand in the path of change; it checks the challenge of
intelligence by a religious order circumscribing it on all sides.
Bergson, a scholar of solid merit, illustrates his thesis by the
spirit-world of India, China and Japan, and of the Greeks and
Romans. He rightly points to this as the primal and popular
religion of Greece, and as the continuing basis of Roman religion.
Literary, and indeed literate, evidence in general tends to depict
the life of the city rather than the life of the country, and when it
portrays the latter, to romanticize it. But in the country ancient
religions persist when the more sophisticated town-dwellers have
outgrown them and the less sophisticated have strayed to novel-
ties. Of this the very name of 'pagan' reminds us, meaning, as it
does, 'a countryman'.

We start then from the countryside. 'For the consciousness of
the Greek,' wrote Zielinski long ago, 'dead nature did not exist;
all nature was life, spirit, divinity.' Scratch a spring and find a
naiad, scratch a river and find a god, scratch a tree and find a
dryad, dive below the sea's surface and find the nereids. Beware
how you walk in the country: you may encounter Pan—to
Vergil a shepherd's god, to Servius the whole of nature (his horns

standing for the rays of the sun and the crescent moon, his red face the celestial fire, his dappled fawnskin the stars, his hairiness trees, shrubs and wild animals, his goat-feet the solidity of earth, the seven reeds of his pipe the harmony of the spheres, and his boomerang the cycle of the year), but to the casual passer-by, nature in the raw, the very spirit of the wild, the cause of panic fear. So with the Romans: Catullus, Vergil, Tibullus, Ovid are instinct with the power of the divine in the countryside. There is among ancient writers less enjoyment of beautiful scenery than is sometimes thought: there is appreciation of shade and comfort, there is a sense of the dangerous strength of nature and consequent relief when she proves innocent, there is a solid sense of utility, and there is the divine, the numinous, *das Heilige*. Mountains were places of worship, the throne of Zeus, the place from which to pray for rain. On the Little St Bernard Pass P. Blattius Creticus, with his own hand guiding the metal punch, stamped an inscription POENINO SACRVM, 'sacred to Poeninus'. Apollonius in Philostratus' fantasy lifts up his eyes to the mountain-summit because it is the home of gods. Trees were sacred: Pliny the elder has a long section on the subject. There was a sacred fig-tree on the Palatine. Augustus put a palm-shoot among his household gods; the emperors had a grove of laurels at Veii, plucking a branch to carry in triumph and replanting it; the Flavians had their own oak. Groves were especially sacred; witness Vergil or Ovid or Lucan.

> In this grove, on this hill with its leafy summit
> some god lives—though I do not know who it is.

For rivers and other waters the evidence is overpowering, and James R. Smith compiled a truly monumental volume on *Springs and Wells in Greek and Roman Literature*. Here is the younger Pliny on the source of the Clitumnus:

Near it there is an ancient and venerable temple. In it stands Clitumnus himself, clothed, and draped in a crimson-bordered robe: the oracular lots around him show that his divinity is present and can foretell coming events. Around this temple there are several smaller shrines, each with its own god. Every one has its own cult, its own name, and some even their own springs.

Many inscriptions testify gratitude to the nymphs for the discovery or rediscovery of springs. (*Pls.* 33, 34)

In general the frescoes portraying country scenes show us an aspect of the countryside which is sometimes forgotten. Nearly always there is a shrine, or a sacred tree; often there is a procession of worshippers. In *Paris on Mount Ida* there is a statue of Priapus, an arch crowned with two vases, and the mountain-god of Ida reclining in the distance. Another painting, also in Naples, shows a pastoral scene with a gorge. A shepherd is pushing a reluctant ram into a sacred precinct for sacrifice; across the gorge is an indistinct statue, perhaps of Diana or Silvanus. A fresco from Boscotrecase shows a rocky island, with a deity seated by a lone tree, a tall column decorated with shields and topped with a bronze vase, a cylindrical shrine covered with shields and garlands and roofed in red tiles, an ithyphallic herm on a pedestal, and two shrines in the distance. From the same villa comes *Polyphemus and Galatea* in New York, a pastoral landscape with a goddess on a column bearing a horn of plenty, a sacred tree, a porphyry column decked with shields and topped with a bronze vase, and a distant shrine. In the House of Livia at Rome one can hardly see the landscape for shrines and statues. When all allowance has been made for a standardized 'sacral-idyllic' style of painting, there must be some basis in fact; the countryside was littered with holy places. So Strabo describes the mouth of the Alpheus: 'The whole tract is full of shrines of Artemis, Aphrodite, and the nymphs, in flowery groves, due mainly to the abundance of water; there are numerous herms on the road, and shrines of Poseidon on the headlands by the sea.' As Martin Nilsson says in commenting on this passage, one could hardly have taken a step out of doors without meeting a little shrine, a sacred enclosure, an image, a sacred stone, or a sacred tree. He rightly calls it, not the highest, but the most persistent form of Greek religion.

Roman religion had a rare proliferation of spirits or *numina*. German scholars called them *Sondergötter*, gods of a special function, or, more picturesquely, *Augenblickgötter*, gods of the twinkling of an eye. They are powers, involved in or presiding over a limited but necessary operation, and having no existence apart from that operation. These powers are found chiefly in the life of the family and the work of the fields. They were especially important in those difficult transitional periods which Van Gennep has taught us to call *rites de passage*. Birth is one. Alemona looked after the foetus, Nona and Decima watched the critical months of gestation, Partula was responsible for parturition. Lucina, Candelifera and the Carmentes helped to bring the child to the light. A magical ceremony followed in which an axe, stake and broom were used to drive away evil spirits, and appeal was made to Intercidona, Pilumnus and Deverra, 'Cleaver', 'Staker' and 'Sweeper'. Cunina guarded the cradle; Vagitanus induced the first cry; Rumina watched over breast-feeding; Edusa and Potina were in charge of eating and drinking; Fabulinus induced the first lisping words, Statulinus the first attempts to stand; and it was Abeona and Adeona who preserved the child's going-out and coming-in. Marriage was another dangerous period; we need mention only Cinxia who had to do with the proper girding of the bride, and Unxia who was concerned with the anointing of the bridegroom's door. 'Would these gods have no names if the bridegrooms' doors were not anointed with fat by the brides?' asked the Christian Arnobius with some sarcasm. Among these family powers we may note some who enjoyed a more continuous existence: the Genius of the man and the Juno of the woman were regarded as present through the whole period of fertility, not just in the act of procreation, and the Lar Familiaris was an ancestral spirit brought into the house from the land around. (*Pl. 35*)

For the agricultural *numina*, Fabius Pictor tells us that the *flamen*, in sacrificing to Tellus and Ceres, invoked the following powers: Vervactor for the first ploughing, Redarator for the second, Imporcitor for the harrowing, Insitor for the sowing, Obarator for the top-dressing, Occator, Sarritor, Subrincator, Messor, Convector, Conditor, Promitor for the later operations. We can add to the list Spiniensis for uprooting thorn-bushes, Sterculius for manuring, Puta for pruning, Nodutus for grain-stalks, Mellonia for bees. The name Saturnus looks as if it may have original associations with sowing, and Neptunus with watering. Family life and agriculture were of predominant importance, but when in the reign of Commodus an intrusive fig-tree had to be removed from a shrine, the Arval Brethren invoked Adolenda, Commolenda and Deferunda, 'Burner', 'Smasher' and 'Carter'. The evidence for this pattern of religion extends from republican times to Augustine, and Pater did well to draw it sympathetically in *Marius the Epicurean*, where he calls it 'a religion of usage and sentiment rather than of fact and belief', and 'a sense of conscious powers external to ourselves, pleased or displeased by the right or wrong conduct of every circumstance of daily life'. It was a relevant religion; it dealt with the things which matter in life and revealed a desire to be right with the powers behind the universe in life's central concerns.

Of Celtic religion we can here give only the briefest summary, but it will be useful to place it alongside the Graeco-Roman systems. There are many unsolved problems in the study of the Celtic gods. They show a complex polytheism with many strands. Thus we have a thunder-god Taranis (the name is found in different forms); a hammer-god Sucellus; Esus, probably a tree-god in origin; Teutates (again various forms are found), probably a god of the tribe organized for war, Mars as opposed to Quirinus; Maponus, a god of youth; Belenus, a sun-god; Grannus, a god of healing springs; Ogmius, a god of speech. There are war-gods too numerous to name. There are some gods with animal connections: Tarvos Trigaranos, the bull with the three cranes or three horns; Moccus, a god of pigs; Artio, a bear-goddess; Epona, a horse-goddess; and a stag-god whose name is unknown. There are deities of rivers, springs and wells, like Nemausus, the spring at Nîmes, Icauna, the Yonne, and Sequana, the Seine; it is notable that Patrick found the Irish of his day making offering to a well called Slan, 'health-giving', and that Columba did battle with the spirits of a spring in Scotland. There are other tree-gods besides Esus; inscriptions from the Pyrenees speak of the Divine Beech and of the Six Trees. There are sea-gods like Manannen. All of nature was divine. In Ireland oaths were taken by the elements— heaven, earth, sun, fire, moon, sea, land, day, night and the like. So Gildas proclaims that mountains, fountains, hills and rivers which once received divine honours are subservient to man, and Kentigern rebukes the Cambrians for worshipping the elements which are divinely appointed for man's use. There is a mysterious three-headed divinity, who has been identified with Cernunnos, apparently a god of abundance. The exact significance of the triplicity is controversial, but the number three was sacred in Celtic thought, and triads recur with schematic frequency. Nor must we forget the popular Mother-goddesses. The total impression, whether from the inscriptions of Gaul or the myths of Ireland and Wales, is of a sprawling, vital complexity, close to life and functional (*Pls.* 8, 37–39, 73, 81–83)

When we come to the Graeco-Roman pantheon the general picture is more familiar. The Homeric poems, if not exactly the Bible of the Greeks, certainly were more instrumental than any other single factor in shaping the picture of the gods, and for the average person continued to do so throughout the ancient world. Already the subordinate gods are assuming specialized functions. Hera has become the guardian of marriage; Poseidon's realm is the sea; Apollo is a sun-god (not all would accept this) whose rays spread pestilence like arrows; Artemis is the goddess of wild nature, the mistress of animals; Hermes is the messenger of the gods, but retains his ancient association with the cairn, with travellers and thieves, with success in business and the lucky chance, a popular lively trickster, like Ananse in West Africa or Coyote in America; Ares, whatever his origin, is the war-god; Aphrodite is the goddess of love; Athene is something of a warrior-maid, a Valkyrie, but wise and the patron of craftsmen; Hephaestus, the god of fire, is naturally associated with smiths and technology. In Greece the Olympians became from early times state-gods. In 405 BC a decree giving Athenian citizenship to Samians is illustrated by Hera and Athene shaking hands. Athene is the divinity of Athens, Hera of Argos and Samos, Apollo of Sparta, Miletus and Cyrene, Artemis of Ephesus, Heracles of

Thasos, Priapus of Lampsacus. But this is only one functional aspect. In general they are and remain universal, each with his own sphere of reference, and it is not unjust to think of them as divine functionaries.

In Rome the *numina*, asexual in origin (the shepherds' god Pales is found in the masculine and feminine, and even the name of Venus is neuter in form), began to take on personalities. Some of them were inherent in an object rather than a process, Janus in the door, Vesta in the hearth, the Penates in the store, Ceres in the corn, Terminus in the boundary-stone. Contact with the Greeks led to the assimilation of the Greek and Roman pantheons, and Greek myths began to attach to Roman gods; by their very nature the *Sondergötter* had no myth. Jupiter was already Zeus. Juno, the power of fertility in women, became Hera with all her attributes and myths. Mars, perhaps a storm-god, though the matter is highly controversial, became involved with agriculture and war, identified with Ares, and in literature and art though not in ritual was solely associated with war. Minerva, an Etruscan craft-goddess, was counterpart to Pallas Athene. Diana, a power of the wildwood, was assimilated to Artemis. Venus, a garden-*numen*, because of her association with growth, was one with Aphrodite, the power of sex. Neptunus became Poseidon, Volcanus (a volcano-*numen*) Hephaestus. Mercurius, a mercantile power, was deemed equivalent to Hermes, and so became messenger to the gods. Others who had no obvious link, acquired personality without myth, and remained shadowy. Such was Silvanus, a power of the wildwood on the fringes of the farm, or Janus. Quirinus is an interesting case. He was the power of peaceful assembly; the Romans in their civil capacity were called Quirites. He might have been identified with Apollo, but this was not done, and he was left stranded. But he was too important for such lack of definition, and at a quite late stage became identified with Romulus, the legendary founder of Rome. By the imperial period the familiar pantheon was long established. Each god or goddess had his particular sphere of reference, and the worshipper would approach the divinity appropriate to his need. A trivial instance may drive the point home. At Lyons there was an inn,

'The Mercury and Apollo'; over the door was the hexameter *Mercurius lucrum hic promittit Apollo salutem*, 'Apollo for health; from Mercury wealth'. In addition each god had a variety of cult-titles. It is hard to be sure how far a worshipper might regard, say, Mars Gradivus and Mars Ultor as different beings, or whether he merely thought that a different title, ritual and shrine were appropriate in approaching the same god for a different purpose. (*Pls.* 4, 7, 29–32, 78)

The habit of looking for *numina* died hard, and in a more sophisticated age took new forms. This has been termed the worship of divine abstractions; a clear enough definition, yet misleading if it leads us to think of a process of ratiocination rather than a sense of immediate power. The practice goes far back into republican times; thus the temple to Salus, Health, on the Quirinal is dated to 302 BC. Already in the second century BC Plautus is making fun of such abstractions—Munditia, and Sancta Saturitas, and Iocus, Ludus, Sermo and Suavisuaviatio (the power of Delight in Kissing). But it was greatly intensified in imperial times and fostered through imperial propaganda by association with the emperor's 'virtues'. Now Pietas, who had a temple in 191 BC, reappears as Pietas Augusta; a name like Antoninus Pius is a religious name; Pietas (not quite our 'piety') is pressed into propaganda so as to foster family solidarity and patriotism. Pax, Peace, is scarcely found before Augustus; now Pax and Pax Augusta are invoked. From the time of Tiberius, Providentia, Forethought, who is a divinity in her own right by the second century AD, and Liberalitas, Generosity, who becomes by the second century the spirit of the emperor's donative, are important powers for imperial propaganda. Salus achieves a revived prominence as Salus Augusta. Libertas is filched from the republicans and made to stand for constitutional government. Fides, Faith or Loyalty, had a temple from 254 BC; in imperial times coins commemorate the Loyalty of the emperor, and the Loyalty of the legions—religious slogans; the symbol of Loyalty is a pair of covered hands. Disciplina is also important for the legions. Virtus escapes from the philosophers and reverts to its old meaning of Military Prowess. Victoria is closely associated; she is also close to Jupiter. A number of powers relate to prosperity including Moneta, the spirit of the Mint, Abundantia and Ubertas and Felicitas, all standing for agricultural prosperity, and Aequitas, the principle of fair dealing. Clementia is a reminder of the emperor's absolute power and his kindness in not using it. It passes to the phrase CLEMENTIA TEMPORVM, 'the mildness of the times', an expression found under Hadrian and later; Probus is shown receiving the orb of power from a divinity, with this inscription. But its personal element was not lost. Diocletian and Constantine were addressed as *tua clementia*. Some of these, notably Pax and Victoria, found their place in Christian thinking; Victoria became the type of the Christian angel, and the inscription AVGVSTA IN PACE relating to Gallienus' Christian wife Salonina is a skilful blend of pagan and Christian language.

We may see the persistence of the pantheon in the cities of Asia Minor. Consider remote Iconium, where we can trace the worship of Zeus-Jupiter, Apollo (whose temple was re-equipped at private expense), Demeter (almost certainly), Dionysus, Hera, Pluto and the Dioscuri, as well as Dike and Nemesis, and the heroes Heracles and Perseus; no doubt these were fusions with local gods, but it is in their Greek form that they appear. It was at nearby Lystra that Barnabas and Paul were identified with Zeus and Hermes; from the third century AD comes the dedication of a statue of Hermes the Great and a sundial to Zeus. In the Troad the great temple belonged to Apollo Smintheus; Athene Ilias and Aphrodite were also prominent. At Sardis we have Artemis as the Mother; Zeus, who grew in prominence during the Roman period; Dionysus, who patronized the theatre, and whose statue was found somewhat oddly in the Christian 'House of the Bronzes'; Athene, less prominent in the Roman period; Apollo, with subsidized worship under the Romans. Coins of the Empire add Demeter, who is also attested by a letter of Apollonius, Aphrodite, Nike (Victory) and the river-god Hermus. At Ephesus we meet in Roman times, apart from Artemis and Zeus, Demeter, Pluto and Kore, Dionysus and Hephaestus, Apollo in various guises, Hermes, Poseidon, Athene (whose statuette was presented to the Artemisium by C. Vibius Salutaris) and others. At Magnesia-on-the-Maeander coins and inscriptions identify for us cults of Aphrodite, Athene and Hephaestus, Hermes, Helios, Pan and Demeter. Idle to elaborate further; there is no evidence here of cult in decay.

If we would see something of the hold which the traditional polytheism retained in Rome itself, we may look at the temple foundations and restorations. By the end of the Republic the traditional religion had fallen into neglect, and Horace, the former Epicurean, pleaded that the favour of the gods, *pax deorum*, would not be renewed until the shrines were rebuilt. Augustus set about this. His new foundations were to the Divine Julius, Apollo on the Palatine, Jupiter the Thunderer, Mars the Avenger, and Vesta. Other foundations of the period are the Pantheon, and the temples of Concord and of Castor. Augustus claims in *Res Gestae* to have restored eighty-two temples, and Livy attests his personal interest in the work: among the eighty-two deities were Diana, Flora, Juno Regina, the Lares, Minerva, the Penates, Hercules and the Muses, Jupiter on the Capitol, Juventas, Jupiter the Supporter (Stator), and Consus. His successors followed the policy: under Tiberius we have foundations to Augustus himself, Fors Fortuna, Flora, Ceres Liber and Libera, Janus and Spes, under Caligula to Isis, under Claudius to Jupiter Depulsor on the Capitoline, and a restoration of the temple of Salus. (*Pl. 31*)

After the disasters of AD 69, and with the centenary of Augustus, Vespasian appeared as 'the restorer of the temples and of public ceremony'. Apart from the restoration of the Capitol there were temples to Claudius, Glory and Courage, Peace, and Jupiter the Preserver. Domitian, a great supporter of religion, restored the temples of Palatine Apollo and of Augustus, and the Atrium of Vesta, and built new foundations to Janus Quadrifrons, the gens Flavia (on the Quirinal), Isis, Jupiter the Guardian, Minerva (whose Quinquatria he celebrated with great splendour), Minerva Chalcidica, Fortuna Redux. It will be noted that new deities are coming in alongside the old, but the old remain.

The second century AD saw fewer foundations; there was far more building in the provinces, less at Rome. Still, Hadrian's reign saw a foundation to Venus and Rome on the Via Sacra (a temple which was actually renovated in the early-fourth century

AD), as well as the monumental elaboration of the Pantheon. His biographer says that his scorn for foreign religion was matched by his care for the traditional Roman. The plaques which found their way on to the Arch of Constantine show appropriate sacrifices to Apollo, Diana, Silvanus and Hercules. Under Antoninus Pius, to take another example, there was a temple to Juno Sospita, the goddess of Lanuvium, restoration of the temples of Bacchus, Aesculapius and Augustus, and an extension of the Atrium of Vesta; this last was further elaborated under the Severan dynasty. Outside the foundations we have the rituals of the Arval Brethren. These are used, rightly, as indirect evidence of early religion at Rome; it is not always remembered that they are direct evidence of what was going on up to AD 241. Thus it was in AD 183 that a fig-tree broke through the roof of the temple of Dea Dia. The Arval Brethren offered atonement to Mars, Dea Dia, Janus, Jupiter, Juno, the divine Virgins, the divine Famuli, the Lares, the Mother of the Lares, any god or goddess protecting the place and grove, Fons, Hora, Mother Vesta, the Vesta of gods and goddesses, Breaker, Burner, Carter and sixteen divinities from the imperial house; the ancient ritual has been extended, but it is the ancient ritual still. Again, the survival of the hymn of the Arval Brethren, one of the most famous pieces of archaic Latin, is in fact based on a protocol of AD 218. (*Pls.* 30, 32)

The Severan dynasty are sometimes regarded as archorientalizers. There was no doubt a broadening of horizons, but the Secular Games of AD 204 were celebrated in a traditional ritual which actually prayed for the loyalty of the Latins to Rome and thus went back to the early days of the Republic. The ritual carefully echoes the Augustan ritual, which we know so well; there was a hymn corresponding to Horace's hymn, and sung in the same way by twenty-seven girls. Another interesting piece of evidence is a Latin papyrus from Dura-Europos, which may be dated within a year to AD 226. It is a part of a list of festivals, and although the document comes from the eastern fringes of Roman penetration it shows little trace of orientalization, and does not even mention the Attis March festival. Restorations under Severus include the temples of Peace, Vespasian, Jupiter the Supporter and Juno Regina, and the House of the Vestals and Temple of Vesta. Severus Alexander's biographer tells us that he was jealous for the ancient priestly colleges of Rome, and our evidence is that the traditional polytheism remained strong well into the third century AD. Lucian's conservative might complain that the trusted gods were being ousted by upstarts and interlopers, but the evidence of inscriptions confirms the continuing popularity of the old and familiar gods.

CHAPTER V

TYCHE

ONE OF THE MORE INTERESTING DEITIES of the Greek-speaking world is Tyche, Chance or Fortune. It is sometimes said that she was a product of the Hellenistic age and its uncertainties, but this is not true. She appears as a Nereid already in the Homeric hymn to Demeter and as a daughter of Ocean in Hesiod's *Theogony*. Archilochus says that *tyche* and *moira*, chance and fate, control our destiny, though these are not necessarily personified. In a fragment Pindar calls Tyche one of the Moirai. In one of the Olympian odes the poet prays to Tyche as the saviour-goddess and daughter of Zeus the Deliverer, but in another passage suggests that such prayers are idle as the goddess has a 'double rudder'. Similarly in the dramatists the thought of chance or fortune naturally recurs, sometimes personified. It is perhaps significant of a contemporary popular belief that many of these references are put into the mouths of relatively humble speakers. So the herald in Aeschylus' *Agamemnon*, describing the storm:

> *Some god—no human hand—gripped our helm*
> *and Fortune, our saviour, sat smiling on our deck.*

So again the sentinel in Sophocles' *Antigone*:

> *... but whether*
> *he's caught or not—Fortune will decide that—*
> *you won't catch me coming here again in a hurry*

or the messenger of the final disaster:

> *From day to day Fortune raises and Fortune humbles*
> *the fortunate and unfortunate alike.*

In Euripides such references are extremely frequent. (*Pl.* 40)

That fortune was a problem for the philosophy of the thought-
ful is obvious. They stood aside from her deification, and ration-
alized. This can be seen clearly among the philosophers. By a
curious quirk, in natural philosophy Tyche comes very close to
physical determinism, for it is the realm where purpose—divine
or human—does not operate. Plato actually has the phrase 'in
accordance with Chance out of necessity'. In human events
Aristotle has an acute discussion, which remained Peripatetic
orthodoxy. A chance event takes place when a man, performing
an action purposively, achieves a result which he might have, but
did not in fact, seek purposively, as for example when a man digs
his garden to plant some vegetables and happens on a buried
treasure. Epicurus rejected this conception of Chance as a 'fickle
cause', as he rejected the popular notion of Chance as a fickle goddess, and substituted, for Democritus' random movement of the
atoms, a movement governed by scientific law combined with an
indeterminate swerve governed not by Chance but by free will.
Equally the Stoics with their pantheistic determinism had no
place for Chance, though the Roman Stoics, influenced by the
Italian goddess Fortuna, did make some distinction between Fate
and Fortune. In Seneca Fortune appears in relation to external
goods, and is treated almost as Satan in the book of *Job*, a divine
servant whose task is to test and assay. In Lucan Fate is the impersonal working-out of the divine law, Fortune is the direct intervention of God; Fate is deistic, Fortune theistic. An exceptionally
interesting comment on the Stoic position comes from Servius,
the fourth-century AD commentator on Vergil. On Vergil's line

Omnipotent Fortune and ineluctable Fate

he comments: 'He was writing in accordance with Stoic views;
they attribute birth and death to Fate and everything in between
to Fortune. For everything in human life is uncertain. That is why
he put the two together, to show the complete doctrine, so to
speak. In fact nothing is so opposite to Fate as Chance (*casus*), but
he was writing according to the Stoic view.' In this passage we see
something of the problems of the rationalists. As late as the fourth
century AD the problem was still there. Sallustius, Julian's friend

and associate, in a statement which forms a kind of manifesto of the pagan revival, turns away from his predominant neo-Platonism to make a concession to popular belief. He has been discussing Providence and Fate. He proceeds,

> Further, as there is Providence and Fate concerned with nations and cities, and also concerned with each individual, so there is also Fortune, which should next be treated. The power of the gods which orders for the good things which are not uniform, and which happen contrary to expectation, is commonly called Fortune, and it is for this reason that the goddess is especially worshipped in public by cities; for every city consists of elements which are not uniform. Fortune has power beneath the moon, since above the moon no single thing can happen by fortune. If Fortune makes a wicked man prosperous and a good man poor, there is no need to wonder. For the wicked regard wealth as everything, the good as nothing. And the good fortune of the bad cannot take away their badness, while virtue alone will be enough for the good.

A good example of the popular view under the Empire may be seen in a passage of the elder Pliny. All through the world, he says, Fortuna alone is invoked; she is the one defendant, the one culprit, the one thought in men's minds, the one object of praise, the one cause. She is worshipped with insults, courted as fickle and often as blind, wandering, inconsistent, elusive, changeful, and friend of the unworthy. 'We are so much at the mercy of Chance (*sors*),' he concludes, 'that Chance is our god.' Pliny is here plainly drawing on his knowledge of the Greek world; he is speaking of Tyche. Another interesting witness is Plutarch, who wrote three lectures, one on the Fortune of the Romans, and two on the Fortune of Alexander. Where Pliny views Tyche under the guise of Fortuna, Plutarch views Fortuna under the guise of Tyche. In all three lectures he is wrestling with the problem of the parts played by Chance and Excellence in shaping our lives. He at one point makes an amusing distinction: Excellence is noble but un-profitable, Chance is irremediable but good. His analysis does not wholly bear this out. In fact he sees Alexander as fighting against

Tyche all through his career; we might almost say that Alexander's *fortuna* consisted in his mastering *tyche*. But in speaking of the Romans he suggests that it was the benignity of Tyche which led to the death of Alexander and left the world open to Rome. There's the rub; it so often happens that one man's good fortune is another man's misfortune. Plutarch concludes that to produce the triumph of Rome Chance and Excellence have combined. Again we find the popular view, as might be expected, in Seneca. His little essay on *Providence* is really an attack on the power of Chance, and his distinctive affirmation is that good men are not dragged on by Chance; they follow her, keep pace with her, and would outstep her if they could. Herskovits, the distinguished anthropologist, writing of Africa, once spoke of 'the deification of Accident in a universe where predetermination is the rule'. Exactly.

In the novelists Tyche appears as a hostile force holding the lovers apart. Thus in Chariton's *Chaereas and Callirhoe*, written in the second century AD, Fortune causes the troubles and disasters, but Aphrodite reunites the lovers. In the first book Callirhoe is sold as a slave, and blames Fortune; when pregnant she blames Fortune for letting her produce a slave-child; by the waters of Babylon she blames Fortune for persecuting a solitary girl. Mithridates tells Chaereas that his position springs from the whims of Fortune. Queen Statira in captivity blames Fortune for her enslavement. The author reinforces the words he puts in the mouths of his characters by his own comments. Tyche here is not blind chance, but a malevolent power. In Achilles Tatius' *Leucippe and Clitophon* the attacks on Tyche are less frequent, but they are there, as when Leucippe in disguise pleads with Melitte to spare her since she is 'through Fortune's will a slave'.

In Apuleius' *Metamorphoses* the theme is at its strongest, especially in the last part. 'Relentless Fortune gave me (*sc*. Lucius) over to new torments.' 'Fortune, that could not have enough of my torments, had devised a new pain for me.' 'Fortune, ever bent on my distress, put an end with hideous swiftness to my happy escape, and set new snares for me.' 'But that savage Fortune of mine, from whom I fled through so many lands but could not escape, and whom all the miseries I had undergone did not appease, once more turned her blind eyes upon me.' The illogical and contradictory nature of the concept is nowhere clearer than in those words, but popular thought, which Apuleius is expressing, is not logical and does not boggle at contradictions. 'Assuredly, if Fortune is against it, nothing good can come to mortal man.' In the end he is rescued by Isis, as Chariton's lovers are rescued by Aphrodite, and in a long and moving speech she expresses her supremacy over Fortune, as in the well-known aretalogy from Cyme she expresses her supremacy over Destiny. She describes Lucius as 'driven by the violent storms of Fortune and buffeted about by her highest winds'. But Fortune, in her blindness, by his very ordeals has only brought him to religious felicity. Now he is safe under the protecting care of another Fortune, one who is not blind. Lucius triumphs over his Fortune by the providence of Isis. This is a magnificent and illuminating passage. In all these novels Fortune is blind because she does not favour the good; she is personal; she is malevolent; she is close to Destiny or Fate, conceived as hostile.

In the extraordinary magical papyrus preserved in Paris and expounded by Dieterich in *Eine Mithrasliturgie* we have a vivid expression of the persistent power of Tyche in various guises. The opening invocation is to Pronoia (Providence) and Tyche, and in the course of the document there is reference to the seven Tychai of the sky. These are plainly the sun, moon, and five planets which are seen as presiding over human destiny.

As a final example of the popular view we may take the evidence of epitaphs. Their tone is one of almost unrelieved hostility to the goddess. She is incalculable, mightier than hope, utterly unjust, bitter, envious of all that are good, inescapable. 'Here I, Phileremus, lie a dead body, the object coveted by Tyche's tyranny, dragged from life by the very spirits.' The mood extends widely in both space and time. Tyche is described as jealous of goodness, as mightier than hope, as an incalculable divinity, as committing every crime. Time and again it is said to be impossible to escape from her and her 'gifts'. The testimony ranges from Marseilles to Asia, and from the classical period of Greece to the late Empire. In all there is only one favourable acknowledgment of the goddess.

But it was difficult for Tyche to remain as mere chance; she acquired other associations. The Agathos Daemon was, it seems, a primitive fertility spirit, and honoured in the form of a snake. No doubt, like other primitive *numina*, the spirit was originally not differentiated sexually, but in classical times on the mainland of Greece it tended to appear as male. It was natural that the male spirit should acquire a female consort. This was Agathe Tyche, Good Fortune. We meet her at the curious oracle of Trophonius at Lebadeia in Boeotia, where enquirers had to lodge in a building sacred to Agathos Daemon and Agathe Tyche. Sometimes the Agathos Daemon is identified with Zeus; at drinking-parties, according to *The Suda*, unmixed wine was drunk to Agathos Daemon till the stirrup-cup which was in honour of Zeus the Saviour. Zeus was beginning to claim the place of the ancient *numen*. This helps to explain a very remarkable Athenian relief of the fourth century BC, now in Copenhagen, where Zeus Philius is depicted with the cornucopiae and Agathe Tyche is his consort; Philia is described as the god's mother. It also helps to explain the association at Elis between Tyche and Sosipolis; Sosipolis is Zeus Soter under a variant name, and he is also associated with the snake as Agathos Daemon. Here Tyche appears as mother rather than wife, and the god was represented as a child. Similarly at Thebes Pausanias saw a more sophisticated statue of Tyche carrying the child Plutus, Wealth; the child is either a substitute for the Agathos Daemon, or his offspring, or both. On the island of Melos a relief showing a similar scene was recovered from the hall of the Dionysiac Mysteries: there the goddess has her full title, in this aspect, of Agathe Tyche.

In Asia, where the great Mother-goddess was long established, Tyche naturally tended to become yet another of her manifestations. In this she is associated, as A. B. Cook has shown, with a mountain peak, appropriately to a nature-goddess in mountainous country (we may remember how the initiates of Cybele in Catullus' poem rush to the mountain-heights). The Tyche of Antioch is depicted seated on a mountain throne, alike on coins and in the

famous statue. A coin of Barata struck by Otacilia Severa shows
Tyche with ceremonial basket, branch, and cornucopiae, seated
on a rock, with a river-god at her feet. A long inscription of
Antiochus I of Commagene (c. 69–38 BC) confirms this view of
the goddess. He identified himself with Zeus Oromasdes, and
resolved to be buried on top of the Nemroud Dagh, the highest
mountain in his territory. He aimed, according to the inscription,
which appears on the back of a rock-cut throne, to sanctify the
place as

> the sacred seat of all gods in common, that so not only this
> heroic company of my ancestors which you see might exist
> established by my orders, but also the divine shapes of mani-
> fest deities sanctified on a holy summit, and that they might
> have this place as a witness by no means bereft of my piety.
> For this reason, as you see, I have established these godlike
> effigies of Zeus Oromasdes and Apollo Mithras Helios
> Hermes and Artagnes Heracles Ares and my all-nurturing
> country Commagene. Moreover, made of the selfsame stone-
> work with gods that answer prayer and throned together
> with them, I have set up the fashion of my own likeness, and
> have caused the ancient honour of great deities to become
> coeval with a new Tyche, thereby preserving a just represen-
> tation of the immortal mind which has many a time been
> seen to manifest itself in my support and to lend me friendly
> help in the carrying out of my royal projects. . . .

The figures were colossal, carved out of limestone, and were on
each of three terraces. Zeus Oromasdes, with a beardless figure of
Antiochus on his left, and Commagene on his right, depicted in
the guise of Tyche with ceremonial basket, in her left hand a
cornucopiae, in her right fruit and a sheaf of corn-ears, and on her
head a corn-wreath. The other two syncretistic deities also appear.
Cook suggests that Commagene is identified with Tyche, who
was in turn identified with the great mountain-mother, and that
this is why Antiochus is careful to link himself with the new
Tyche. Additional evidence for Tyche as a form of the nature-
goddess and associated with mountains is seen in the identification

of Zeus Hypsistos with Tyche at Panamara and with Agathe Tyche at Mylasa. The important fact is that Tyche inherits the emotional aura of the Mother-goddess.

In the public life of the Hellenistic and Roman period Tyche became a city-goddess; Simplicius points out that the Tyche of cities is not found in the older period, though Tyche is. Once the Greek *polis* was seen as an organism with (almost) its own individual personality, this was sooner or later inevitable. Already in Pindar Tyche controls the destiny of Himera. But it is in the Hellenistic age that the concept takes on new life. This, not earlier, was the golden period of the Greek *polis*. Political independence was gone, but there was a large measure of local autonomy, and civic pride, loyalty and involvement. It was perhaps in the new foundations that Tyche attained her new status. Early in the third century BC Eutychides fashioned a bronze statue of the Tyche of Antioch, which Pausanias refers to and which survives in replica in the Vatican. The goddess is seated on a rock which represents Mount Silpion; at her feet is a young man who personifies the River Orontes; she bears a sheaf of wheat, symbolizing prosperity, in her right hand; and on her head she wears the turreted crown whose battlements stand for the protection of the city. This statue became the type of all subsequent representations of the Tyche of a city. Such city-goddesses are attested on numerous inscriptions right through the Roman period. We may mention Athens, where the wife of Herodes Atticus was priestess of the Tyche of the city; Thera, where the Tyche of the city appears in the middle of a dedication of public works in AD 149–50; Selgae, where the high-priest of the Tyche of the city held office for life; Mytilene, where the goddess is the Great Tyche of Mytilene; Trapezopolis in Phrygia, where she is the great goddess in defence of the city; Thasos; Stratonicia; Rome, in Latin Fortuna Romana; Syllium in Pamphylia, where there was a most elaborate shrine; Rhodiapolis, where there were two shrines, to Tyche and Nemesis; and, attested by coins, Sicyon, Olbia, Smyrna, Ephesus, Adraene, Edessa, Medaba and Bostra. Sometimes the actual name of the city is appended, sometimes the goddess is called 'the Tyche of the *polis*'. At Opramoa the name Tychopolis is coined out of this.

It is a clear deduction, confirmed in particular instances, that a dedication to Tyche is likely to be a dedication to the city-goddess. (*Pl.* 40)

The Roman Fortuna was originally a goddess of fertility (the name is probably derived from *ferre*, 'to bear') introduced into Rome from outside at an early date. Her fertility function may be seen in the title Fortuna Muliebris (Women's Fortune). In her great centres of Praeneste and Antium she was an oracle-goddess; the method of consultation at Praeneste was to draw a billet of wood inscribed with a helpful motto. But the 'bearer' is also the 'bringer', and an oracle deals in more than fertility. Fortuna did not wholly lose her original character. She retained such titles as Muliebris and Virgo, associating her with womanhood, and Columella shows her as a patron of garden growth. But from the early contact with the Greeks she took on the identity of Tyche. So Pacuvius:

> *Philosophers assert that Fortune's mad, blind, crude,*
> *say she stands on a slippery, round rock,*
> *prophesy that Fortune falls where chance drives the rock,*
> *mad because cruel, fickle, unstable,*
> *blind because she does not see where she is applying herself,*
> *crude because she cannot distinguish good from bad.*

It was an easy identification, and it gave to Fortuna a new lease of life, especially under the Empire: we have seen Pliny's comment. Juvenal was scornful: 'Fortune, it is we, we, who make you a god.' There were many factors which encouraged the widespread belief: the mood of the times, Stoic ideas of destiny, the onset of astrology, the association with Isis, and the like. One of the commoner, though bitterer, of Roman epitaphs runs:

> *I've escaped, I've got clear. Good-bye, Hope and Fortune.*
> *You've nothing on me. Play your tricks on others.*

But, as Kurt Latte has shown, there is one marked distinction between the Roman Fortuna and the Greek Tyche. Tyche is a universal goddess, though she may have particular manifestations; she is 'the bearer of the inexorable fate that is linked to all events'.

But Fortuna is in essence particular. The Fortune of individual cities and of individual people (Fortuna Seiana or Fortuna Flavia) can be paralleled from the Greek world, but not phrases like the Fortune of This Day.

Rome was full of monuments to Fortune. Many were believed to go back to Servius Tullius. But they were there in the imperial period, as Plutarch testifies. Among those of imperial foundation we may mention a temple of Fortune built by Nero within the Golden House; the temple of Fortuna Redux in the Campus Martius, built by Domitian to celebrate his triumphs in Germany, which is probably to be seen in a coin of AD 174 and on a relief incorporated into Constantine's Arch; and a shrine to Fortuna Stata, dedicated in AD 112. The Christian writers attack her under various titles: Tertullian and Augustine make some play with Bearded Fortune; Lactantius also with Fortune the Commander, and Fortune on Horseback.

The chief symbol of Fortune is the wheel, and she stands unstably upon it. In an exquisite Gallo-Roman bronze in Autun she is seen half-mounting. In Gloucester Museum she may be seen with three of her attributes: the cornucopiae indicating the prosperity she diffuses so unpredictably, the rudder symbolizing the direction of life (our word 'governor' comes from the Latin for 'steersman'), and the globe, an ambiguous symbol, conveying the power of Fortune in the totality of the universe, the orb of authority, and at the same time lubricity and instability. Other typical emblems are the ship's prow, wings, the fruit-measure, the corn-ear and the libation-bowl. Here we see the fertility-goddess, giver of prosperity, and we also see an assimilation to Victory. When she is sitting, she is plainly less mobile than when standing. One particularly interesting representation comes from Palestine. It is a marble statue dedicated by a priest named Mercurios and datable to AD 210–11, and represents a winged griffin seated with one paw on an upright wheel. This is the wheel of Fortune, but the griffin is associated rather with Nemesis. The lines are not so much crossed as interwoven; the symbolism is clear. (*Pls.* 41, 78)

The persistence of Tyche is remarkable. Julian sacrificed in her temple at Antioch during his visit of AD 361–62; plainly, whatever temples had been closed, Tyche and Zeus had not suffered. A few years later Libanius petitioned the emperor Theodosius to protect the pagan temples; he mentioned as untouched those of Tyche, Zeus, Athene, and Dionysus. Palladas, writing at Alexandria at the end of the century, found a statue of Tyche in a café and played with the theme.

> *I see the world's all topsy-turvy:*
> *I've seen Fortune in misfortune.*

For him Fortune's a whore drifting with the stream. But he believes in her.

> *A toy of Fortune—*
>> *that's human life, pitiable, all over the place,*
>>> *tossed between*
>>>> *poverty and plenty.*

> *Some she throws down*
>> *then tosses high like a ball;*
>> *others she throws down*
>>> *from heaven to hell.*

Macrobius identifies Tyche with the moon; that he does so shows that she is still there to identify. With Martianus Capella Fortuna is the last in the council of the gods, identified with Tyche, the Etruscan Nortia, Sors (Luck) or Nemesis. But before this, when Constantine built his Christian city of Constantinople he set in it a temple of Fortune, and in that temple a statue of the Fortune of Rome; for the city we call by his name he thought of as New Rome. We see the Tyche of the new city, with cornucopiae in hand and turreted crown on head, enthroned, on silver medallions struck in Constantinople itself. In bronze medallions from Rome she is seen with turreted crown, cornucopiae, wings, and feet on the prow of a ship. Here the Tyche of the new city is assimilated to Victory, and even appears as the Victory of the emperor, VICTORIA AVGVSTI. She was there to protect the New Rome, as the old.

CHAPTER VI

THE SACRED FIGURE OF THE EMPEROR

SACRAL KINGSHIP is widely found in all parts of the world. The sovereign is a mediator between the divine and life on earth; his regalia, the crown, sceptre, orb and throne, proclaim his cosmic function. Upon him the fertility of the harvests depends, his touch heals, he has power over life and death, as representative of the divine order he dispenses justice and is the arbiter of peace and war. In some systems he is ritually killed before his powers can wane; the legendary stories of Osiris and Romulus show the pattern; in each the body is divided and buried in the fields. In others a substitute is provided.

In Rome the ancient kingship had been sacral, as the survival of the Regia as a sacred building (with shrines of Mars and Ops, and religious ceremonies associated with the October horse and the worship of Janus) and the existence of the *rex sacrorum* as a priestly office, may remind us. Elements of sacrosanctity attached to the person of the consul and especially of the tribune. In Egypt the divine kingship was open and unabashed. In the Greek world there had long been a tendency to the heroization of prominent individuals. In legend the hero was in the strict sense a demi-god, the son of a god by a mortal mother. Heracles and Asclepius are good examples. It is important that the hero did not receive divine honours: sacrifice was made so that the offering poured down to the ground rather than ascending to the sky: the link is with the ancestral dead. Such cult was offered to the founders of cities, or at Athens to the victors of Marathon. There were in Greek piety two strains: one emphasized the distance of man from god, the other aspired to equality with the divine. For the Greek world, however, the decisive change came with Alexander. He enlarged the horizons, and his miscellaneous empire demanded new perspectives. In Egypt his divinity was a matter of political necessity: it was made slightly more palatable to the Greeks by his foundation of Alexandria: nowhere in the world could Alexander be denied the title of city-founder. In Persia he was honoured by prostration: whatever this implied to the Persians, to the Greeks it meant divinity. In 324 BC he demanded the recognition of his deity by the Greek states: they acceded, not very seriously. At Sparta the decree ran, 'Since Alexander wants to be a god, let him be a god.' Probably these moves were political. But Alexander is important, a model for ambitious Romans from Pompey to Caracalla.

The Hellenistic age is also important. The mood is now very different. The Athenians received Demetrius with the most fulsome flattery, calling him the only true god, all the others being asleep, absentees or non-existent; they gave him the Parthenon for his palace. There had been no cult of Alexander during his lifetime; now Ptolemy introduced one; the motive was political, the result religious. Ptolemy II deified his predecessor and Berenice, and instituted a festival in their honour; this practice became regular except in Macedon; after their deaths Seleucus became Seleucus Zeus Victor and Antiochus became Apollo Saviour. By the late 270s BC a cult of the reigning monarch was established in Egypt for the Greeks, though it was not identical with the Egyptian ritual. The great divine titles were Saviour and Benefactor. Jesus alludes to the latter: 'The rulers of the Gentiles exercise dominion over them, and those in authority are called Benefactors. But not so with you.' Important too to see that John, the most politically alert of the gospel-writers, is claiming for Jesus what earthly rulers have claimed when he calls him Saviour, as when he calls him Lord and God.

This was the world the Romans encountered, and they succumbed to it. In 212 BC Marcellus was hailed as Saviour of Syracuse and a festival established in his honour. In 195 BC a priesthood to Flamininus was set up at Chalcis, which still survived in Plutarch's day, and a paean composed to Titus, Zeus and Roma, ending: 'Hail Paean Apollo, hail Titus our Saviour.' Roma, a divine creation of the Greeks, was worshipped at Smyrna in 195 BC, and her name was often coupled with the consul or proconsul. At Ephesus there was a shrine of Roma and P. Servilius Isauricus, proconsul from 46 to 44 BC. M' Aquilius received a priest at Pergamum. The notorious Verres was honoured in Sicily. Cicero and his brother were offered honours but refused them. Paullus Fabius Maximus is an interesting case; he was proconsul from 9–4 BC and was associated in the Troad with Apollo in a festival, Smintheia Pauleia, which was still kept in the third century AD. In 167 BC Prusias of Bithynia came to Rome and greeted the senators: 'Hail, Saviour gods.' The Romans were not unaffected. Gaius Marius was hailed as the third founder of Rome and worshipped with offerings of food and drink. Marius Gratidianus received sacrifices of incense and wine. Pompey called himself 'Great' in emulation of Alexander, adopted Alexander's hairstyle, emotional expression, and fashion in clothes, and appeared on coins as Janus. Caesar temporized: the evidence is difficult of interpretation, but he was flirting with the idea of the divinization he received after death. Sextus Pompeius called himself Neptune's son. Mark Antony was openly the oriental divine monarch, Dionysus-Osiris, consort of Cleopatra-Isis, queen of Egypt, and their children were Helios (Sun) and Selene (Moon).

It was Augustus who with his exceptional political flair set the general pattern for the future. In Egypt for practical purposes he had to be the divine ruler; he appears as the inheritor of the Pharaohs with all their honours; to the Greeks of Egypt he is one with Zeus Giver of Freedom, is invoked in oaths, receives temples. Elsewhere he was more cautious. The Greeks had established societies (*koina*) for various purposes, and these became adapted to the ruler-cult; the initiative came in 29 BC from Asia and Bithynia. Normally Augustus did not permit altars or temples to be erected to himself alone; his name must be coupled with Roma, or the Lares, in Cilicia with Poseidon. About 27 BC at Mytilene a decree conferred privileges on him, with allowance for future additions, 'so that he may be deified as much as possible'. At Rome he took the title *divi filius*, son of the Divine Julius—a title, by comparison with Hercules, looking to future deification. The name Augustus with its religious overtones was a master-stroke. His birthday was declared a public holiday, his name was used in hymns, the day of his entry into the city was honoured with sacrifices, quinquennial vows were made in his name, a month was named after him, the emblem of Jupiter put on his house, the Shield of Virtue dedicated to him, a decree passed that at every banquet a libation should be poured to his Genius. This last became the centre of a widespread cult, and in 12 BC was included in official oaths. Other divine abstractions are Concordia Augusta, Pax Augusta, Salus Augusta; Numen Augusti was worshipped at Narbo.

Throughout the reign there is an expectation of apotheosis, in Horace's poems, in the symbol of the eagle on coins, and elsewhere; at Puteoli in AD 14 some sailors (from Alexandria) made a spontaneous act of veneration. After his death, on 17 September AD 14 the senate decreed that the Divine Augustus be accepted among the gods of the state. Augustus, in other words, was not among the *di Manes* in the underworld, but the *di superi* in the sky; a senator claimed to have seen him bodily ascending, and an eagle was released from his pyre. As so often, the structure of heaven is a reflection of the structure of earth; there is a celestial super-senate with co-option on a basis of merit. Cicero related immortality to personal achievement, and explicitly spoke of rulers and preservers who proceed from heaven and return to heaven. This might too easily lead to the assertion of divine origin as a basis for divine right. A better model was the Hellenistic Benefactor, or Hercules labouring for mankind. Tiberius made this last comparison in his oration at Augustus' funeral, and in a rescript based Augustus' divinity on 'the magnitude of his benefactions to the whole world'. (*Pl.* 42)

The pattern was set, and the saner emperors followed it, though from time to time a megalomaniac with an inferiority complex would appear and demand worship in his lifetime, Caligula, Nero, Domitian, Commodus. The cooler policy is seen in Tiberius, who rebuked a flattering speech about his sacred office, by suggesting that 'laborious' might be more appropriate; Claudius, who tried to refuse divine honours in Alexandria, though the governor in publishing the refusal called him 'Caesar our god'; Vespasian, who, feeling his death-agony approaching, remarked with blunt humour, 'Oh dear, I think I'm becoming a god.' The mood continued; in the second century AD, as one able ruler followed another, he deified his predecessor, sometimes, as with Hadrian, dragging a reluctant senate with him. When Marcus Aurelius deified his colleague Lucius Verus, the subject was less worthy, but one feels that the burden of Lucius dead was somewhat less than the burden of Lucius alive. The process became cynical. Caracalla murdered his brother Geta, and acceded to his deification with the words *sit divus, dum non sit vivus,* 'he can be in heaven, provided that he is not on earth'.

The identification of an emperor with a god is an ambiguous feature of the scene. Plainly it represents some kind of pretension to divinity, but although it is found extravagantly on the part of those who asserted their divinity in life, it is by no means solely theirs. Thus Antony's propaganda told of a banquet of the twelve gods in which the future Augustus played the role of Apollo, and Apollo has clearly affected his appearance in statues; Horace sees him as Mercury incarnate, and again the statues offer an echo. Caligula appeared variously as the Dioscuri, Dionysus, Mercury, Apollo, Mars, Neptune, Juno, Diana, and Venus; he ordered his own likeness to replace the head of Zeus at Olympia; he prolonged his palace so that the temple of Castor and Pollux might become its vestibule. Nero was identified with Zeus the Giver of Freedom, Hadrian with Zeus Olympius; Julia Domna was identified with Cybele and portrayed on Juno's throne. Severus Alexander and his mother Julia Mamaea were associated with Jupiter Dolichenus and Juno Regina, and represented as such. At Carnuntum statues of the divinities wearing imperial cloaks establish the identification; we may safely take a similar figure found at Chesters as similarly representing the imperial deity. The whole process is an interesting one and repays scrutiny. We can see in the first place a method of association: Augustus with Apollo; the emperors taking over a share of Zeus' festival at Laodicea, or of Aphrodite's temple. Alongside this we can see the process of identification. From these two together there is a tendency, though it must not be more strongly stated, for the imperial cult to displace the Olympians. (*Pl.* 46)

The imperial cult is found most vigorously in the Asiatic provinces. A city which was given official permission to be the centre of the provincial cult was styled *neokoros* or 'temple-warden' and the cities vied with one another for the title. A quick survey of some of the principal sites will illustrate.

At Smyrna long before Roman times Queen Stratonice had appeared as Aphrodite Stratonicis. It was here that Roma first became a goddess, and she appears as such on coins of imperial date. By 10 BC the assembly of the *koinon* met in Smyrna, and we find the Asiarchs paying for a special coin-issue; one such was associated with Polycarp's execution. Under Tiberius the cities of Asia applied to set up a temple to Tiberius, Livia and the Holy Senate. Pergamum already had a temple, and Ephesus and Miletus had their world-famous temples of Artemis and Apollo; the new temple was granted to Smyrna, and with it the title *neokoros*. Through the offices of Polemo, Hadrian was induced to allow a temple in his honour; the city again took the title *neokoros* and, in gratitude, the name Hadriane. In the third century AD it actually became temple-warden for the third time.

Pergamum was the first meeting-place of the assembly of the *koinon*. It had a temple of Augustus and Roma and a festival Romaea Sebasta. In the second century AD it became *neokoros* for the second time with a prominent temple of Trajan. Here too there was a statue 'to the god Hadrian'.

At Ephesus under the Republic there was a cult of P. Servilius Isauricus and Roma. It was in Ephesus that the representatives from Asia joined in declaring Julius Caesar god manifest. Within the precinct of the great temple of Artemis was a shrine of Augustus, but that was only a city-cult. The cult of Gaius and Lucius Caesar was centred here, and under Tiberius we find a priestess of Livia as Augusta Demeter, and a priest of Tiberius' twin grandsons, and even a dedication to Tiberius himself by the Roman settlers. But it was not till Claudius that the title of *neokoros* was given; it appears on a coin of Nero but seems to pertain to the previous reign. It may relate to a temple of the emperors. Nero was worshipped with Artemis, and had no temple of his own. There was a second temple under the Flavians, perhaps dedicated to Domitian, but the second title of *neokoros* then claimed was withdrawn by Trajan in view of Domitian's unpopularity. It was restored in honour of the new temple of Hadrian in his guise as Zeus Olympius; the festival was the Hadrianeia Olympia.

Tarsus was twice temple-warden, once under Hadrian and once under Commodus. Sardis became temple-warden under Hadrian; here the emperor was identified with Dionysus, and the actors formed themselves into the Sacred Hadrianic Stage Guild. Philadelphia was a centre of the imperial cult, but did not receive the title *neokoros* till the reign of Caracalla. Tralles actually received the title without a temple. At Magnesia-on-the-Maeander we meet Asiarchs in Nero's reign; in the late-second century AD there was a great festival of Roma. At Laodicea the assembly of the *koinon* held meetings; by the middle of the second century AD the festival of Zeus had become a festival of Zeus and the emperors. At Thyiateira similarly the festival of Apollo was expanded; there was a shrine to Trajan here, and Hadrian was honoured as Zeus Olympius. At Caesarea the temple of Augustus and Roma dominated the city; here too was a shrine to Tiberius dedicated by Pontius Pilate.

In some remoter corners of empire Augustus was worshipped during his lifetime, at Antioch-near-Pisidia for example, and even Sinope. This last appears to have had a cult of Marcus Aurelius. At Iconium we know that the imperial cult in the second century AD was in the hands of one Q. Eburemus Maximus. The climactic period of the neocorate was somewhere around AD 200; it should be noticed that a temple of the imperial cult alone did not suffice, and Nicaea never received the title of temple-warden. In addition to Pergamum and Smyrna we meet the *koinon* at Ephesus, Sardis, Cyzicus, Laodicea and Philadelphia. Under the Julio-Claudians the title was granted to Ephesus, Pergamum, Smyrna, Ancyra and probably Tarsus; the second century AD adds Pergamum, Smyrna, Ephesus, Cyzicus, Tarsus, and Laodicea; the Severan dynasty Ephesus for the third time, Perinthus, Sardis and Mazaca-Caesarea. A number of the grants (which had to be by decree of the senate) are of unknown date: there were provincial cults at

Tomi, Philippopolis, Thessalonica, Nicomedia, Amasia, Neo-caesarea, Nicopolis, Synnada, Tralles, Anazarbus, Perge, Side, Tripolis, and the Syrian Laodicea as well, and cults are also known from Juliopolis, Hierapolis, Aegae, Neapolis, Teos, Acmonia, Nysa and Abila-Leucas. The associated games at Pergamum were the first of many. The Hadrianeia were celebrated at Cyzicus, Smyrna and Ephesus, the Commodeia at Tarsus, and the Severeia at Perinthus, Cyzicus, Sardis, Caesarea in Cappadocia and Laodicea in Syria.

So far as the government at Rome was concerned, the object of the imperial cult was political. 'The emperor was god,' said Fustel de Coulanges, 'because he was emperor', and Havet called the apotheosis 'merely one form of the adoration which Rome exacted for herself'. This led to a curious paradox: it was more readily introduced into the newer and more backward provinces than into those which were more firmly established within the Roman political system. In the former it was needed as a means of associating the image of Roman power with a religious aura; in the latter it was less necessary as a key to Romanization, and indeed would risk provoking hostile reactions. Hence we have the prominence of the cult from early times in Britain and Germany. It has sometimes been argued with some weight that Vespasian at the beginning of his reign combined his political resettlement with religious measures instituting a provincial cult of the emperor officially in Narbonensis, Baetica and Africa. The priest was called *flamen Augustalis*. At some point in the second century AD, this title was changed to *sacerdos*, perhaps in Hadrian's reign, but we do not know the occasion or the cause. We can trace similar changes elsewhere, as in Sardinia where the *flamen divorum Augustorum* gives way to the *sacerdos provinciae Sardiniae*. From then on the cult flourished; from Africa we have inscriptions identifying fourteen priests in the period from Vespasian to Diocletian, three *flamines* and eleven *sacerdotes*. By AD 183 the list of *divi* comprised Augustus, Claudius, Vespasian, Titus; then Nerva, Trajan, Marciana, Matidia, Plotina, Sabina, Hadrian, the elder Faustina, Antoninus Pius, Lucius Verus, the younger Faustina and Marcus Aurelius. By AD 224 Commodus, Pertinax, Septimius Severus and

Caracalla are added, and this list is confirmed by the *Ferale Duranum* of AD 225–27.

We may illustrate the process by three records relating to Trajan, which we have already noticed. On the Arch at Beneventum Jupiter is actually represented as delegating his power to the emperor: this was before Trajan's death. In a papyrus from Egypt we have the script of a pageant to welcome Hadrian, and Phoebus, the Sun-god, announces that he has escorted Trajan to the heavens, and has now returned to present his successor. Finally, on the relief from Ephesus, now in Vienna, Trajan rises to heaven in the chariot of the Sun, leaving Earth behind. Or we may take the panel in the Capitoline representing the apotheosis of the empress Sabina, in Hadrian's presence, attended by a winged spirit representing Eternity and bearing the torch of eternal light. Or the Vatican Apotheosis of Antoninus and Faustina, presented under the likeness of Jupiter and Juno and thus already deified, swept up to the sky by a winged spirit, with guardian eagles on either side, while the goddess Roma and the god of the Campus Martius look on. On a coin of AD 176–77 we see Marcus Aurelius' wife, the younger Faustina, now dead, translated to heaven on the back of Juno's peacock: she looks back to earth, her veil encircles her head like a nimbus, and in her right hand she bears a sceptre. The main symbols of apotheosis are the eagle and the wreath: these are derived from the East, and found frequently on Syrian monuments. The eagle is the messenger of the Sun, and is entrusted by its master with the task of bringing back the liberated soul to the sky; the wreath is symbolic of the ultimate triumph of the soul. About a hundred such symbolic representations are found on medallions alone from Augustus to Constantine. (*Pls.* 45, 47–49)

The formal process of apotheosis is carefully recorded by Herodian in the third century AD: his words are of sufficient interest to record in full:

It is the custom of the Romans to deify those of their emperors who die, leaving successors, and this rite they call apotheosis. On this occasion a semblance of mourning, combined with festival and religious observances, is visible throughout the city. The body of the dead they honour after human fashion with a splendid funeral, and making a wax image resembling him in all respects, they expose it to view in the vestibule of the palace, on a lofty ivory couch of great size, spread with cloth of gold. The figure is made pallid, like a sick man. During most of the day senators sit round the bed on the left-hand side, clothed in black, and noblewomen on the right, clothed in plain white dress, like mourners, wearing no gold or necklaces. These ceremonies continue for seven days, and the doctors severally approach the bed, examine the patient, and declare him to be growing steadily worse. When they have made believe that he is dead, the noblest of the *equites*, and young men, carefully selected, of senatorial rank, pick up the bed, carry it along the Sacred Way, and lay it in the open in the old forum. Platforms, rather like steps, are erected on either side. On one stands a choir of young nobles, on the other a choir of noblewomen; they sing hymns and songs of praise to the dead, modulated in a solemn, mournful strain. After this they carry the bed through the city to the Campus Martius. Here, in the broadest portion, a square erection is constructed entirely of gigantic timber logs, in the shape of a room, filled with faggots, and decorated outside with hangings interwoven with gold and ivory pictures. Upon this a similar but smaller chamber is built, with open doors and windows, and above it a third and fourth, still diminishing to the top, so that one might compare it to the lighthouses which go by the name of Pharos. In the second storey they place a bed, and collect all sorts of aromatics and incense, and every kind of fragrant fruit, herb or juice; for all cities, nations and eminent individuals emulate one another in contributing these last gifts in honour of the emperor. When a vast heap of aromatics is collected, there is a procession of horsemen and chariots around the pile, with the drivers wearing robes of office, and masks made to resemble the most distinguished Roman emperors and military commanders. When all this is done, the others fire the pile from all sides;

the fire easily catches hold of the faggots and aromatics. Then from the smallest storey at the very top, as from a pinnacle, an eagle is let loose to mount into the sky as the fire ascends; this is believed by the Romans to carry the soul of the emperor from earth to heaven, and from that time he is worshipped with the other gods.

A change was brought in the latter part of the third century AD by Aurelian. It was decisive. He changed the theory of *Gottkönigtum* for the Mazdean doctrine of rule by the grace of God (though, paradoxically, he was himself honoured as *dominus et deus*, 'Lord and God'). To the Mazdeans and to Aurelian god was the Sun-god, but this conception opened the way for the Christian emperor. Constantine might invest his statue with the attributes of the Sun-god, and the emotions appropriate to the divine monarch might still be directed to the monarch who ruled not as god but as his god's vicegerent, but Constantine's grave was set among the cenotaphs of the twelve apostles, not the thrones of the twelve Olympians. (*Pl.* 43)

CHAPTER VII

PERSONAL RELIGION

THE IMPERSONALITIES of state-religion could not satisfy the religious needs of the individual. For these he turned to the Mysteries. A mystery is in derivation something to keep mum about, a secret salvation revealed only to initiates. The Mystery-religions of the Graeco-Roman world were many and diverse, but all show three essential common features. First, all have a ritual of purification through which the initiate has to pass. Second, all involve communion with some god or goddess. Third, all promise to the purified and faithful a life of bliss beyond the grave.

The Mysteries were a Greek creation, and this is important. Many of them were in origin oriental, none was in the strict sense occidental. The difference between the Greek *ecstasis* and the Latin *superstitio*, both of approximately the same literal meaning, may suggest a contrast. So may the psychological difference between the Roman practice of covering the head in prayer to shut out evil omens, and the Greek practice of uncovering so as to expose the worshipper to divine influence. The oriental cults had a strong organization with a professional priesthood, and this must have helped the process of incorporation. But it did not produce it. The initiation, the secret lore, the sacred books—these are not associated with the cults in their native lands, and Nilsson has argued that it was the influence of Eleusis and the Orphics which transformed them. Even Mithraism, which by-passed mainland Greece, seems to have acquired its distinctive form under the influence of Hellenized *magi* from Asia Minor: such at least has been the view of our greatest experts, Bidez, Cumont and Vermaseren.

ELEUSIS

The most famous of the Mysteries remained those at Eleusis, and they were patronized by emperors from Augustus on: a priestess declares proudly on her epitaph that she presided over the initiation of Marcus Aurelius and Commodus. Not all found it so easy: Nero, and even Apollonius of Tyana were rejected. In the background at Eleusis was the myth of the Rape of Kore, the Maid, or Persephone, by the god of the underworld, the grief and wandering search of her mother Demeter, the blight that Demeter laid upon earth, the restoration of the girl to her mother for part of the year only, and the reunion of the goddesses. The myth reflects the burial of the seed-corn underground in storage jars during the dark blight of winter, and its new appearance for the spring sowing, and this in turn becomes a parable of the life of man and the promise of a life which lies beyond death. The great festival took place in September. We have records from the imperial period of the proclamation inviting those 'pure of hand and Greek in speech' to seek initiation; the demands were moral as well as ritual. On the next day the cry was raised, 'Initiates, to the sea,' and the cleansing power of the waves was consummated by the sacrifice of a sucking-pig; it was a baptism of regeneration, as Tertullian admits. Then on 19 September came the procession from Athens, and the initiation. (Pl. 50)

The secret of the Eleusinian Mysteries has been well kept, and we do not know for certain what went on in the Hall of the Mysteries. We can discount the more obscene suggestions of the Christian writers on the offensive in more senses than one. It may be taken as certain that there was some kind of dramatic re-enactment of the myth, and the restoration of the Maid to her mother in the midst of a revelry of torches. There may have been a sacred marriage: the matter is controversial, but the evidence is reasonable and it is a likely aspect of such a cult. The climax of the whole initiation, however, did not lie in the drama or the marriage, but in the visual revelation (epopteia) of sacred objects, apparently with a brilliant light, which must have involved the use of reflectors. These objects will have included crude cult-statues of great antiquity, but the final revelation, the climax of the climax, lay in the display of an ear of corn, the symbol of life. Finally there was some kind of communion in cereal and barleywine. 'I have fasted. I have drunk the barleywine, I have taken things from the sacred chest, tasted them, and replaced them first in the basket and then in the chest.' This must represent some kind of identification with the goddess who is manifested in the grain, and the emperor Gallienus put the feminine *Galliena Augusta* on his coins in commemoration of his initiation. (*Pl.* 44) What this initiation promises is expressed in the Homeric hymn to Demeter:

> *Blessed among men on earth is he who has seen these things.*
> *But he who is uninitiate in the holy rites, who has no lot in them,*
> *does not enjoy a share in like things when in death he lies beneath*
> *the broad-spreading darkness.*

Cicero said of Eleusis: 'We have learned to live and to die with a better hope.' Its finest expression comes from Plutarch:

> When a man dies, he is like those who are being initiated into the mysteries. . . . Our whole life is but a succession of wanderings, of painful courses, of long journeys by tortuous ways without outlet. At the moment of quitting it, fears, terrors, quiverings, mortal sweats, and a lethargic stupor, come over us and overwhelm us; but as soon as we are out of it pure spots and meadows receive us, with voice and dances and the solemnities of sacred words and holy sights.

Similarly Jesus promised: 'Unless a grain of wheat falls into the ground and dies, it remains alone; but if it dies, it bears much fruit.' 'Glorious indeed,' cried an initiate, 'is that mystery vouchsafed by the blessed gods, for death is no ill to mortals, but rather a good.'

DIONYSUS

We pass next to the Mysteries of Dionysus. Dionysus, like Demeter, was a god of nature. Plutarch says of him, 'The Phrygians think that the god is asleep in the winter and is awake in the summer, and at one season they celebrate with Bacchic rites his goings to bed and at others his rising up. The Paphlagonians allege that in the winter he is bound down and imprisoned and in the spring he is stirred up and let loose.' Macrobius too sees the four ages of Dionysus as representative of the birth, growth, decay and rebirth of nature. At this period stress is laid on Dionysus of the Tree. It is readily understandable that such a god of fertility in nature would find in the vine his peculiar emblem, that the phallus would play an important part in his cult, that the ritual dramas of tragedy and comedy would develop under his aegis. It is understandable too that such a god should bear with him the promise of new life extended to those who have offered themselves in a deeper sense. (*Pl. 52*)

Mysteries associated with Dionysus extended over the Graeco-Roman world. We meet them under the name of Orpheus, a kind of double of Dionysus, in Sicily and Greece during the fifth and fourth centuries BC and again in the buried gold tablets found at Petelia giving instructions to the soul of the dead; the phrases became familiar through repetition and are still found in the second century AD. We meet them in the so-called Orphic hymns, from some Dionysiac brotherhood of imperial times with a very different slant from the authors of the tablets. We find them threatening the senate's concept of public order and decency at Rome as early as 186 BC; the initiates are already numerous enough to be called a second people. We hear of initiation, ecstatic prophesying, scandalous behaviour. The movement was checked; it was not rigidly banned but assemblies were limited to five, with no common funds and no priests. Such associations grew again in the imperial period: we know of one from Tusculum during the second century AD. Membership rose to nearly 500, and a woman, Julia Agrippinilla, heads the list. We find them in the power of Sabazios, a great god from Phrygia who was variously identified with Zeus and Dionysus, and who colours all the Dionysiac mysteries. His cult is most clearly seen in the votive offering of bronze right hands decorated with magic symbols, representing the god's benevolent power. These are found throughout the imperial period; inscriptions suggest that the second and third centuries AD were the period of the god's greatest popularity; and even in the fourth century there is the evidence of a curious cycle of frescoes in the tomb of Vibia whose husband Vincentius was a priest of Sabazios. (*Pl. 56*)

The most powerful witness of Dionysiac initiation is the series of frescoes adorning the walls of a room in the villa of the gens Istacidia on the outskirts of Pompeii. The pictures belong to the

early-first century AD, but they may legitimately be taken as
evidence of the continuing nature of the Dionysiac mysteries.
They form a sequence of events, brilliantly painted against a
bright vermilion background, twenty-nine figures in all. The lady
of the house sits, hieratic, immobile, watching the scene which
unfolds. Next stands a neophyte with scarf over her head and
hand on hip listening as a young boy reads the prelude to the
liturgy under the guidance of a seated matron; there is evidence
from elsewhere of a boy reading part of the ritual in Orphic
initiation. A comely maidservant with a tray draws this scene
together with the next. She is carrying ritual offerings from the
neophyte to a priestess or officiant seated at a table with two
attendants; one is pouring a libation or lustration from a small pot.
Next we come to the mysteries. A gross Silenus leans playing the
lyre, a young Pan plays the flute, a charming boyish Panisca offers
her breast to a kid. This is the peaceable transformation of nature
offered by the god; we recall the tranquil scene in Euripides, and
the Orphic catchphrase, 'A kid I am fallen into milk.' Then in the
corner, forming a link with the wall at right-angles stands a
woman starting back in terror. What has startled her? Perhaps the
scene immediately to her left; perhaps the more distant unveiling
or flagellation, or perhaps she is playing a role in some divine
drama. She reminds the worshippers that the road to bliss lies
through suffering. Next comes a curious scene. A Silenus with
head averted is holding a bowl; a satyr is peering inside (he does
not seem, as some suggest, to be drinking); behind him another
satyr holds a grotesque mask. This last seems pointless unless the
mask is somehow reflected, and the scene is probably to be interpreted in terms of *lekanomancy*, a form of ecstatic divination.
Now, presiding over the whole scene are the figures of Dionysus
and Ariadne, and it is they that the worshipper would see first on
entering the room. Next a kneeling woman unveils an object—
undoubtedly a phallus. Beyond her a great winged figure, perhaps
Telete, the very spirit of Mystery-initiation, stands wielding a
long rod, and far to her left crouches our initiate, her finery cast
off, her hair rumpled, a robe of penitence loosely worn, her back
bared for the blows which alike represent the touch of fertility (as

in the Lupercalia), the test of endurance, and the ritual death which must precede resurrection. Her head is in the lap of a woman who comforts her; another stands anxiously by. But immediately, blending with this scene, we see the resurrection. The ordeal is over. The initiate has cast off the robe of penitence, and picked up the scarf which lay ready under her arms during the flagellation, the same scarf which swirls over the head of the sea-queen in so many imperial mosaics, and she is clashing cymbals and gyrating in a great dance of Bacchic victory. So finally to a scene of preparation for mystical marriage in re-enactment of that of Ariadne. It is a unique record of a deep experience. (*Pls. 53, 54*)

This apart, our main record is the sarcophagi which with their radiant hope we must examine presently. The cult was persistent. Diodorus attests it for the reign of Augustus, Pliny for the first century AD, Pausanias in the second and Maternus in the third records its practice in Crete, and in the fifth Nonnus wrote his strangely monumental poem in the god's honour. (*Pls. 61, 62*)

CYBELE

The Great Mother, as is natural to a power of life, had her own Mysteries. The ceremony of initiation is not in fact attested till the second century AD. This was the *taurobolium* or baptism in bull's blood. We have a vivid description from the pen of Prudentius in the fourth century AD—a long passage, put contemptuously into the mouth of a martyr named Romanus, and of great importance.

> *As you know, a trench is dug, and the high priest*
> *plunges deep underground to be sanctified.*
> *He wears a curious headband, fastens fillets for the occasion*
> *around his temples, fixes his hair with a crown of gold,*
> *holds up his robes of silk with a belt from Gabii.*
> *Over his head they lay a plank platform criss-cross,*
> *fixed so that the wood is open not solid;*
> *then they cut or bore through the floor*
> *and make holes in the wood with an awl at several points*
> *till it is plentifully perforated with small openings.*
> *A large bull, with grim, shaggy features*
> *and garlands of flowers round his neck*

or entangling his horns, is escorted to the spot.
The victim's head is shimmering with gold
and the sheen of the gold leaf lends colour to his hair.
The animal destined for sacrifice is at the appointed place.
They consecrate a spear and with it pierce his breast.
A gaping wound disgorges its stream of blood,
still hot, and pours a steaming flood on the lattice
of the bridge below, flowing copiously.
Then the shower drops through the numerous paths offered
by the thousand cracks, raining a ghastly dew.
The priest in the pit below catches the drops,
puts his head underneath each one till it is stained,
till his clothes and all his body are soaked in corruption.
Yes, and he lays his head back, puts his cheeks in the stream,
sets his ears underneath, gets lips and nose in the way,
bathes his very eyes in the drops,
does not spare his mouth, wets his tongue
till he drains deep the dark blood with every pore.
When the blood is exhausted the priests drag away
the carcase, now growing stiff, from the structure of planks.
Then the high priest emerges, a grim spectacle.
He displays his dripping head, his congealed beard,
his sopping ornaments, his clothes inebriated.
He bears all the stains of this polluting rite,
filthy with the gore of the atoning victim just offered—
and everyone stands to one side, welcomes him, honours him,
just because he has been buried in a beastly pit
and washed with the wretched blood of a dead ox.

Prudentius records only the central rite. The evidence of inscriptions reveals a more complex ceremony which might last up to five days. Probably there was ritual preparation of the baptized, but if so we know nothing about it; an altar would be specially consecrated for the occasion; and it seems that the sex-organs of the sacrificial animal were ceremoniously interred after the baptism. The object of the baptism was the purification of the baptized and his rebirth to new life. There appears to have been some question about the duration of the baptism's efficacy. Some of the baptized describe themselves as *in aeternum renatus* 'reborn for ever', but others renewed the baptism after twenty years. Besides the *taurobolium* there was a variant the *criobolium*, which involved a ram instead of a bull. Sometimes they were combined, and then it seems that the ram was associated with Attis, and the bull with the Mother. The *taurobolium* might be vicarious; sometimes it is a public offering rather than a private baptism.

The initiate received milk as one reborn. There was evidently a sacramental meal associated with the cult. The initiate's affirmation of faith included the words:

> *I have eaten from the tambourine,*
> *I have drunk out of the cymbal.*

The familiar musical instruments of the cult become appropriately the plate and cup of communion. This communion was a participation in the life of the god or goddess—probably here the divine consort, since Attis was called 'the reaped ear of corn'. Christian writers drew the parallel with the Christian eucharist, and regarded the Cybele-Attis rite as a demonic parody.

ISIS

In some ways the most important of the Mystery religions was that of Isis. It was during the Hellenistic and Roman period that Isis became a Saviour-goddess with Mysteries of her own. The Mysteries date from Ptolemy I and represent a clear example of a new religious institution meeting the needs of a new age. The main formative influence was Eleusis, as we know from the presence of Timotheus of Eleusis in the court; it is not surprising that Isis was identified in one of her guises with Demeter, or that her image takes on Greek lineaments. In ancient Egypt we have no trace of individual initiation, and only priests in general were admitted to the shrines.

We have to recognize that the Egyptian religion of the Roman period stands at the end of a long tradition. Already in the third millennium BC the *Pyramid Texts* show Osiris as the central figure of a blend of legend and ritual, in which there are two essential

points, first that Osiris has in some sense overcome death, second
that this conquest of death was somehow available to the dead
rulers. By the time we reach the *Coffin Texts* of the early-second
millennium BC the identification of the dead man with the god is
in a sense complete; he is even addressed as Osiris, and called to
resurrection as such: 'Raise thyself to life, thou dost not die'; or
again, 'Osiris, live! stand up, unhappy one who dost lie there! I
am Isis, I am Nephthys.' This is what lies behind the evidence
from the Ptolemaic and Roman periods. Here the Rhind papyrus
is particularly interesting, for there is a contrast between illustrations and text; in the illustrations the dead man stands before
Osiris, in the text he is identified with the god, though there is one
passage where the process of assimilation can be seen, when
Anubis says, 'I lay my hands upon thy body as I did for my father
Osiris.' Later still, now from the Roman era, are some painted
shrouds, showing, it seems, Anubis leading the dead man towards
Osiris, represented as a mummy; we are in fact looking at the
moment of assimilation. It is this hope of new life which was the
basis for the Mysteries.

The great document of Isiac initiation is Apuleius' picaresque
novel, *The Metamorphoses* or *The Golden Ass*, which ends on the
serious note already sounded in the fable of Love and the Soul.
Lucius is in ass's form. By the sea he falls asleep, is wakened by the
full moon, ritually bathes, and invokes the Moon-goddess. She
reveals herself, and her true name of Isis. She will save him, but he
must devote his life to her. He will then know glory in life, and
after death will continue to adore her, as she gives light to the
dead. Next day Lucius watches the procession pass, the women
with heads covered, the men tonsured, carrying the *sistrum*. Then
come the senior priests with white surplices, the first with a
lantern, the second with sacrificial pots, the third with a palm-
branch and the wand of Mercury, the fourth with a token of
equity, an open and deformed left hand, and a gold vessel in the
form of a breast, full of milk, the fifth with a winnowing-fan, the
sixth with a wine-jar. Then come the gods, Anubis with his dog's
head, and a cow standing for Isis, followed by a man with a closed
box, another man with a symbol of gold, and the High Priest with

sistrum and roses. Lucius eats the roses and is restored to his natural shape. The priest calls upon the irreligious to look and recognize their error, and on Lucius to become a soldier of Isis. The procession now proceeds; at the temple a scribe offers prayer and spring is declared here, for Isis is the power of fertility. (*Pls.* 9, 55)

Lucius now takes up residence in the temple. He adores the statue of the goddess with a rare intensity. The goddess appears to him in dreams (a practice attested by Juvenal and Pausanias). He must have a clear call for ordination (as Pausanias again attests). Eventually he accepts and is accepted. Sacred hieroglyphs are shown to him, he is baptized for the remission of sins, verbal mysteries are revealed, and a fast is imposed. After ten days the full initiation begins: the ceremonies are not to be spoken, and all he says is that he trod the threshold of death, saw the sun at midnight, and approached the gods; there is clearly a cataclysmic experience, a ritual death, and a vision and illumination. He now emerges wearing twelve stoles, a linen shirt and a 'cloak of Olympus' with embroidered animals (like that of the Lion grade of Mithraists). He is set on a dais and revealed to the people; this is an epiphany; the initiate is one with the divine. Later he has further initiations into the Osiris-cult and the priestly college. The whole story is in its way a rare record of personal devotion. Festugière put it well, when he said that Lucius felt himself to be loved, and so offered his love in return.

HERMES TRISMEGISTOS

Coming, like the worship of Isis, from Egypt is the mystic literature of Hermes 'Thrice-Greatest', the Egyptian Thoth. The interpretation and dating of the eighteen books which comprise the *Corpus Hermeticum* is extremely controversial, but there are indications that they were brought together in a single publication at the very end of the third century AD, and that they were written across the three preceding centuries. They are the papers of a distinct sect, which offered to its initiates the experience of rebirth, through a fusion of Egyptian, Greek and oriental approaches. Of the eighteen tractates two are of outstanding importance, the first, *Poimandres,* and the thirteenth, *The Secret Discourse on the Moun-*

tain. From these and other references we can reconstruct something of what initiation meant. There was first a call to repentance; the seventh tractate is precisely this. Similarly in *Poimandres* we hear the call: 'Repent, you who have journeyed with error and joined company with ignorance; rid yourselves of darkness and grasp light; forsake corruption and partake of immortality.' From the readiness to repent came personal instruction, and many of the tractates are concerned with this; these two stages correspond closely with the Christian *kerygma* and *didache*. The initiate was expected himself to take the initiative, in contemplation, asceticism, and ritual and moral purity, controlling the senses. The ultimate experience was religious ecstasy, and this ecstasy brought rebirth; the vision it produced was knowledge of God, and therein lay salvation. For knowledge, as Plato said long before, is of likes. 'We must not be frightened of affirming that a man on earth is a mortal god, and that a god in heaven is an immortal man.' This is the paradox of salvation. And, for all the paradox, to put on divinity is to put on immortality. The promise of Hermes is the promise that the initiate shall be 'admitted to the company of the gods and the souls that have attained bliss'. At the end of *Poimandres* comes a mighty prayer:

> *Holy is God, the Father of all!*
> *Holy is God, whose will is performed by his own Powers!*
> *Holy is God, who wills to be known, and is known by those who belong to him!*
> *Holy art thou, who by the Word hast created all things that exist!*
> *Holy art thou, of whom all Nature has produced the image!*
> *Holy art thou, whom Nature has not formed!*
> *Holy art thou, who art mightier than all power!*
> *Holy art thou, who dost excel every excellence!*
> *Holy art thou, who art above all praise!*
> *Accept our spiritual and pure sacrifices, which are offered thee from heart and soul which yearn after thee.*

The Hermetic sect was probably a small one, whose scriptures have survived through the accidents of history, but they form another element in the mosaic.

ASCLEPIUS

Hermes was identified with Asclepius, the Greek god of healing, and three of the tractates bear the latter name as title. But Asclepius attracted personal devotion in his own right; indeed the identification could scarcely have been made otherwise. A god who healed the body might easily be seen as a god who healed the spirit. So in a mime of Herodas we hear of the 'gentle touch of his hand'. Over the divine hospital at Epidaurus stood the inscription: 'The man who enters the sweet-scented shrine must be pure: purity is concentrating on holy thoughts alone.' The devotion the god inspired can be seen in the prayer:

> Asclepius, child of Apollo, these words come from your devoted servant. Blessed one, god whom I yearn for, how shall I enter your golden house unless your heart incline towards me and you will to heal me and restore me to your shrine again, so that I may look on my god, who is brighter than the earth in springtime? Divine, blessed one, you alone have power. With your loving kindness you are a great gift from the supreme gods to mankind, a refuge from trouble.

The god was much honoured by the Romans. He may be seen on intaglios from the Roman period in the Metropolitan Museum in New York, bearded and compassionate, with his snake-staff. A fine marble group in the Vatican shows him seated, with Hygieia-Salus, the goddess of health, standing at his side, caressing the snake and looking adoringly at the god. Another statue in the Vatican allows a beardless young doctor the attributes of the god he loves and seeks to emulate. Apuleius, the devotee of Isis, wrote in his honour, though the treatise entitled *Asclepius* is a later Hermetic compilation. But the great document of faith in Asclepius is the *Sacred Stories* of Aelius Aristides, which Festugière treated with such perspicacious charm in his Sather lectures. A lecturer and *littérateur* by profession, an invalid, genuinely but with hypochondria as well, and suffering from acute religiosity, Aristides made a dreadful journey to Rome in the depths of the winter of AD 143–44; he was suffering from toothache, earache, asthma and fever; the standard remedies proved useless. He

returned to Smyrna, and in AD 146, still an invalid, visited the
sanctuary of Asclepius at Pergamum. He catalogues his ailments,
using the overt desire to praise the god, whose healing power
proved so versatile, to cover the tolerably widespread delusion
that our hearers will be fascinated by our symptoms and sufferings.
But something happened. As he slept the Saviour spoke, and he
answered in his sleep with the traditional cry: 'Great is Asclepius!' We know from other sources of Asclepius' standard remedies: walking barefoot, riding, and taking cold baths. They tell us
something of the physical and spiritual condition of the patients
who needed such prescriptions; Aristides was spending much of
his time wrapped up in woollen blankets in an airless and therefore dark room. The new remedies were prescribed for him, as
were ointments and poultices, diets, warm baths, purges and the
letting of blood. In some instances, though not with Aristides,
who needed no encouragement in that direction, the god prescribed literary exercises. What is so interesting about the case of
Aristides (as we may legitimately say) is not the cure. No doubt
the prescriptions did do him good, but he remained something of
an invalid, and we may suspect that he remained an invalid to be
near his god. For what is fascinating is the faith. This is personal
devotion to a personal Saviour. Even this prosy orator had his
mystical experiences. Once in the sanctuary he saw the statue
brilliantly illuminated (a common mystical experience) and seem-
ingly with three heads, suggesting a power of heaven and the
underworld as well as earth. He called, 'One,' a formulaic cry,
here implying Zeus-Asclepius-Sarapis as one, and he heard the
god's voice: 'That is you' (*Tat tvam asi*). This is mystical communion, and with this experience he cared nothing about his
illnesses; it gave him the will to live. Aristides is a reminder that
personal religion was not confined to the Mysteries. (*Pl.* 57)

MITHRAS

Mithraism was a Mystery-religion in the full sense. The chapels
were technically called 'caves'. The main sanctuary was oblong
with a vault representing the sky and symbolic motifs on the wall.
The relief of Mithras and the bull stood at the end, sometimes with

devices for effective lighting. Only men were admitted, though there were fraternal relations with the women of the Cybele-cult. The initiates sat on benches, costumed according to their several grades. There were seven grades: the planetary number seven has mystical significance, and we find seven steps and seven altars also. In the Mithraeum of Felicissimus at Ostia we can trace in mosaic the symbols of the seven grades associated with those of the seven planets: Mercury, Venus, Mars, Jupiter, the Moon, the Sun, Saturn. The lower grades were, in ascending order: Raven, Bridegroom, Soldier; these were collectively known as Servitors. The upper grades, or Participants, were Lion, Persian, Courier of the Sun, Father. (*Pls.* 26, 27, 51)

We know that the whole process of initiation involved real or symbolic tests of endurance. We hear of branding, ordeals by heat and cold, fasting, scourging, journeying. The Soldier was offered a crown across a sword; this he had to win and then renounce with the words, 'Mithras is my crown.' The Lion had his tongue and hands purified with honey. It is likely that there was some dramatic representation of the journey of the soul for the neophyte. There was a regular routine of public worship, with fire perpetually burning, and daily offices. There was also a communion service in memory of the farewell banquet of Mithras and the Sun; this included the drinking of communion wine, and in a relief from Konjica we see something uncommonly like hot-cross-buns. We may reasonably suppose that the Father and the Courier of the Sun presided at this meal, re-enacting the roles of Mithras and the Sun, and, more speculatively, that the liturgy included sacrifice, coronation and covenant before the meal in re-enactment of the myth. The place of the *taurobolium* in the religion of Mithras is controversial. It belongs properly to the cult of Cybele, but the cults had a close fraternal relationship. It may be taken as certain that the majority of chapels do not have the space for such a rite, but those at Trier or in the Baths of Caracalla do, and there are a few inscriptions of Mithraic initiates who do not claim the Cybele-initiation but who are *tauroboliati*; it looks as if it were a ritual occasionally practised but not universally observed. There were however always baptismal lustrations.

29 Diana, originally a spirit of the wildwood, became readily equated with the Greek Artemis. She appeared in three roles, as the moon in the sky, Diana on earth and Hecate in the Underworld. In this fine statue of Diana Lucifera from the Capitoline Museum, Rome, the crescent moon appears as a tiara, and the torch in her hand proclaims her as Light-bearer. The swirling scarf assimilates her to the sea-goddesses (p. 71).

30–33 *Above*, a reminder of the varied power of the Roman pantheon. Three coins with the temples of, *left to right*, Vesta, called VESTA MATER, spirit of the hearth (p. 71); Janus, power of the gate (p. 74); and Venus (the garden-spirit who became goddess of love) and Roma (p. 75). *Below*, Pan (p. 65) (or the Celtic Cernunnos) with Apollo and Mercury (p. 72), in Rheims.

34–36 *Above, left*, a stele in Brussels showing Dionysus hunting, as a power of wild nature. His vine is in the background (pp. 65, 102). *Above, right*, a Lar, a Roman household god: perhaps originally an ancestral spirit guarding the fields round the farm, later brought inside (p. 68). Metropolitan Museum of Art, New York. *Below*, the Suovetaurilia, a sacrificial procession of a bull, sheep and pig (p. 156). It was offered to Mars, a god of agriculture as well as of war (p. 71). Louvre.

37 A relief of Cernunnos, a Celtic power of abundance, no doubt appearing in stag form (p. 70). Compare Pl. 33. Musée de Cluny, Paris.

38, 39 *Left*, Epona, the Celtic horse-goddess, in St Germain-en-Laye; *below*, Artio, the bear-goddess, in Berne (p. 69). Here the animals, which were originally themselves the divinities, have become attendant on the goddesses.

40, 41 Two aspects of Fortune.
Above, Tyche in her guise as a
city-goddess (p. 84). This is a copy
of the famous Tyche of Antioch by
Eutychides. She sits on Mt
Silpion, with the river-god of the
Orontes at her feet. The turreted
crown is on her head, and a sheaf of
corn, representing the prosperity
of the city, in her hand. *Right*, the
Roman goddess Fortuna, with her
attributes, the rudder and
cornucopiae (p. 85). Both statues
in the Vatican.

42–44 Aspects of Imperial religion. *Above*, a cameo in the Bibliothèque Nationale, Paris, with the apotheosis of Germanicus. Tiberius is seated as Jupiter and Livia as Ceres: Augustus reclines in heaven. *Below, left*, a bronze antoninianus of Aurelian, showing Victory crowning the emperor as 'restorer of the world'. *Below, right*, a gold aureus of Gallienus, wearing a corn wreath, after his initiation into the Eleusis mysteries. The inscription gives his name in the feminine (p. 101).

45, 46 *Above*, the apotheosis of Trajan on the Arch of Trajan at Benevento (p. 96), dating from AD 115. Here the emperor is crowned by Victory. In other scenes the Olympian gods receive him, and in one Jupiter is actually handing over the thunderbolt of power to him. In all the emperor is the main figure *Left*, a statue of Commodus as Hercules, in the Museo dei Conservatori, Rome (pp. 91–92). Commodus also identified himself with Mercury and with Liber Pater, but Hercules was his favourite identity, and he had his own *flamen Herculaneus*.

47–49 The apotheosis of Antoninus Pius and Faustina. *Left*, a panel from an ivory diptych in the British Museum. Although late in date, it celebrates the centenary of an apotheosis, perhaps that of Antoninus three centuries earlier. *Above*, a sestertius of Antoninus, with the temple of Faustina. She died in AD 141, and Antoninus was later joined with her in the dedication. *Below*, the apotheosis of Antoninus and Faustina in the Vatican (p. 96).

The central mystery revealed related to the journey of the soul. The soul is immortal, and its sojourn in an earthly body is a time of trial. At birth it descends from the home of light through the gate of Cancer, passing through the seven planetary spheres, and becoming tainted at each stage by the appropriate vice (sloth from Saturn, anger from Mars, lust from Venus, greed from Mercury, ambition from Jupiter). On earth the initiate has the opportunity to shake off the weight of these impurities by a combination of moral effort and the knowledge revealed to him in the Mysteries. After death there is a struggle between the devas and angels for the soul, with Mithras as arbiter. If the good qualities have out-weighed the bad, the soul rises again through the gate of Capri-corn, passing the planetary spheres in reverse order, and finally shedding all taint of impurity. On the way it meets divine officers called (quaintly) Customs-Officials, who must be intimidated, cajoled or tricked into letting it pass. This journey of the soul is of central importance. It will be clear that there is a deal of astral symbolism in the cult. Here we must mention the figures of Cautes and Cautopates which flanked the bull-slaying relief. Their origin is obscure, their symbolism clear. Cautes carries his torch held upwards, and is associated with the sign of the Bull; he stands for the rising sun, morning, spring. Cautopates holds his torch pointing down, and is associated with the sign of the Scorpion. He stands for the setting sun, evening, winter. For this is what Mithraism is about, the battle between light and dark, day and night, life and death, summer and winter, good and evil. The Mithraist was in the most literal sense on the side of the angels.

One of the most important documents of Mithraism is also one of the most controversial. This is an Egyptian magical papyrus dating from about the year AD 300. There is a mass of occult hocus-pocus in this weird hotch-potch, but it seems that it does incorporate some material from Mithraic cult, and enables us to reconstruct something of the mood and meaning of the final grade of initiation. The liturgy contained in the papyrus consists entirely of invocations, but through them we can confirm that the Mysteries of Mithras were concerned with the death and re-birth of the initiate. The first prayer is for initiation and rebirth;

throughout the liturgy there is a contrast between physical birth and spiritual rebirth; and the closing words show a lofty exaltation of spirit: 'O Lord! I have been born again and pass away in exaltation. In exaltation I die. Birth that produces life brings me into being and frees me for death. I go my way as thou hast ordered, as thou hast established the law and ordained the sacrament.'

The doctrine of hope of blessedness through Mithras was held by the emperor Julian in some fusion and confusion with other ideas. He was urged on by an oracle: 'But when you have pursued the Persian people as far as Seleuceia and reduced them under your sway, then a fiery chariot shall bear you to Olympus, tossing in a whirlwind; you shall be free from the curse and weariness of your mortal limbs. You shall reach your father's courts of aetherial light, from which you wandered to enter a human body.' He makes the Sun tell the young man in his myth that he has an immortal soul, and if he follows obediently will be a god and see the father; and at the end of *The Banquet* Hermes tells him to obey Mithras, and so to prepare for himself a safe anchorage; then when he leaves he will leave with a god to lead him and with a good hope.

CABEIRI

One other religion of initiation is of particular importance. This is the cult of the Cabeiri, recorded as the oldest of the Mysteries after those of Eleusis. Their great centre was Samothrace, but it was by no means the only one. The country round Pergamum was their special province, and there is evidence of the cult late in the imperial period; the city of Pergamum dedicated an altar to the Cabeiri at Sestos. Aelius Aristides calls them the oldest of spirits, with control of mysteries giving protection against storms. They had a cult in Boeotia near Thebes, doubtfully said to have been founded from Athens. They appear on coins at Thessalonica and on a relief from Hierapolis in Phrygia. From these representations where they carry hammers on their shoulders they appear to have been volcanic spirits. This would make them smiths; it would also associate them with the underworld. They are linked with divinities with strange archaic names, Axieros,

Axiocersa, Axiocersus, Cadmilus; the Greeks identified these with
Demeter, Persephone, Hades and Hermes, from which we may be
sure that a religion of the dead has become fused with the cult of
the Mother. The Cabeiri themselves are generally, but not always,
two in number, and identified with the Dioscuri. At Samothrace
the cult was international, and representatives came from all over
the Aegean world; the greatest support, even in Roman times,
was from Thrace and Macedonia.

Initiation was as near classless as imaginable. Roman governors
and their staffs were initiated, travelling bureaucrats or business-
men, the crews of ships, wives with their husbands, slaves with
their masters, all seeking the same hope. Initiation took place at
night; the initiate wore a crown, carried a lamp and shared in a
sacramental meal. After initiation the initiate wore an iron ring
and a purple scarf as talismans against danger; and particularly
shipwreck. There were two grades of initiates, the *mystae* who
received the secret and the *epoptae* who had seen the spectacle. We
still say 'Seeing is believing', and these last were the deeper
believers; far fewer were admitted to this grade. There is evidence
of a confessional before admission to the higher grade. The
spectacle may have been a mystical marriage; at least we know
that it concerned Earth and Sky, that it explained the ithyphallic statues of Cadmilus-Hermes, and that there was music and
dancing. Such a story bears with it the promise of life, a promise
which might extend beyond the grave. The sanctuary was heavily
damaged by an earthquake about AD 200, but was rebuilt, and the
cult prospered for a while; then a decline set in, and from AD 400
there was a steady process of destruction.

JUDAISM

The Jews were a peculiar people in many senses. Coming out of
a polytheistic background they had associated themselves in a free
covenant with Yahweh, a sky-god of the Kenites worshipped on
the mountain, and passed from monolatry to monotheism. From
the first the covenant had imposed moral obligations, nationally
and individually, and a succession of prophets kept this challenge
before the people. Yahweh was for his people Lord of history

who had delivered them out of the hands of the Egyptians and would deliver them from other oppressors, finally through his anointed Messiah establishing the kingdom of righteousness and peace. He too was Lord of nature and it was treacherous idolatry for them to turn to other fertility-gods. After their conquest by the Mesopotamians and during the greater flexibility of the Hellenistic age the Jews spread over the Near East and the Mediterranean. Their hopes remained centred on the temple at Jerusalem till its destruction by the Romans. Yet their vision was world-embracing. Yahweh was the Lord of all history, not just of Jewish history. The prophet proclaimed Yahweh's judgment upon atrocities committed in a conflict between Moab and Edom; it was he who brought the Syrians from Kir and the Philistines from Caphtor, and at the last all nations should flow to the hill of the Lord. Judaism therefore was a proselytizing religion, and, because of its peculiar nature, it appeared to the outsider as another of the Eastern Mysteries. A. D. Nock has brilliantly summarized its appeal to the prospective God-fearer: 'You are in your sins. Make a new start, put aside idolatry and the immoral practices which go with it, become a naturalized member of the Chosen People by a threefold rite of baptism, circumcision, and offering, live as God's Law commands, and you will have every hope of a share in the life of the world to come.' The august vision of God combined with stern moralism was the special appeal of Judaism. We have occasional glimpses of its impact in strange places: in the household of Pollio in the Augustan age, in the work *On the Sublime* which singles out the creation-narrative from *Genesis*, in Numenius, who in the second century AD described Plato as 'Moses speaking Greek'. (*Pl.* 84)

CHRISTIANITY

Christianity grew within the Roman Empire. Its immediate context was Judaism, but a Judaism already aware of the Graeco-Roman world, and nowhere more so than in the Decapolis where much of Jesus' ministry lay. Jesus was the village carpenter at Nazareth who at the age of thirty set out upon a three-year ministry, calling men to repentance and to accept Yahweh as their king. Jesus claimed a unique relationship with Yahweh, with whose authority he spoke, challenging the religious authorities with their conventionality, and illustrating his teaching with varied wit and stories. As the attitude of the authorities stiffened, popular support fell away. He still hoped with his immediate followers to establish the New Israel, which he personified as the Son of Man, but soon came to see that the triumph of the new community would be won only through suffering. Hence much of his teaching is 'eschatological'; it looks to the ultimate triumph of God; yet in one sense the eschatology is 'realized', for Jesus saw Yahweh's kingship as fully realized in his own obedience. Some of his support came from those who looked for a military leader against the Romans, and it may have been in an effort to force his hand that a misguided follower betrayed him to the authorities. Jesus accepted the betrayal and, left in his full obedience the sole representative of the kingdom, allowed himself to be executed.

Then something happened. The disciples (the word really means apprentices) who had run away in cowardice found a new lease of life. They declared that Jesus had appeared to them visibly after death, and that even after those appearances had ceased they had been lifted out of themselves by a power they called impartially the Spirit of God or Spirit of Jesus. So they went out with a pro-clamation (*kerygma*) which in its simplest form ran something like: 'Jesus of Nazareth, a man attested to you by God with mighty works and wonders and signs which God did through him in your midst, as you yourselves know—this Jesus, delivered up according to the definite plan and foreknowledge of God, you crucified and killed by the hands of lawless men. But God raised him up, having loosed the pangs of death, because it was not possible for him to be held by it.' The book we call *The Gospel according to Mark* is simply an expansion of that affirmation; it is not a biography of Jesus but a preachment of Christ. (*Pls.* 86–87)

Those who came in shared in the teaching (*didache*): this was based upon 'love', a concept so new that a virtually new word (*agape*) had to be coined for it. It was the dim reflection of the love they had experienced from their God; it was the cement of the new society; it was the secret of their out-reaching to the afflicted and their relations with their enemies. The behaviour it implies may be seen in the collection of sayings called 'The Sermon on the Mount', or in Paul's letters to the Romans or Galatians, or the moralizing letter of James. Or, from the second century AD, we may cite the anonymous letter to Diognetus with its picture of Christians exercising their citizenship of heaven through their citizenships on earth, obeying the laws, and going far beyond the laws in their standard of behaviour, free with their hospitality but not with their chastity, like others in having children, unlike others in not leaving children to die. Besides, each week they shared in the sacrament of a common meal, in the course of which came the Thanksgiving or Eucharist, in which they broke the bread and poured the wine in commemoration of their founder's broken body and blood shed, and shared the power of his life as they ate and drank.

Wherein then lay the appeal of Christianity? It was first in the personality of the founder. This has been doubted, because it is not stressed by the apologists. It is not stressed because it was taken for granted: no need to repeat in the second century what was in the gospels. That the person of Christ was central is seen in the critiques of Celsus and Porphyry, in the exaltation of Apollonius by Philostratus and Hierocles as a counterblast, in the heroic witness of a Polycarp: 'I have been his servant for eighty-six years and he has done me no wrong; how can I blaspheme my King who saved me?' It was secondly in the way of love revealed, in the witness of community (*koinonia*), in a fellowship which took in Jew and Gentile, slave and free, men and women, and whose solid practicality in their care for the needy won the admiration even of Lucian. 'How these Christians love one another!' was a respectful affirmation. There was a curious gaiety about the Christians; years later it was this warmth which attracted Augustine. The women were a particular power: Mithras, for example, did not admit them. It was thirdly in the very strength of conviction, in the simple directness which cut through the multitudinous choices offered by the ancient world, above all in the courage which faced martyrdom without flinching and wrung a grudging recognition from Celsus and Marcus Aurelius, and secured the conversion of Justin and Tertullian. It was finally in a message of hope for all, for from the first the resurrection of Christ had meant for his followers the certainty of victory over death. As Nock put it pungently, 'it was left to Christianity to democratize mystery'.

Christianity spread at first chiefly among Jews; even in the records of Jesus we can discern a certain tension between the mission to Israel and the encounter with a wider world. That same tension was acute in the early Church, between the Juda-izers as represented by Jesus' brother James who led the Jerusalem Christians, and those whose horizon was wider, such as Paul. Ultimately Paul's party won, and Christianity spread geographi-cally. By the beginning of the second century Christian com-munities are found, perhaps in India, widely in the Near East, on Crete and Cyprus, in Egypt, in Cyrene, in the main centres of Greece, at Puteoli, Pompeii and Rome, and perhaps in Spain. 'We are but of yesterday,' claims Tertullian a hundred years later, 'and we have filled everything, cities, islands, camps, palace, forum— all you have left is the temples'—and he claims that Christ has conquered areas of Britain which the Romans have failed to reach. As it spread geographically it also spread socially. At first the care the Christians showed for the needy and oppressed meant that it was among those groups that the faith chiefly spread. This long continued and was never wholly forgotten; there is a striking passage in Celsus' indictment where he declares that where other mystery-religions invite the pure and righteous, Christians invite crooks and simpletons, yes, and women and children, and the very teachers are wool-workers and cobblers and laundry-men. It was a group which tended, as Max Weber saw, to congregational religion, religion of salvation, rational, ethical religion. But others were there from the first. Most of the disciples of Jesus were relatively obscure, but Joseph of Arimathea and Nicodemus were men of wealth and distinction. *Luke* and *Acts* were directed to a high Roman official, who was expected at least to be sympathetic. By the end of the first century there is strong evidence that Flavius Clemens, a member of the imperial family, and his wife Domitilla were Christian converts. By the second century converts are coming in from all classes: philosophers, scholars and lawyers; soldiers (who were not given full membership till they left their bloody trade); a few, though still only a few, of the governing classes.

Tertullian may be taken as an example. He was born in or near Carthage somewhere round AD 150. His parents were not Christian: his father was a centurion. He was well educated, taking the groundwork of medical courses before transferring to law. He is one of the great masters of Latin—rhetorical, but Latin is a rhetorical language. It is clear enough that it was the witness of the martyrs which converted him to Christianity; it is he who coined the phrase 'the blood of Christians is seed'. From then his brilliant wit and warm, irascible temper were at the service of the Church, and directed alike against non-Christians and fringe-Christians. The finest work of his large output remains *The Apology*, penned in AD 197 during a period of persecution. His indictment of the persecutors is magnificent. Other men are tortured to force them to confess, Christians to make them deny. Trajan said, 'Don't look for Christians, but punish them if you find them.' If Christians are guilty why should they not be hounded down; if innocent, why should they be punished? The charges against Christians are preposterous. If the Nile does not overflow its banks, if the Tiber does, if the earth moves, if the sky fails to move, if there is famine or pestilence, the cry goes up: 'The Christians to the lion!' All those Christians to one lion? The sarcasm is superb. Of course there were disasters before Christ came. Christians may be condemned by men; 'we are acquitted by God'. Later Tertullian became a Montanist, unorthodox but never heretical. A rich personality, vigorous, domineering, unfair, yet with his heart in the right place, knowing that conduct is the criterion of creed, pleading that man naturally reaches out to God, the soul is naturally oriented to Christianity (*animae naturaliter Christianae*).

GNOSTICISM

Finally, there are the Gnostics. The problem of the origins of Gnosticism is highly controversial, and cannot here be argued at length. There are four main theories of its origin: (*a*) Eastern, perhaps Egypt, Syria, Iran or even India; (*b*) Greece, especially

Platonism and some Hellenistic thought; (c) Jewish; (d) Christian. That all four contributed to the Gnostic systems seems clear: the dualism is Persian, much of the language Platonic, the mood Hellenistic, the system anti-Judaic and therefore belonging to Judaic thought, and we encounter the Gnostics in the second century as Christian heretics. Syria and Egypt were the melting-pot. Before the second century we can see tendencies which we may, if we will, call Gnostic: no more.

Gnosticism is a religion of revolt. It offers a fresh interpretation of the universe: first of God and things ultimate, then of the formation of the world in its contrast between height and depth, then of the state of man, and lastly of salvation. The picture of the universe is dualistic. God stands in opposition to the world which was formed by an anti-god (who is identified with the Old Testament Yahweh). We may put alongside the God-world contrast three others, spirit-soul (*pneuma-psyche*), light-darkness, life-death. The soul needs redemption. As *The Hymn of the Pearl* puts it: 'They mixed me drink with their cunning and gave me their meat to taste. I forgot that I was a king's son, and served their king. I forgot the Pearl for which my parents had sent me. Through the heaviness of their nourishment I sank into slumber.' Salvation comes through *gnosis*, knowledge, but in the sense of certainty rather than of intellectual cognition; this is contrasted with *pistis*, faith, which offers only partial or limited salvation. The salvation offered is a secret revelation: in this sense Gnosticism may be classed with the Mystery-religions. It comes from a divine Saviour who is often seen as Christ, but, because the material world is evil, there is a strong tendency to distinguish between the spiritual Christ and the material body of Jesus of Nazareth. Gnosticism thus offers a pessimistic view of the world, but the opportunity to escape. Man is a being with a divine spark, fallen into the world of matter, estranged and needing to be awakened by a divine call so as to be restored to his highest state.

Perhaps the first great exponent of Gnosticism was Valentinus, who worked in the cosmopolitan centre of Alexandria towards the middle of the second century AD. Valentinus seems to have begun his *Gospel of Truth* with a relatively straightforward reinterpretation of Christian doctrine. The Word, the Logos, has come from the Thought and Mind of the Father. Men are drunk and in darkness, dreaming nightmares, oblivious of their origin and destiny. Salvation, through knowledge, is offered by Jesus Christ; Error tried to destroy him, but Truth and Knowledge cannot be destroyed. But behind this relatively simple statement lies a system of inordinate complexity. The *pleroma*, or fullness of the godhead, consists of thirty *aeons* or spiritual beings, arranged in pairs or *syzygies*. First come the *Ogdoad*: Abyss and Silence, Mind and Truth, Word (*logos*) and Life, Man and Church. From Word and Life come the *Dekad*, five more pairs, and from Man and Church the *Dodekad*, six more pairs, completing the *pleroma*, in which all love and joy and harmony and praise is to be found. The thirtieth and weakest aeon is called Achamoth, *Sophia* or Wisdom. She has an incestuous desire to know the Father of all; in her passion she produces formless Matter. Now Abyss and Mind produce the first Redeemer, Horus (*Limit*), who fences off Wisdom from heaven, though she does not lose her heavenly origin. Now she produces Ialdabaoth, Child of Chaos, the creator-god.

To Valentinus, the creator, the demiurge, brings together Yahweh in *Genesis* and Plato's divine craftsman in *Timaeus*. He tries to imitate the perfection of the *pleroma* in the realm of matter, and the eternity of the *pleroma* in the world of time. The world and the living things in it are thus ultimately of heavenly derivation, but in need of redemption. Mind counters by bringing out two more aeons, the perfect offspring of the *pleroma*, Jesus and the Holy Spirit. The divine Saviour comes down to redeem and wed Wisdom and bring her back to the *pleroma*, and to redeem the souls of the Gnostics, who are the true children of their mother, from the realm of matter. Mankind is divided into three groups—the *carnal*, who are beyond redemption, the *psychic*, who live by faith and good works but not by light, and who are redeemed from this world without attaining the *pleroma*, and the *pneumatic*, the illuminated, the true Gnostics, who have perfect knowledge and a brighter destiny, and whose feminine souls will be united in the *pleroma* with male angels. With Freud behind us we can evaluate Valentinus more justly than any previous generation. Consciously or unconsciously he has anticipated Freud in linking religion and sexuality; the double meaning of 'knowledge' is important. The story of Sophia is the story of the repression of incestuous desire; Horus is the censor, the super-ego. Perhaps William Blake is our closest parallel; among those who have in this way constructed their own thought-world Valentinus stands high.

Contemporary with Valentinus, also at work at Alexandria was a man of equal but different genius, Basilides. Valentinus tried to explain everything; Basilides followed the *via negativa* and claimed that it was misleading to make any statement about the deity. His conclusion is that the non-existent god made a non-existent cosmos out of the non-existent. But this is not mere playing with words. Basilides is trying to bring together a Semitic religion of salvation, Buddhist concepts of Maya and Nirvana, and some of the acutest speculations of Greek linguistic philosophy. A child of his time, Basilides could hardly avoid letting his thought emerge in a revealed myth ending in cosmic annihilation when those who remain below will neither be saved nor know of their need for salvation. In his fundamental thought he has a philosophical profundity beyond any of the other Gnostics.

These may stand as representative of a wider movement. They claimed, Basilides most forcibly, to stand within the Christian tradition, and others have echoed the claim for them. But their attitude to matter could not be reconciled with an incarnational theology, and they were bound to take a docetic view that the Logos did not in any real sense become flesh. The dualism is even clearer in Saturninus, for whom the Christ descends incorporeally from heaven to destroy the god of this world and to save men from women. Further, already in the first century Paul had warned against an emphasis on knowledge rather than on faith and still more on love. Hans Jonas has called the Gnostics the first speculative 'theologians' in the new age of religion superseding classical antiquity. In some ways they seem as precursors of scientology. Yet they were speaking to a real hunger.

CHAPTER VIII

BEYOND DEATH

IN THAT SAME WORK to which we have already referred, *The Two Sources of Morality and Religion*, Bergson argues that in the Closed Society religion, as a corollary to its function of social preservation, is a defensive reaction against the thought of the inevitability of death. In the pattern of belief about what lies beyond death the Romans showed a wide variation of belief.

First we find as a commonplace the immortality of fame. Already at the end of the Republic Cicero had subjected this concept to a quizzical examination: politicians, poets and artists commend their fame to posterity, and even philosophers, who ought not to care about such things, take pains to fix their names on their books. But Cicero himself feels that the terror of death is for those who lose everything with life, not for those whose fame cannot die. It is ironical that Epicurus, who believed that death was extinction, stipulated in his will that his birthday should be commemorated every month; this was still done by his disciples under the Empire. Seneca makes play with the survival of fame beyond death, and at the end of the first century AD Tacitus uses it in his funeral oration for Agricola. It is more blatantly seen in the desire of emperors and other conquerors to leave some visible mark of their memory: the building programme of Augustus, Caligula's palace, Nero's plan for Rome, the Arch of Titus, the Flavian amphitheatre, the forum, market and Column of Trajan, Hadrian's Pantheon and the Castel S. Angelo and all the buildings in every outpost of empire ('Games and buildings everywhere,' says his biographer), the Column of Marcus Aurelius, the great buildings of Septimius Severus, the Arches of Constantine and Galerius, the refounding of Rome in the east by Constantine. Or it can be seen in the vast structures at Athens financed by Herodes Atticus. Or at Ephesus in all the wealthy citizens who left names attached to buildings, Celsus with his library, Verulanius with his portico, Vedius who built a sumptuous gymnasium and whose wife, not to be outdone, countered with a music-hall, right on to the Christian Scholasticia who combined cleanliness with godliness by restoring the baths with stone taken from pagan buildings and erected her statue in the middle. Or in the fancy of the Roman soldier who served in Egypt and planted a pyramid for his sepulchre near the city walls, or in some of the other elaborate tombs which line the Appian Way. Or, more humbly, in the simple sepulchral inscription MEMORIAE AETERNAE 'to a memory which does not perish'. It will be observed that though a desire to be remembered on earth is not incompatible with a belief in a life of another sort beyond the grave, it is not likely to be strong in those in whom such a belief is strong. It will be remembered, too, that to many their children would be their memorial.

Secondly, there remained some fear of punishment, torment, or a life of deprivation in the underworld. At the end of the Republic, Lucretius felt that such fears needed extirpating. The cultured Cicero thought this was tilting at windmills, but our knowledge of the horrors of Etruscan demonology, and of the way simpler and cruder beliefs survive in circles which a Cicero would hardly know, leads us to think that he was wrong. The suggestion that such beliefs are childish is repeated by Seneca, and in the second century AD by Juvenal. That men of culture need to go on protesting is sufficient proof that men without culture went on professing them. Furthermore, the very survival of literature with its allusions to the fate of Tantalus, Tityos, Sisyphus and the Danaids, the eleventh book of The Odyssey and the sixth of The Aeneid helped to colour the picture of the after-life and through education to perpetuate it. It is an ironical fact that the Christian picture of Hell is precisely pagan. The Hebrew She'ol was a realm of nothingness, and Gehenna a fire for burning rubbish: the idea of punishment in the after-life, though not without justification in the Christian scriptures, has been filled out with the beliefs of Graeco-Roman mythology, another fact which proves the effective survival of those beliefs.

Thirdly, there was widespread belief in an after-life within the tomb. Lucretius claims that to be torn to pieces by wild animals is no worse than to be cremated, embalmed, or pressed down by a weight of earth, and epitaph after epitaph with the simple STTL (*sit terra tibi levis*, 'may the earth be light for you') testifies to this very attitude to burial in the imperial period; it is not found before the first century BC. The tomb is the house of the dead. Petronius' Trimalchio points the fallacy of decorating the homes we occupy when alive and not the one we shall spend far longer in. The oriental phrase *domus aeterna*, 'eternal home', recurs on the tombstones. 'This is our fixed home; we had better look after it,' says one inscription, and another, 'This is my eternal home; here I have been put, here I shall be for ever.'

Hence of course the practice of interring the dearest properties of the dead: the soldier has his arms, the craftsman has his tools, the woman her toilet-apparatus, the child its toys; in Egypt bedside books were even provided. In the Royal Archaeological Museum in Leyden may be seen an astonishing third-century AD sarcophagus from Simpelveld. The dead woman was provided with jewelry and toilet-articles: rings, ear-ring, a brooch and a gold necklace, a mirror, scent-bottle and stand. These can be paralleled elsewhere. But in addition the interior of the sarcophagus is carved to give a passable imitation of a furnished room, with a fine three-legged table, cupboards and sideboards, arm-chair, couch, a large chest, a bath-house and a heating system. Flowers were then as now set on tombs, not in pursuit of a cult of beauty nor even as an expression of growth, but, as Servius tells us, red in imitation of the blood which is the life. The Rosalia was a festival when roses were strewn on the tombs. (*Pls.* 58, 59)

Hence too sacrifice to the dead. This is what the gladiatorial shows were in origin. Animal sacrifice continued; in seventh-century Syria Christians were still sacrificing bulls and sheep on tombstones. But sacrifices also meant food, and the dead man needed food to maintain his life in the grave. Hence the funeral feasts, one, *silicernium*, immediately, one, *cena novendialis*, eight days later. These were renewed on anniversaries and at the Rosalia. Large monuments often have a dining-room and even a kitchen attached, and rich men would by will endow such feasts in perpetuity: 'I ask you all, my friends, to refresh yourselves without stint.' For in this the dead and the living joined:

*Here in my tomb I drain my cup more greedily
because here I must sleep and here must stay for ever.*

Not all were endowed: one grave calls to the passer-by not to soil it, but pour its owner a drink. The Christians attack these practices. Tertullian accuses the banqueters of using the dead man as an excuse to get drunk themselves. Augustine is using the same language two centuries later of the sort of people who 'drink extravagantly over the dead and in offering banquets to corpses bury themselves on top of the buried and set their own greed and drunkenness to the score of religion'. It will be noticed that the inscriptions which address the passer-by imply a local habitation and a yearning for human society: 'Lollius has been placed by the side of the road so that every passer-by may say to him, "Hello, Lollius."'

In general the inscriptions show little hope. There is occasional thought of the chain of life: 'I am ashes, ashes are earth, earth is a goddess. Therefore I am not dead.' One inscription recalls *The Ballad of Reading Gaol*: 'May the passer-by who has seen these flowers and read this epitaph say to himself, "This flower is Flavia's body."' Others pray for their ashes to become violets and roses or for the earth above them to be fertile. Occasionally we meet a philosophical formulation. From Cologne: 'The holy spirit which you bore has escaped from your body. That body remains here and is like the earth; the spirit pursues the revolving heavens; the spirit moves all; the spirit is nothing else but God.' But these are exceptional. Any note of hope tends to be hypothetical. So Tacitus over Agricola: '*If* there be an abode of the spirits of the righteous. . . .' So the tombs: '*If* there be any sensation after death . . .'; '*If* the dead have any faculties. . . .' Often, as in Horace's poetry, the lost pleasures of life are contrasted with the emptiness of the grave: 'All I've got is what I ate and drank'; 'What I ate and drank I have with me; what I left behind I have lost'; 'While I lived I drank freely; drink on, you who are still alive.' So a set of silver cups found near Pompeii show the philosophers and poets among skeletons, with the injunction: 'Enjoy life while you are alive.' A frequent formula on tombstones is *es bibe ludi veni*, 'eat drink sport come.' Often too the troubles of life are contrasted with the peace of the grave—no hunger, no gout, no disease, no financial problems, and free hospitality: 'Life was a penalty, in death there is thought of rest for me.' Often and often death is simply 'eternal sleep'. The thought of annihilation may be expressed with a touch of philosophy:

> We are nothing, as we were before. Reader, consider
> how swiftly we mortals drop back from nothing to nothing.

The idea becomes so trite that it is expressed in a formula NF F NS NC: *non fui fui non sum non curo*, 'I was not: I was: I am not: I care not.' It is important to note that this nihilism is scarcely to be found either in Greece or Rome in the epitaphs before the imperial period or the later Hellenistic age. In general the note of lamentation sounded in so many epitaphs does not imply great hope.

One feature of many inscriptions which suggests an absence of hope in an after-life is the meticulous recording of the exact age of the dead person. There are innumerable examples: it will be convenient to quote from Britain. Thus at Horsley in Gloucestershire, Julia Ingenuilla lived for 20 years 5 months 29 days; at Bath Successa Petronia lived for 3 years 4 months 9 days. There is an elaborate example from Ribchester, put up by Julius Maximus; it honours his wife Aelia who lived for 28 years 2 months 8 days, his son M. Julius Maximus who lived for 6 years 3 months 20 days, and his mother Campania Dubitata who lived for 50 years; with older women, as still in Africa, the records tend to be vague. The preoccupation with exact age arises from the importance of life on earth as the only one we have; there is a notable contrast with Christian epitaphs which tend to be indifferent to the age but precise about the date of death, the birthday into new life.

Some time in the early part of the second century AD there was

and rebirth, and to take this as representative of the rebirth open to individuals through the power of Dionysus. Some interpreters consider that the general picture is of a new Golden Age, like that of Vergil's fourth Eclogue. The pursuit of lizard by snake runs counter to this, and we have rather an indication of the power of the god in the forces of nature: the strongest animal, the elephant; the swiftest of predators, the panther; the king of birds, the eagle; the subtlest of reptiles, the snake.

Next comes the Ariadne scene: she lies abandoned and asleep; the rout approaches, saving her from the winged approach of Death; a small Pan twitches at her robe, a little Eros reaches a lighted torch towards her. An arched gateway seems to represent the door of death. The god has in fact gone into the world of death to rescue Ariadne into new life. We shall not be altogether wrong if we assimilate Ariadne here to Psyche and see Dionysus as the supreme manifestation of that Eros with which some of his attendants are identified. There is a variant of this scene in the Gardner Collection in Boston; here the Bacchic procession discovers Ariadne asleep—only Bacchus is not obviously present. There is however an infant on Silenus' back, and it is likely that we have a conflation of themes; this conflation must have had a practical purpose, and it is easy to discern. On the one hand we have the soul awakening to new life at the divine presence; on the other the god himself appears new-born and the soul in its state of rebirth is one with the god. (*Pls.* 61, 63)

The story is drawn out by a sarcophagus in the Ashmolean Museum in Oxford, on which Dionysus and Ariadne make an epiphany in glory with centaurs drawing their car, and maenads dancing in attendance. The portrait of the dead man is also carried by centaurs. In a similar example in the Louvre it is an Attis-like figure who holds the medallion; he carries a winnowing-fan in his right hand and an upturned torch in his left. In this too there is a butting contest between a goat and Pan, urged on by Cupids: here is a whimsically delightful reference to the *agon* which is life.

The Metropolitan Museum in New York contains a very interesting variant on the Ariadne theme. The sarcophagus shows three scenes from the Theseus-Ariadne saga. In the first we see the labyrinth, and its door is the door of death; in the second we have the killing of the Minotaur; in the third the familiar Dionysus-Ariadne scene. Here there is a 'double-take', a transfer of identity from Theseus to Ariadne. One suspects a strongly masculine male, not content to be represented by the figure of Ariadne, yet unable to drop it because it was already hallowed, and insisting therefore on the scenes where Theseus breaks through the door of death, and through all trials to victory.

The triumph of Dionysus is well seen in a superb sarcophagus in the Fitzwilliam Museum at Cambridge. At either end are trees, an elm with vine at one, and a laurel at the other, and there are pine-trees along the route. At the head of the procession is a panther; then a young satyr with a full wine-skin on his shoulder; next comes a huge elephant with rich trappings, carrying two maenads and a satyr on his back; then a satyr with a child on his shoulders. In the centre is Silenus drunk, wearing a wreath of ivy, dropping an empty wine-cup, and supported by a satyr and maenad; he is followed by Pan clashing a tambourine and dancing with some sprightliness. Now at last comes the chariot, drawn by two centaurs, one male, one female, with drinking-vessels, pine-branch, garlands, panther-skin. The chariot has a lion's head on the wheel-hub, and on the body reliefs of a panther, a young satyr with a torch, a *putto* with a thyrsus, and a scene showing Eros teasing Pan. In the chariot the god stands, still, resting his arm on a crouching satyr, with a thyrsus in his left hand, ivy in his hair and a skin over his shoulder; finally a dancing maenad follows with tambourine. The ends of the sarcophagus show a scene from the infancy of Dionysus, and two Erotes carrying a drunken ithyphallic Pan. The total effect is a mighty testimony to the power of a god of life. It is a particularly interesting sarcophagus, both for the skill of its carving and because it is an early example of scenes which can be amply paralleled elsewhere; it seems to date from before the mid-second century AD.

The Fitzwilliam Museum contains another, much simpler, Dionysiac sarcophagus dating from the third century AD. Here much of the front consists of the characteristic undulating fluted ornament, but there are three relief-panels. At one end stands a satyr, with ram, goat and panther at his feet, and the infant god on his shoulder, at the other a maenad, dancing with cymbals. In the centre is the god himself, garlanded with ivy, fruit and flowers, leaning on a satyr with his left arm while he uses his right to pour a libation over a ram's head on an altar; he is attended by Pan; a panther eases its way between his legs and places its paw on a basket from which a snake is emerging.

Heracles-Hercules was the divine son who laboured for mankind, and, for his services, which ended in death, was granted a place among the immortal gods. He was, as we have seen, a model adopted by the emperors. The theme of Heracles occurs frequently on the sarcophagi. One common pattern, slightly adapted, may be seen in a magnificent second-century AD example from the Palazzo Torlonia at Rome. The dead couple recline, Etruscan-wise, on the lid of the tomb. The long sides show in a series of niches ten of the twelve Labours: parallel examples have all twelve, but there is a reason for the difference. The short sides are much more difficult of interpretation. Each has three niches. One shows the door of death, on one side a young woman with a casket, on the other a young man with a staff in his right hand and a ram's head in his left. It is hard to know whether these are divine or human figures; perhaps they are the son and daughter come with offerings to the tomb. At the other end two figures of Heracles stand on either side of a divine figure with cornucopiae. The two figures complete the Labours symbolically: they represent the cleansing of the stables of Augeas, and the securing of the golden apples of the Hesperides. But they do more than that. One holds his club up, one down; they stand like the figures of Cautes and Cautopates on Mithraic monuments, representing night and day, winter and summer, death and life, and they flank a goddess laden with the fruits of life. Here is hope and promise through the strength of Heracles who cleansed life and conquered death. (*Pl.* 68)

There is a particularly interesting example of the Heracles-motif in the Louvre. It shows a bearded man standing between two women; the scene has been identified as Homer between *The*

Iliad and *The Odyssey*, but it is clearly the fable of the Choice of Heracles retailed by Prodicus, only the dead man stands in the place of Heracles. One more example may be taken from the elaborate family tomb erected at Igel near Trier by some prosperous drapers named Secundinii, a monument which won the admiration of Goethe. The tomb is richly sculptured, and the sculpture is full of symbolism. The rape of Hylas represents the rape of death, the rescue of Andromeda the liberation of the soul, the baptism of Achilles the entry into new life. The climax is the scene, at the rear of the tomb, of Heracles' apotheosis.

The appearance of the Muses on sarcophagi has recently been the subject of an extended study by Max Wegner. A good example in the Louvre has love-scenes above, and at either end a bearded man seated, under an arch or tree, and expounding to a woman, in one instance veiled and in the other unveiled; this is the symbolism of the soul. There is no call to enter here into the details of the Muses' individual iconography. Sometimes they appear on their own, sometimes with Apollo, or Apollo and Athene. Often they display the tools of their trades, books and musical instruments, tragic and comic masks. The figure of a poet which appears with them in some representations suggests that these scenes too are to be interpreted in terms of the divine touch upon humanity; here however the theme is compatible with a glory achieved in this life only, and an immortality on the lips of men, such as older Roman poets from Ennius to Horace had claimed. Sometimes the figure of Marsyas appears in association with the Muses: he is indeed a theme in his own right. This is the crucifixion of the lower nature by the divine power, but again it has no necessary consequences beyond the grave. (*Pl.* 67)

The round of the year naturally suggests the passage from life to death, but it also offers hope of the passage from death to life. One characteristic way of representing this is through the depiction of the Seasons. There is a convenient example at Boston, datable on grounds of technique to about AD 260. The dead man stands centrally, and on either side of him are four *putti*, each group representing the four Seasons. Those nearest him are warmly dressed, and plainly and appropriately represent winter.

But all the cherubic figures carry emblems of life, thyrsus-wands, or grapes, and the panthers which are depicted among the flocks and flowers in the background show that the passage of the year is to be seen in the context of the redeeming mysteries of Dionysus, and the ploughman portrayed at each end of the sarcophagus shows that the tomb is a preparation for rebirth. (*Pl. 62*)

Another fine example in the Dumbarton Oaks collection was the subject of an extended study by George Hanfmann. It is of uncertain date, but was perhaps made in the reign of Constantine. A large medallion displays the images of the dead couple; it bears the signs of the zodiac. Winter has the attributes of Attis, an obvious type of the death of the year; he is wearing a one-piece under-garment and a cloak. Spring is wreathed with flowers; he carries a basket of flowers in his right hand and supports the medallion with his left. Summer, who also supports the medallion, is wearing a crown of corn-ears. Autumn is crowned with vine-branches; he holds in his hand some game which a leaping dog is trying to secure. At their feet are portrayed agricultural scenes, a shepherd milking a goat, an excellent vintage scene, and a harvester. Here there are no Dionysiac associations, and it is possible that they merely represent the blessings of life and the passage of time, as in the epitaph:

May spring grant you his welcome gifts of flowers,
may the joy of summer, welcome with his foliage, smile on you,
may autumn always bring you the gifts of Bacchus
and may a light season of winter be decreed for you in the earth.

But the signs of the zodiac adorning the medallion may suggest something more. When a Christian convert, like Minucius Felix or Tertullian, sees the pattern of nature re-enacted in man, who is saved by being lost and comes to a new springtime, he is putting forward a thought familiar to his pagan audience.

The creation of man by Prometheus is a fairly frequent scene: there is a good second-century AD example from Arles in the Louvre, and a most elaborate representation from the third century in the Capitoline. In these we have the human saga from life to death; yet surely the creation of man for life symbolizes the new creation for new life beyond the grave; indeed we can see Athene-Minerva supplying the newly-fashioned human with a winged soul. It was the Capitoline relief in an engraving by Montfaucon which gave Goethe his image of Prometheus:

> Here I sit, shaping man
> After my image,
> A race that is like me,
> To suffer, to weep,
> To rejoice and be glad,
> And like myself
> To have no regard for you!

That is a romantic interpretation. But there may here also be a return to Dionysus. The Titanic element in man is the body; but he has a soul as well. (Pl. 67)

One of the most frequent forms of decoration on sarcophagi is Nereids and Tritons; like the Seasons, they are also a common feature on mosaics. There they are commonly associated with sea-born Aphrodite or the sea-goddess Galatea, or the nuptials of Poseidon-Neptune. On a Louvre sarcophagus we can see the birth of Aphrodite, surrounded by Nereids and sea-centaurs. Generally on tombs they probably represent the journey to the Isles of the Blest; Rumpf dissented (wrongly) on literary grounds. The symbolism is extended widely; it may be simply dolphins or other sea-creatures appearing in a convenient corner of the lid. At Carnuntum we actually see a boat inscribed FELIX ITALIA transporting the dead woman. Many sarcophagi are decorated with series of wavy lines in parallel on each side of the centre. It seems that these originated in the sea-waves of the Nereid scenes and were a symbol of the journey to bliss. We cannot be certain that their origin and function were not lost, and they may not have meant more than an attractive (and relatively inexpensive) decoration vaguely associated with funerals. Interestingly they are among the pagan motifs to appear on Christian sarcophagi. (Pl. 65)

A common decorative theme is the garland. Flowers are a symbol of life, and the practice of laying flowers on the grave originated with the use of red flowers as blood-surrogates, and

has always had its links with life; it is not to be seen as a mere
prettiness. This interpretation of the apparently purely decorative
sarcophagi is supported by examples where figures support the
garlands. Where these figures are Victories it is hardly to be
denied that they represent the triumph of the soul over death.
More frequently they are Erotes, Cupids, Amorini; the theme
goes back to Hellenistic art and is found at Rome from the early
Empire or even before; sometimes the Erotes appear in their own
right. It seems clear that they represent the soul, and that in the
hunting and racing scenes we have the *agon*, the trial or struggle
of the soul. On sarcophagi in Sparta and Athens they appear in
Bacchic revelry, a sure sign of links with immortality. In the
Palazzo dei Conservatori they are in a sea scene with dolphins;
again we have the association with the journey to bliss. In an
excellent garland-sarcophagus in Naples they encircle the dead
pair with wonderful festoons of flowers and fruit; on the lid a
chariot-race shows the symbol of struggle and victory.

Battle-scenes are one of the most important types of sarco-
phagus-relief. They begin about the middle of the second
century AD, but they are clearly based on Hellenistic sculptures of
the Pergamum school. A fine early example is the Ammendola
sarcophagus in the Capitoline Museum at Rome, a wonderful
elaboration of prancing horses, one with head foreshortened as
a Roman soldier gouges at its eyes; there are prisoners in the
corners, fierce sword-fighting in the centre, and horses' manes
and Gaulish hair flow freely in the wind. Similar, though less
successful, because the figures are less clearly organized to the
theme of conflict, is a rather later sarcophagus in the National
Museum at Rome showing Romans and Germans fighting. In
the Trojan War cycle we have curiously few scenes of general
fighting between Greeks and Trojans, though the sack of Troy
appears. More characteristic, and the most typical battle-scenes
of all, are the conflict of Greeks and Amazons. These are found in
very large numbers; there is a particularly magnificent example in
Vienna. We may include also under battle-scenes the Giganto-
machies and Centauromachies, though here an additional
allegory is the overcoming of the lower nature by the higher. In

all these the theme is rather glory in death than life through death. Life is a struggle; victory may come for a time, but death lies round the corner. The strong sexuality of the Amazon theme concerns us less than the representation of the soul as feminine; this is the rape of death, and the battle-scene leaves no hope which the Persephone theme allows. The centrality of Achilles and Penthesilea to many of these scenes only adds poignancy: even love cannot halt death. (Pl. 60)

Linked to battle-scenes are hunting-scenes. Sometimes these too are straightforward without any obvious mythological content. Probably therefore they represent the struggle and adventure of life, no more. Mythological scenes of hunting are associated with Adonis, Actaeon, Meleager and Hippolytus. There is a good example from Arles in the Musée Rolin at Autun. The main panel shows the boar-hunt at Calydon; one of the end-panels seems to be Meleager and Atlanta; the other shows two men facing a lion—one has been knocked down but is protecting himself with shield and short sword, the other stands firm meeting the shock of onset on his spear. I find it hard not to think that there is some assimilation, at least of Meleager and Hippolytus, to Adonis. Yet we have the problem of interpretation which recurs in so many of these tombs in different forms. Is this the man who dies, even though he is beloved by the goddess; or is this the semi-divine being who dies to rise again? The fierce beast is an obvious symbol of death; we may probably so interpret the appearance of great lions' heads on some coffins, as that of Arria and Aninia Hilara, once in Warwick Castle, now in New York, itself carved with the Selene-Endymion scene. These lions' heads were taken over on to Christian sarcophagi—there is a superb example at Tipasa on the Algerian coast—where they are seen in the context of the myths of Samson and (especially) Daniel.

Achilles is another sarcophagus theme. The example in the Fitzwilliam Museum at Cambridge shows the episode where he is tricked out of his woman's disguise by the sound of the war-trumpet. He is shown in the centre of the relief in his woman's clothes, brandishing shield and spear. The ends of the sarcophagus display subsequent scenes at Troy, the victory over Hector and the killing of Penthesilea. It is hard to say what is the symbolic purpose of these scenes. Achilles in *The Odyssey* reveals the emptiness of death to the Homeric hero; but that is hardly the point here. Rather, there is association with heroic endeavour; the scenes at the ends are of victorious struggle; the sphinxes on the lid suggest the power of death but the magnificent corner-masks of Pan remind the viewer of Dionysus and life. The central scene may well be an affirmation of power: just as Achilles' true nature asserted itself through the woman's guise, so the true nature of the soul will assert itself through the guise of death. Achilles on Scyros is a frequent theme on the tombs. Other episodes from the saga are the forging of the arms, in the Capitoline at Rome, the dragging of Hector behind the chariot shown with ghastly realism, Priam's ransoming of Hector. (*Pl.* 69)

Odysseus appears in various scenes, of which the most frequent depicts the temptation of the Sirens. These happen to show very clearly the problems of interpretation. The Sirens are spirits of death, and it might seem that such a scene represents the power to overcome death. Clearly in some examples it does: we see Hermes on the left touching the dead man's left eye; the family mourn. Then comes the scene with the Sirens; then Heracles with Cerberus, a Bacchic scene, and two river-nymphs. Heracles overcoming death, and the Bacchic scene show clearly enough that this is a representation of life through death. Yet in another example, from the Villa Albani, the tomb of a girl named Severa, the scene with the Sirens (but without the adjuncts) is accompanied by a Greek inscription beginning: 'None among men is immortal: Severa, Theseus, the sons of Aeacus, bear witness to the fact.' Here then the Siren scene represents the successful passage through the temptations of life: no more.

We pass to some scenes familiar through drama. The killing of Clytemnestra and Aegisthus by Orestes receives a number of portrayals; there is a particularly good example in the Lateran from the Hadrianic period in memory of C. Cominius Proculus. The central scene of the killing is vigorously portrayed, with the Furies bursting in on the murder; it is sandwiched between the scene at Agamemnon's tomb and the scene at Delphi as Orestes

leaves his pursuer asleep. The ends of the sarcophagus show the
spirits of Clytemnestra and Agamemnon being ferried over the
Styx by Charon, and one of the Furies with snake and torch.
What is significant about this sarcophagus is the lid, which adds
scenes from Euripides' *Iphigeneia among the Taurians*. The Orestes-
theme can be variously interpreted; the other does look like an
escape from death. The Iphigeneia story is in fact found as the
main scene in its own right. A fine sarcophagus in the Louvre,
closely paralleled by another in Mantua, shows the Medea saga:
the opening-scene of Medea with the children, the death of
Creusa in torment, the killing of the children, and Medea's escape.
There is death and terror in the theme, but there is also escape
from death and power over death. Hippolytus is found on several
sarcophagi. There is an outstanding example in the Louvre from
the Antonine period. It is difficult of interpretation. Phaedra
seated at the left with an attendant Eros is balanced by Theseus
on the right plucking his beard as he hears the news of Hippolytus' death. On one side of the centre stands Hippolytus in the
fine nakedness of youth, with horse and hound, on the other an
old man is talking to a young girl with a child; he may be the
old huntsman from the opening scene of Euripides' play. Alcestis
offered an excellent theme especially for the tomb of a girl:
witness that of Ulpia Cyrilla from Château St Aignan. The finest
(from the Vatican) however commemorates a man, C. Junius
Palatina Euhodus; it dates from the second century AD. Here the
theme of triumph over death is inescapable. Another play represented is Aeschylus' *Seven Against Thebes*. A third-century AD
sarcophagus in the Lateran has as its main theme the legend of
Adonis; but the lid shows the life of Oedipus: Laius at Delphi,
the birth, the exposure, Oedipus in Corinth, the killing of Laius,
Oedipus and the Sphinx, and the final dénouement: the theme
may be progress through external achievement to self-knowledge.
These and similar scenes are the work of artists who know the
plays intimately: they are closely linked to the tragedies and are
not based on a general mythical tradition. Patron of the tragedies
was Dionysus. Dogmatism is not possible, but it may not be
wrong to see a link with the Dionysiac hope.

A few other scenes occur from mythology, none of great moment or frequency. Such are Bellerophon, Daedalus, Phaethon and the Niobids: these are all cautionary tales, of the presumption of mortals. Here we discern no note of hope: only 'remember you too are mortal'. It is evident, not merely from the recurrence of themes but from the recurrence of precise designs, that the sculptors worked from handbooks offering a limited number of designs suitable to sarcophagi; of course originality of interpretation might creep in. This in itself suggests that we are right to look for symbolism. Some of the symbols are ambiguous, some are negative, some may merely indicate heroic endeavour. We do well to remember that the function of a symbol may be lost; and a visit to Forest Lawn in Los Angeles will convince anyone that a depressingly large number of people will accept the replica of a great work of art, however irrelevant, or, worse still, some simpering sentimentality as a suitable memorial to the Loved One. Interpretation must be cautious. But there are enough sarcophagi where the symbolism is clear, the Dionysiac especially, but not only those, to make it certain that the richer classes had moved away from the nihilism of the late Republic to some kind of faith or at least hope.

Yet one wonders how deep the promise went. Witness the Orphic hymns, where in this once other-worldly religion the votaries pray for health and wealth in life, and a good end long delayed, and Death is expressly said to bring sleep without end. Witness a second-century AD inscription from Nicopolis in Egypt: 'Heraclides the handsome lies here, just like Osiris, or Aphrodite's Adonis or Selene's Endymion, or Alcmene's son Heracles with his twelve Labours, utterly.' Witness Hadrian, initiate though he was of Eleusis and Samothrace:

> Fleeting, winsome little spirit,
> guest and mate of the body,
> for what regions will you now leave,
> pale, stiff, bare,
> and no longer produce your familiar jests.

CHAPTER IX

THE MENACE OF THE FUTURE

ORACLES

INDIVIDUALS AND STATES seek supernatural sanction for their actions. The imperial age however saw a period of decay in the great Greek oracles. Dodona had been crushed by the Romans, and its oaks were silent. Even Delphi was comparatively dumb, and Strabo commented on its decay, and Juvenal on its silence. Plutarch, who held the office of priest of Apollo, wrote a piece *On the Decline of Oracles*. Local oracles, such as those of Apollo at Tegyrae or Ptoion, have disappeared. Delphi itself uses one prophetess where three were once needed. Yet Plutarch does not seem unduly worried. The situation suits the reduced population of Greece, and he is content to speculate, with much irrelevance and much digression, on possible explanations in the drying-up of mephitic vapours and the gradual decay of the intermediate spirits or *daemones* who operate the oracles. A later treatise *On the Oracles of the Pythia* is concerned with the question why the oracular responses are no longer given in verse. This does not suggest a drastic decline in consultations, but a change of emphasis. The peace brought by Roman rule has put an end to the great public consultations of the past; states are concerned with questions of economics or public health, private enquirers ask, 'Shall I get married?', 'Shall I take a journey?', 'Shall I put out a loan? and the like, trivial questions demanding curt answers. In fact the oracle enjoyed a brief period of revived prosperity owing to the patronage of Hadrian; and even he did not ask any great political question but a literary riddle about Homer's birthplace and parents; he was told in pompous verse that the poet was Odysseus' grandson, born in Ithaca, a surprising piece of information. The prosperity was short-lived, though the oracle intervened politically to back Severus at the end of the second century AD, and it was still active in Origen's lifetime.

However, the Greeks of Asia Minor, ill content now with dependence on the mainland, had shrines of their own, also in the name of Apollo. That at Didyma certainly went back to the sixth century BC, and is mentioned by Herodotus. It had thus a long tradition and seems to have retained the confidence, or at least the patronage, of some of the Asiatic cities well into the imperial period. But it was partially eclipsed by the remarkable upsurge of the oracle at Claros. In the early Empire its procedure was relatively simple. The medium was male, from Miletus and largely illiterate; he was told the enquirer's name but not his question. He then retired to a cave, drank sacred water, and on emerging gave his answer in hexameters.

Recent excavation has revealed a much more elaborate procedure by about the year AD 200 recorded in inscriptional records. Now the oracle has a large staff, there are rites of initiation, and a formal choir sings special anthems. Responses are offered in a wide variety of metres. There are consultations from Macedon and Thrace, the shores of the Black Sea and Asia Minor. Evidently the oracle had a high reputation, as is evidenced by the fact that its fame was known as far away as Dalmatia, Sardinia, Numidia and Britain. The responses seem to have been stock, and the Cynic Oenomaus reasonably poured scorn on the delivery of stock obscure answers to all sorts of men in all sorts of need. Replies such as

> *There is in the land of Trachis a garden of Heracles,*
> *harvested by all every day, with all in blossom,*
> *yet not diminished but replete with rain continually*

or

> *A man shoots stones from a whirling sling*
> *and kills with his casts gigantic grass-fed geese*

roused his anger. In fact the Ifa oracle of West Africa works similarly. The diviner, who may be technically illiterate, has by heart a corpus of traditional verse known as the Odus of Ifa. His divining tells him which of the poems in the corpus is appropriate to the enquirer, and he recites this in answer to the enquiry. Thus different people will receive the same response. But each will be stressed in such a way as to suggest to the individual a particular appropriateness to him. The oracle at Claros must have operated thus; Oenomaus' rationalistic scorn was not wholly justified.

From Oxyrhynchus in Egypt we have a list of questions to an oracle from the late-third century AD: (72) Shall I receive the allowance? (73) Shall I stay where I am going? (74) Shall I be sold? (75) Am I receiving benefit from my friend? (76) Has it been permitted to me to complete a contract with X? (77) Am I to be reconciled to my son? (78) Am I to get a leave-pass? (79) Shall I get the money? (80) Is my wandering boy alive? (81) Am I to get a profit out of the deal? (82) Is my property to be put up for sale? (83) Shall I find a means of making a sale? (84) Am I able to carry off what I have in mind? (85) Am I to become bankrupt? (86) Shall I become a refugee? (87) Shall I be made an ambassador? (88) Am I to become a senator? (89) Is my escape to be prevented? (90) Am I to be divorced from my wife? (91) Have I been bewitched? (92) Am I to get my rights? These are the personal questions of an age of political and economic stress. It is important to realize that the questions about the status of ambassador or senator arise not from political ambition but from economic insecurity; these were expensive offices to hold.

Oracles remained and were consulted, but their great days were gone. The reason is simple; it is seen in the oracles set up by Julianus and Alexander. People were not content with the old certainties; they wanted magic and mumbo-jumbo. Milton's suggestion that the birth of Christ turned the oracles dumb is picturesque but without foundation. But they gradually lapsed into speechlessness. Already in the third century AD Nicaea tried to consult Delphi, and were told that the spoken oracle could not be renewed, but they should continue to sacrifice to Apollo. From the next century a pathetic story is told of a consultation by Julian:

> Tell the king: the monumental hall has fallen to the ground.
> Phoebus has no longer a hut, has no prophetic laurel,
> no speaking spring. Even the water which speaks is quenched.

The story has been doubted, but the situation is sure. It came from the weakness of paganism, not from the strength of Christendom.

ASTROLOGY

Astrology came west from Babylon; it was fostered by the formidable learning and dominant personality of Poseidonius. Augustus, who had little religion except when it suited him, but plenty of superstition, espoused it. Under Tiberius, ensconced in Capri 'with his Chaldaean gang', it cut loose: it was now that Manilius wrote his poem, which may be called *Astronomica* but which contains more astrology than astronomy. Astrology is concerned with the effect of the heavenly bodies on human destiny: we still speak of people as martial or jovial, mercurial or saturnine, or even lunatic. The elder Pliny writes of the kinship between men and the stars. 'We share powers and passions with the planets,' says an astronomical writer. Interpretation was a mixture of astronomy and myth. The planet Saturn's slow course led to the belief that it made men sluggish; on the other hand Venus blessed lovers, and the constellation of the Snake helped the healing process. Astrological thought was fatalistic; those who consulted astrologers were seeking to know the future not to change it. There were many such. The abacuses rattled as the horoscopes were cast, for the calculations were abstruse, and the astrologers were known as *mathematici*, mathematicians. Boll called astrology 'the scientific theology of paganism in decline'.

Perhaps it was not officially discouraged, though there were times which saw the astrologers banished from the capital. Casting of horoscopes too close to the imperial family might be subversive; but those who blamed the stars for their fate were less likely to blame their rulers. At any rate it flourished with imperial connivance and despite imperial opposition alike. Hadrian's great-uncle was an expert astrologer, and Hadrian himself was interested. Vettius Valens wrote under Marcus Aurelius: to him astrology was the supreme subject of study and carried with it the highest blessings, and he sees the astrologer as enjoying a mystical communion with the gods. In the fifth century AD Stephanus of Byzantium is still using much the same language.

In the fourth century, before his conversion to Christianity, Firmicus Maternus was following out the thought of the sympathy between man the microcosm, and the macrocosm around him, in defence of astrology.

Modern writers have tended to concentrate upon these moderately respectable interpreters, rather than on the abject mass of pullulating superstition, but a glance at the great magical papyrus from Paris will remind us of this tyranny of superstition. Stoics and Platonists fostered it; Epicureans and Christians fought a losing battle against it. Only for the Epicureans it was a battle of reason against illusion, but for the Christians it was a battle of rival gods; they believed in the astral powers but asserted that their Christ was stronger. When Paul speaks of being freed from the elements, or from principalities and powers, depth and height, he is speaking of the astral bodies and their declination and ascension. So Tatian claims that the Christian is above Fate, above the Sun and Moon. Fate, the Christians assert, may hold them before baptism, but baptism frees them. So Eusebius calls his hearers to pass from the heavenly bodies to the creative mind behind them. But it is still a battle which Augustine had to fight, and even he did not win it.

HARUSPICY

Astrology was an increasingly popular means of divination, but it was by no means the only one. Interest in dreams and their interpretation never decays, and in the fourth century AD Synesius and Macrobius write on the subject; this was the most frequent form of 'natural divination'. Under the Republic the most characteristic form of 'artificial divination' was augury; Roman rationalists like Cicero (himself an augur) had long since scorned the whole business, but it remained part of the apparatus of state. Haruspicy, quicker and simpler than augury, tended to oust it. This was borrowed from the Etruscans. Prominent under the Republic, it seems to have lapsed in the early period of the Empire, and to have been revived by Claudius for antiquarian reasons. It was by no means dead, and we have an excellent representation of a consultation on an early-second-century AD relief in the Louvre. The discovery at Piacenza nearly a century ago of a bronze model of a victim's liver on which are inscribed the Etruscan names of a large number of deities indicates something of the method of interpretation; there is a link with astrological lore, for there seems a parallel with the divisions of the sky found in Martianus Capella. Once it was re-established the practice proved persistent. In the fourth century the Christian emperor Theodosius decreed that if the imperial palace were struck by lightning the *haruspices* were to be consulted. In AD 408 the Etruscans offered their services to Pompeianus, the city prefect, to save the city from the Goths. Pompeianus consulted the Christian bishop, Innocent, who said that he would not oppose the wishes of the people provided that the rites were kept secret. The outcome is uncertain; Christian writers claim that consultation was tried and was useless; pagans that it was never tried. Haruspicy remained: it was still seriously discussed in the time of Laurentius Lydus in the sixth century AD. (*Pl.* 73)

OMENS

Haruspicy, with a sheep as the most popular victim, was still moderately expensive. It was cheaper to attend to omens; Pliny passes on a deal of folklore about animal omens, and Julius Obsequens was interested enough to compile a volume of prodigies from the pages of Livy: no difficulty in that. The *Historia Augusta* is full of prodigies and omens: in the reign of Antoninus a Tiber flood, a comet, a two-headed child, quintuplets, a crested serpent which ate itself, barley growing from the tree-tops, a pride of naturally tame lions; under Commodus footprints of the gods leaving the forum, a blaze in the sky, a sudden darkness on 1 January, firebirds. The brief glory of Maximinus and his son was foreshadowed by a snake coiling round his head as he slept, a vine with clusters of purple grapes, a shield blazing in the sun, a lance split clean in two by lightning; Severus Alexander's death by a victim escaping from sacrifice and splashing him with blood, by falling trees, by the words of a Druid, and by some words of his own. We must remember that omens were not necessarily world-shaking portents. There must have been many who, like Augustus, put their right shoe on first, or thought it a good omen to set out on a long journey in a light drizzle, and few who did not think it good to have incense, salt-cake or the sort of leaves and wood which would make a fire crackle and spurt with good omen. But even accidental omens might be dangerous, and Gibbon makes much of the part that birthmarks of the right shape or the accidental contact with purple might play in shaping the ambitions of parents in an age when emperors appeared from the most improbable corners.

One of the most fascinating survivals of the ancient world was discovered at Pergamum in the early years of this century. It consists of a sorcerer's professional equipment from the third century AD. It includes a three-legged bronze table, elaborately engraved with a full-length image of the triple goddess of magic, Hecate, and inscriptions invoking her; a round dish, carefully divided into sections, and displaying magical symbols from Egyptian and eastern sources, and two magic rings. This is evidently equipment for divination; the dish will be set on the table in a magic ceremony, and the rings, hanging from a thread, induced to indicate the significant symbols as they swing. (Pl. 74)

Lastly we may mention the random consultation of books. The *sortes Homericae* were followed by the *sortes Vergilianae*, which are found no less than eight times in the *Historia Augusta*, and they in turn by the *sortes Biblicae*. After all, was not this the final turning-point for Augustine? Meditating in a garden, still un-committed, still in tension, he heard the voices of children at play. 'Pick it up and read it,' said one voice (*tolle*, *lege*). A Bible was at his side, and the text at which he opened it spoke to his condition.

SACRIFICE

It is just to say that though the theory of divination, like that of astrology, might imply a fixed destiny, those who used divina-tion were usually not seeking to discover a determined fate but the approval or disapproval of the gods on a course of action. For those who believed in personal gods a further way to securing that approval lay through sacrifice. There have been many elevated theories of sacrifice, and no doubt Hebrew sacrifice was immeasurably subtler; we should not forget the elements of communion and of self-offering. But it is hard not to think that the general principle behind most sacrifices is in fact *do ut des*; the god, like the judge in *The Caucasian Chalk-Circle*, begins by saying 'I receive'. This is certainly the view of ancient writers, though Iamblichus tries to establish that it is an expression of friendship not a bribe. At Rome the process went through two stages, the *nuncupatio*, or promise of a sacrifice in requital of favours received, and the *solutio*, or fulfilment of the promise if the god did his part.

The largest and most welcome sacrifices were nearly always of animal victims. Each divinity had his preference. A white victim was suited to Zeus and to the Olympian gods generally, a black one to the deities of the underworld. Poseidon liked horses, Priapus asses, Dionysus goats. The earth-goddess might receive a pregnant sow. At Rome Robigus, the spirit of rust in wheat, received a red dog. But not all sacrifices offered animals: there might be fruit, beans, milk, cheese, honey, oil. Often there would be a promise rather than a gift, and the gift would follow the favour received. Hence the common VSLM *votum solvit libens merito*, representing the free fulfilment of a promise. Here again what survives is naturally the gifts of those who could afford expensive permanent offerings, statues and altars, statuettes of bronze, inscriptions, even whole buildings. There will have been countless simpler, humbler gifts which have perished, in money or kind or even service: the healing sanctuaries with their model limbs in memory of the part healed are but one reminder. In all this there is a personal relation between worshipper and deity; the worshipper is establishing for himself the *pax deorum*, the favour of the gods. (*Pls.* 36, 72)

MAGIC

Magic and religion have always existed side by side; it is an error to try to isolate a period of magic before a period of religion—or vice versa. We may make a theoretical distinction; in magic a ritual is performed and if it is correct in every detail the desired result must follow unless countered by a stronger magic, whereas in religion the result depends upon the will of a personal god. But we are not so coldly analytical even today, and the man who says, 'I'm not doing badly, thank God, touch wood' is amply paralleled at all times. Thus on the one hand in a clearly religious ritual every word must be precise and in place; if the officiant stumbles he must go back to the beginning. On the other hand a piece of magic is often buttressed by invocation and prayer; as Max Weber put it, 'in prayer, the boundary between magical formula and supplication remains fluid'. We may note for example that the proper spells associated with herbs include the name of the god who discovered their powers: 'You powerful plants, whom the Earth-Mother has created and given to all the peoples of the world'; 'Castor-oil plant, in the name of the almighty god who gave you being'; 'Betony, the discovery of Aesculapius or Cheiron.' As Christianity spread, the name of Jesus or Mary was invoked in the same way. More widely, the power of magical science may, as Apuleius puts it, be ineluctable and the divine powers under compulsion, but its practitioners still invoked Hecate, Night and the gods of the underworld.

The essence of magic rests on two principles: Frazer identified them as 'homoeopathy' and 'contagion'. Both have been challenged, and require restatement, but broadly the analysis can stand. On the one hand there is the principle of sympathetic magic, that a parallel action will produce parallel results. The Kouretes or the Salii leap for taller crops; ritual prostitution secures the fertility of the earth; melt a wax image and your enemy will waste away with fever; clash spear on shields to produce thunder; bathe a statue to produce rain. The other principle is the extended personality: if you can secure some part of a person, his hair-clippings or nail-parings for instance, or something he has worn or used, or the impress of his body on a bed, or the mark of a pot he has used, or ashes, or even his name (as we are reminded by sources as various as the story of Jacob's wrestling with Yahweh, and *Old Possum's Book of Practical Cats*), you have power over them. It is easy to see the symbolism which underlies much magic; it is important to remember that to the practitioners the power is not symbolical at all, but direct.

WITCHCRAFT

Witchcraft does not greatly change. Horace's Canidia seeks a love-philtre. She seizes a young boy and removes from him the phallic amulet (*bulla*). Then with hair streaming, garlanded with small snakes, she orders her attendants to bring wild fig trees uprooted from a cemetery, funereal cypresses, the eggs and feathers of a screech-owl smeared with toad's blood, herbs from Thessaly and Colchis, and bones snatched from a hungry bitch: these are to be burned. Sagana, a second witch, sprinkles the house with water from Avernus. Veia scoops out a hole in the ground where the boy is to be buried alive and die lingeringly gazing on food which he cannot reach. After death they will remove his marrow and liver for the love-philtre. Folia stands by, she who can charm the stars and moon down from the sky. Canidia gnaws her long clawlike nails, and invokes Night and Diana (that is, Hecate), but breaks off because her spells are not working: there must be a more potent witch operating against her.

In another poem Canidia comes with black cloak tucked high, bare feet and streaming hair, howling in concert with Sagana, greater than herself, each terrible to see. They first dig the ground with their nails, then tear a black ewe-lamb to shreds with their teeth; the blood is allowed to gather in a trench so that they can draw up the spirits of the dead (like Saul or Macbeth) to give oracular answers. They have two effigies, one of wool and one of wax, representing Canidia and her lover, the woollen one larger so as to dominate the other which is shaped in a suppliant attitude. They call on Hecate and Tisiphone; snakes and hell-hounds circle round; the witches bury a wolf's beard and a spotted snake's tooth, and melt the wax image. It is interesting to compare the love-magic here with the love-magic in Vergil. In an eclogue derived from Theocritus we meet the main ingredients of love-magic: love-spells; water; soft fillets and an altar; the burning of perfumes; a charm repeated as a refrain (songs have been known to bring down the moon, to produce metamorphosis and much else); the figure three; the use of colour; knots of love; images of clay and wax; bay, bitumen and salt-cake

to sprinkle on the fire (causing the fire to flare up and crackle);
clothes forming a link with the man; herbs and potions.

We meet other witches in the Augustan and post-Augustan
writers. In Tibullus there is a witch who can draw down the stars,
turn the course of nature and raise the dead; she uses a dark victim
by night, herbs, and the number three; chanting and spitting are
important ritual acts; milk is an essential feature, ambivalent
since it is a minister of life which, like the blood in the trench,
may give life to the ghosts, but which is white, a colour repug-
nant to the dead and therefore apotropaic. Ovid, as might be
expected, is fascinated by witchcraft. A Madam named Dipsas
tries to attract Corinna away to more lucrative customers. Ovid
accuses her of being a witch: she can reverse the flow of water,
she knows herbal lore, she spins the magician's wheel, deals in
love-philtres, controls the weather, alters the face of moon and
stars, transforms herself into an owl by night, traffics with the
dead. It is a revealing passage, precisely because we are dealing
with a witty, trivial poem; this is not a mythological echo of the
past, but a curtain casually drawn from the present. In *Fasti* we
meet a witch named Tacita, and see her as with three fingers she
puts three cloves of frankincense under a mousehole in the door,
binds enchanted threads with a dark spindle, turns seven black
beans over in her mouth, roasts the head of a pilchard sealed with
pitch and pierced with a bronze needle, pours a few drops of
wine on it (drinking the rest herself), and goes off muttering,
'We have set a curb on evil tongues and inauspicious lips.'
Medea especially gripped Ovid: he wrote a tragedy on her, and
one of the *Heroides* letters is hers. In *Metamorphoses* (which is
chock-full of magic) we see her at work. She invokes Night, the
stars, Hecate (who controls spells and magic), Earth (giver of
herbs), breezes and winds, mountain, rivers and lakes, gods of
groves and gods of night. She then gives a vivid account of what
she has accomplished 'with your help when I have willed it':
turning rivers back in their courses, stirring up the sea, controlling the weather, breaking the jaws of snakes, uprooting
trees and rocks, making the earth groan and quake, drawing up
the dead, and pulling the moon down from the sky. As she sets

about her spells the moon is full; Medea is barefoot with no fastening on her dress or hair; it is midnight; she turns three times, three times asperses herself with river water; three times utters wailing cries.

Medea is also the subject of a long magical excursus in Seneca. Indeed Seneca and his nephew Lucan are both absorbed, in a way quite unfitted to professing Stoics, by the witches' power to change the course of nature. In Lucan's epic, which is, after all, something of an essay in the Stoic interpretation of history, there is an astounding sequence where Sextus Pompeius seeks the help of a Thessalian witch named Erichtho. There is a long, gory description of the witch. She offers no prayers to the gods above; she knows the houses of Pluto and Styx; she is pallid with unkempt hair; she specializes in stealing dead bodies, and especially those of criminals; if she wants living blood she commits murder; and she uses her left hand. Sextus finds her and asks her to call up Death. She replies that this is difficult; it is better to call up one dead man. She then redoubles the darkness, hides her head in a cloud, and wanders among the bodies of the unburied dead. She finds a body, and takes it to a gloomy wood unpierced by light, under an overhanging mountain. She puts on a multicoloured dress, pushes her hair back from her face, and dons a garland of snakes. She then opens the breast and pours in blood, adds *virus lunare* (presumably a juice believed to emanate from the moon), the foam of a rabid dog, a lynx's entrails, a hyena's spine, a stag that has fed on snakes, a barnacle, snakes' eyes, eagle-stones, a winged snake from Arabia, a Red Sea snake, the slough of an African horned snake, the ashes of a phoenix: she adds nameless horrors, herbs magicked and spat upon, distillations of her own invention. She calls in various animal sounds, on the gods below: the Furies (oddly called by the euphemistic name Eumenides), the abomination of Styx, the goddess of Vengeance, Chaos, Dis, Styx itself, Persephone, Hecate, Aeacus, the Fates, Charon. In a second wild invocation she threatens to add to these Demogorgon. He is not named; indeed his name was not to be known, though we know it from other sources. He was the great god of the magicians, dangerous to call up; he was invoked girdled (so that his power bound the invoker) and wearing iron (a modern invention belonging to the new world, not the past). The threat is enough; the life returns; the destiny is proclaimed; the corpse asks for death again, and spells and herbs grant this. It is of course sheer fantasy; but it was the sort of fantasy which might appeal to a sophisticated audience.

These literary examples come from the early period of the Empire. But they are echoed in the late-second century AD by Apuleius. In *The Golden Ass* there is a thrilling account of a Thessalian witch named Meroe, who could call down the sky, hang the earth up in heaven, freeze up springs, melt mountains, raise the dead, send gods to hell, put out the stars, and light up the underworld; she had turned people into beavers, snakes and rams, and transported a house a hundred miles. In the course of the adventure she and her associates murder a man, steal his blood and his heart and substitute a sponge. More important to the story is Pamphile, who knows all the spells sung over tombs, can pull the moon's light down into the underworld by breathing upon sticks and stones, is mistress of love-potions and metamorphoses. She is in love with a young man, and tries to get hold of some of his hair to magic him through it, but fails and is fooled. For her laboratory she has a room on the roof, reaching up towards the sky. Here she goes after dark. She has herbs, hieroglyphics, remnants of dead creatures of ill omen. She chants a spell over quivering entrails; then she offers fresh spring-water, milk, honey and mead; she twists the young man's hair (as she supposes), knotting it fast, and throws it with perfume on to the fire. She also transforms herself into an owl by the use of ointment and a magic lamp: the antidote is to bathe in and drink spring-water with anise and bay-leaf. Lucius tries to emulate her, but makes a mistake and becomes a donkey with decidedly errant wings; his antidote is the rose.

Apuleius' story stands in a line of Greek narratives, but its mood is contemporary. Two centuries later Augustine was not certain that his compatriot had not really been turned into a donkey. Apuleius himself was actually put on trial for marrying a rich wife by magic. In the previous century the elder Pliny records an anecdote about a man who was tried for sorcery because he obtained better crops than his neighbours; he won his acquittal by exhibiting in court the quality of his tools. Apuleius' defence is more elaborate, and highly amusing. The first part deals with his cleanliness (unexpected in a philosopher), the small number of his slaves, and his general way of life. When he comes to the specific charge of magic he makes three main points. First, he asserts that magic is simply the Persian for religion. Second, in answer to the accusation that he bought peculiar fish, he replies (*a*) that he was interested in natural history, (*b*) that a magician would use herbs not fish, (*c*) that if he was distilling medicine from the fish, that was science not magic and (*d*) that anyway he had not done so. Third, in answer to the charge that he chanted spells and sprinkled perfumes over epileptics in order to use them for clairvoyance, he replies that an unhealthy person would be a bad subject, and that in one case he was seeking a cure, in another he had only asked about a buzzing in the ears. The prosecution was futile, but Apuleius may well have dabbled in magic: Augustine certainly thought that he did.

There is a certain consistency in these tales of witchcraft. The power of the witch was to change the course of nature, to control the power of love, to foretell the future, to produce metamorphosis, and to raise the dead. It is interesting to see necromancy surviving into Christian tradition: thus Spyridon calls his daughter Irene out of the tomb to reveal the hiding-place of a valuable entrusted to her; Severinus calls up a dead presbyter and asks him to consent to come and serve his congregation again, but he implores to be left in eternal rest. Over their methods we note the use of darkness, midnight, thick groves, and black victims; cutting across this, however, the mysterious power of the full moon. We note the power of the knot: the witch must have no knots about her person, no laced sandals, belted dress or tied-up hair, for then her spells might fetter her; but knots may be used to bind a spell on someone else. We note the use of effigies, identified with the people concerned, or of clothes or clippings from their body; a spell put on these will bind them; Pliny confirms the use of hair and nail-parings in magic, and some of the tabus observed by the Flamen Dialis point the same way: his hair and nail-parings (clipped with bronze) must be buried under a lucky tree for fear they be used for magic. Bronze is important; it belongs to the old order, which witchcraft invokes. Spitting is apotropaic, as Pliny again tells us. The symbolism of all this is straightforward. The mixture of binding incantations and prayers of invocation is especially noteworthy.

SIMPLES AND AMULETS

Plants are important in magic. This arises partly because they are an example of living power, partly because of the healing properties—and fatal properties—of various herbs. So in West Africa today the *babalawo* or *dibia* may be an expert herbalist; yet there will always be incantations and magical ritual associated with his work. Thus in the ancient world herbs used for magical purposes had to be cut with a bronze knife, for the reasons we have noticed; so Dido's priestess uses herbs slivered in the moon's light by bronze. Again, Pliny tells us that the herb *reseda* (Linnaeus' *reseda alba*) will cure inflammations, but for the cure to take effect the sufferer must spit three times (apotropaically) and on each occasion say: 'Reseda, alleviate [in Latin *reseda*] these diseases. Do you know, do you know what chick it is that has torn up these roots? Let them have no head or feet.' In the Paris papyrus there is a fascinating invocation:

Thou wast sown by Cronos, picked by Hera, preserved by Ammon, produced by Isis, nourished by Zeus, the giver of rain; thou hast grown, thanks to the Sun and the dew. Thou art the dew of all the gods, the heart of Hermes, the seed of the first gods, the eye of the sun, the light of the moon, the dignity of Osiris, the beauty and splendour of heaven. . . . Thy branches are the bones of Minerva; thy flowers the eye of Horus, thy seeds the seed of Pan. . . . I pluck thee with Good Fortune, the Good Spirit, at the lucky hour, on the day that is right and suitable for all things.

As late as AD 1608 a similar formula is prescribed for the picking of vervain 'for in the Mount of Calvary, there thou wast first found'. Sometimes it is the magic which is all, and the properties of the herb nothing. Pliny again tells us of a cure for headache, which involves finding a herb growing on a statue's head, wrapping it in a cloth and tying it round the sufferer's neck with a piece of red string.

Magical amulets were a protection against disease. A medical scientist of Galen's calibre can recommend an engraved stone as a protection against dyspepsia, and Caracalla instituted legal action against those who wore amulets to protect them from malaria. Campbell Bonner in an exemplary study identified the main diseases warded off by amulets. Malaria is curiously infrequent, though there are a number of papyrus charms against it. Digestive troubles are the most frequent, a suddenly revealing insight into the everyday life of the ancient world. Among the others are various eye-disorders, gynaecological complaints (symbolized by a stylized uterus), sciatica, hydrophobia ('Flee, demon hydrophobia, from the wearer of this amulet') and consumption ('Rescue me from the wasting and the disease').

A good example, relating to a womb complaint, is a haematite amulet found at Welwyn; it dates from the late empire, and was lost perhaps in the reign of Gratian and imported some fifty years before. The obverse is framed by an *ouroboros*. Within the area are Isis with a *sistrum*, a lioness, and the Egyptian divinity Bes with a tripartite head-dress, a conventional womb, a seven-toothed key and the letters $AE(H)IOY\Omega$; outside are the letters $A(E)MEINAE(BAP\Omega)\Theta EPE\Theta\Omega PABEAENIMEA$ which is interpreted as an invocation to Typhon. On the reverse is a scarabaeus, with a uterine symbol, and the letters $OP\Omega PIOY\Theta IAH\Omega IA\Omega A\Omega I$, an invocation to Ororiouth, a protector-spirit of women's diseases, and Yahweh named three times in different forms.

Pliny records some spells and charms against ailments of various kinds. To those against headache and inflammations already noticed we may add two more. One is a cure for impetigo: its basis is a common stone found near rivers and covered with a dry moss; this must be moistened with human saliva and rubbed by another stone; that stone is now laid on the impetigo while apotropaic words are recited. Less plausible is a cure for toothache. The sufferer must stand with his shoes on under an open sky on the living earth at a lucky hour on a lucky day. He must then grasp a frog, open its mouth and spit into it, asking him to take away the toothache with him, and then let him go.

CURSES

Curses are frequently found. They were often inscribed on lead and buried. The simplest form is a name pierced with a nail: this is parallel to the melting of a wax image. But many are more elaborate. An amusing one comes from Carthage. On the tablet are Greek magic symbols. There is an oval, and ten lines, with nine dots between them. Then follow the names of thirty-two horses and a Latin curse, calling on the spirit (*demon*) to check the horses named, entangle them and prevent them from moving. Plainly we are dealing with a four-horse chariot race with nine competing teams; some punter is trying to use supernatural dope to nobble all the teams except his own.

Three examples from Britain, all as it happens from the southwest. At Bath a formidable curse with each word reversed for additional power: 'May he who carried off Vilbia from me become as liquid as water. May she who obscenely devoured her become dumb, whether Velvinna, Exsupereus, Severinus, Augustalis, Comitianus, Catusminianus, Germanilla, Jovina.' There is a promising beginning to a detective-story, with eight suspects ready provided. In the fascinating temple at Lydney a man named Silvianus who has lost his ring asks Nodens to curse the thief, and offers the god half the value in a *do ut des* transaction; he evidently suspects a certain Senicianus. At Caerleon a mysterious curse is addressed to Nemesis: 'Lady Nemesis, I give thee a cloak and a pair of boots: let him who wore them not redeem them except with the life of his blood-red charger.' Here there seems to be rivalry in a cavalry regiment, perhaps in the regimental horse-race. One rival has secured some of his rival's clothing from the lockers or changing-rooms: a curse on the clothing is by sympathetic magic a curse on the person. The combination of prayer and magic is to be noted: they are not easily separated.

It would be possible to go on citing these curses at great length: they give an interesting glimpse of a sometimes forgotten side of Graeco-Roman life. Two more must suffice. Malcio's curse of Nico is so comprehensive that he might have taught even the Cardinal Lord Archbishop of Rheims a trick or two: he curses Nico's eyes, fingers, arms, nails, hair, head, feet, thigh, belly, buttocks, navel, chest, breasts, neck, mouth, cheeks, teeth, lips, chin, eye (again!), forehead, eyebrows, shoulder-blades, shoulder, sinews, bones, marrow, belly (again!), penis, leg, money profits and health. Pleasanter altogether is Felix's attempt to 'fix' Vettia to do his desire, to become sleepless and hungry for love of him, to forget father, mother, relatives and friends and fix her mind on him and him alone. There is pathos here, and real love.

MAGICAL FORMULAE

Typical of the use of divine names in magic is a gold tablet discovered at Caernarvon nearly a century and a half ago. Only here and there do the words become lucid, though we must suppose them to be powerful throughout. The author of the tablet, Alphianus, is asking for protection, and among the magical symbols and formulae we can discern in Greek letters the divine names ADONAI, ELOAI, SABAOTH and IAO. IAO was also found on a bloodstone at Silchester associated with the magical figure of the cock-headed snake. Another gold tablet appeared in York. Only two lines of the writing survive, the first magical nonsense, the second (again in Greek) *PHNEBENNOYΘ*, which has been interpreted as 'the lord of the gods' in Coptic. Perhaps the very unfamiliarity of these Jewish and eastern titles in far-off Britain made them seem more potent. Not only in Britain. Jerome comments with some scorn on how the practitioners of magic (whom he unfairly identifies with the Basilidian Gnostics) father on the Hebrews names like Armazel, Barbelo, Abraxas, Balsamus, Leusiboras, 'terrifying simple folk with barbarous sounds'. The name of Abraxas, or, as it often appears in magic, Abrasax, is of some interest. It does appear in Gnostic systems, and is perhaps the name of some forgotten sun-god. In magical contexts the name is often accompanied by the portrayal of a daemon with cock head and snake feet. This appears to be an attempt to bring together the solar emblem of the cock with the healing symbol of the snake. Another divine name of magical power is Kok Kouk Koul; the three Ks, which are found on their own, are of magical power. On the Paris magical papyrus the name of 'Jesus, god of the Hebrews' is used for conjuration. (*Pl.* 75)

Many of the magical inscriptions seem meaningless. The power is formulaic; some may derive from snatches of liturgy in a foreign tongue, recorded by ear and garbled; if so the original is often irrecoverable. Some take added power from their shape. A magic word is repeated with the subtraction of one letter each time, to form an inverted pyramid. Palindromes are especially powerful: *ABΛANAΘANAΛBA* is the commonest of these, perhaps a garbled version of some Hebrew. Anagrams of a simple sort are also found. In this connection we may mention the Christian word-square found at Cirencester among other places:

R O T A S
O P E R A
T E N E T
A R E P O
S A T O R

The interpretation is controversial, but its discovery at Pompeii does not make it pre-Christian, since there were Christians at nearby Puteoli, and the author of *Revelation* need not have invented the Alpha-Omega formula. Here we have (*a*) a direct meaning which may allude to Ezekiel, (*b*) a palindrome, (*c*) a word-square, (*d*) a form with four Ts (the cross) at key-points flanked by A and O, (*e*) an anagram, since the letters can be rearranged to form PATERNOSTER twice intersecting with a common N in the centre, and the A–O formula twice repeated. Probably all of these are involved. (*Pl.* 70)

Number-magic is sometimes covered by word-magic, since the Greeks and Hebrews used the letters of the alphabet to denote numbers. There is a familiar example in *Revelation*, where the number of the Beast is 666; probably it represents Neron Kesar in Hebrew. The power of the name Abraxas is enhanced by its

50, 51 Two sites of the Mysteries. *Above*, the *telesterion* at Eleusis, a square room with sides over 150 feet long, and 42 columns to support the roof (p. 100). *Below*, the Mithraeum under the church of S. Clemente in Rome. Its cave-like structure can be clearly seen and, on either side, the benches for the reclining worshippers (p. 111).

52, 53 The Dionysiac Mysteries. *Above*, a wall-painting, in the British Museum, of a ritual dance. *Below*, and *right*, two details of the wall-paintings in the Villa of the Mysteries, Pompeii (p. 103). To the left, lekanomancy: the grotesque mask is reflected instead of the satyr's own face. Next: Dionysus and Ariadne, with thyrsus; then a kneeling woman unveils the mystic phallus. To the right: Telete, the spirit of the Mysteries, beats the initiate with a rod.

54 The initiate passes through the ritual death of flagellation, and rises again in a dance of ecstasy: in the original it can be seen that the scarf which swirls round as she dances is the scarf under her arms as she is whipped (p. 103).

55–57 *Above*, a procession in honour of Isis, in the Vatican Museum, Rome. It may be compared with the literary description in Apuleius (p. 107). Here the attributes are, from left to right: *sistrum* and ladle (*simpulum*); a jar of sacred water; falcon headdress and scroll; cobra, bucket (*situla*) – and a lotus in the hair. *Below*, a bronze hand with magic symbols in honour of Sabazios (p. 102). Musée Romain, Avenches. *Right*, a bronze statue from Anzio of Asclepius with a snake (p. 110). Capitoline Museum, Rome.

58, 59 The common wish to make the deceased at ease in his 'eternal home' is illustrated by an astonishing sarcophagus from Simpelveld (*above*) in the Royal Archaeological Museum, Leiden. The interior is carved with a bed, chairs, a table, cupboards and the like, to represent the house of the dead (p. 134).

60 The battle between the Greeks and the Amazons, a favourite sarcophagus theme (p. 145). It is hard to say whether these battle-scenes are seen as victories or defeats. Plainly, at least, they show life – and death – as a struggle. Capitoline Museum, Rome.

61 The discovery of Ariadne asleep by Dionysus and his rout, representing the touch of divinity on the soul (p. 139). Walters Collection, Baltimore. The god stands in the centre with a panther at his feet. The figure of Ariadne was a model for Renaissance artists, as in Titian's *The Andrians* in the Prado, Madrid.

62 Dionysus, thyrsus in hand, riding in triumph on a panther (p. 140). With him are the four Seasons, each with his characteristic gifts (p. 142). The figures are carved almost in the round and there is a great deal of activity to be seen in the small figures rushing between the Seasons. Metropolitan Museum of Art, New York.

63 A different treatment of the discovery of the sleeping Ariadne by Dionysus, from the Vatican cemetery. Here the god comes in a car pulled by a Centaur with a lyre. A little Amorino urges him on. The panthers, the tragic mask, the musical instruments and the dance movements are all magnificently portrayed.

64 Selene, the moon, descending to the sleeping Endymion, urged on by Erotes or Amorini. The scene is parallel, even in the attitude of the sleepers, to the discovery of Ariadne by Dionysus, and equally represents the touch of divinity on the soul. But the great lion heads remind us of the devouring power of death (p. 137). Metropolitan Museum of Art, New York.

65 Sarcophagus from the Tomb of the Egyptians, Vatican cemetery. The curling lines allude to the waves crossed by the dead in their journey to the Isles of the Blest: note the sea-monsters on the lid (p. 144).

66 Prometheus making man. The Titan sits before his prostrate creation, his finger to his lips. Around him are the gods and goddesses of the pantheon (p. 143). Museo Nazionale, Naples.

67 The nine Muses, each with some characteristic emblem or pose. The Muses were originally undifferentiated powers of inspiration, and only in Roman times acquired individual functions. This scene again represents the divine touch on humanity (p. 142). Louvre.

numerical equivalence to 365, the number of days in the solar year. Meithras, a magic spelling of Mithras, is numerically identical. The curious sequence *ΧΑΒΡΑΧ ΦΝΕΣΧΗΡ ΦΙΧΡΟ ΦΝΥΡΩ ΦΩΧΩ ΒΩΧ* which occurs on a number of amulets, generally in association with the Egyptian god Harpocrates, is explicable simply by its numerical equivalence to 9999. Number-magic is important; we have seen the prominence of three in the practice of the witches. Vergil declares that god delights in odd numbers, and Servius comments that an odd number is immortal because it cannot be divided. Curiously, two is sacred to Dis, lord of the dead, and four to Mercury, guide of the dead.

The survival of magical practices into the Christian-dominated fourth century is well evidenced. In the year 319 Constantine decreed that no soothsayer should enter a private house, even of a personal friend: the penalty was the stake, and deportation for the man who received him: informers were encouraged. By the year 320 the force of public opinion, coming, so far as we can see, alike from aristocracy and commoners, forced him to a change of policy. Now it is black magic alone which is proscribed, as for purposes of murder or seduction, and white magic, to cure sickness or protect the crops, is permitted, and even mildly encouraged. Constantius II restored the severity of the law. The death-penalty is imposed on soothsayers, astrologers, and magicians of all sorts; even the aristocracy is not exempt; and those who will not admit their guilt after conviction are handed over to 'the iron claws of the executioner'. Ammianus Marcellinus reinforces the picture. The wearing of an amulet against disease, the mere accusation of walking by a graveyard in the twilight was enough to procure condemnation. Valentinian and Valens reassert a general tolerance, but in fact it does not extend very far. Not merely is the death-penalty invoked on those who practise evil imprecations, magic rituals or necromantic sacrifices by night, but also on astrologers and those who consult them, whether by day or by night, in private or in public: 'it is as criminal to learn these things as to teach them: they are for-bidden'. Ammianus is full of fascinating case-histories. There was the involved trial of those who tried by divination to discover the name of Valens' successor. They made a three-legged table of olive-twigs, like the one discovered at Pergamum, and after due ritual placed on it a circular metal dish with letters round the rim. The diviner pored over this with a special ring hanging from a thread, which spelt out in the approved mediumistic way various messages (in polished verse) and then the beginning of the name of Theodorus. Another case involved the horoscope of Valens; that it was another Valens altogether did not save its possessor from torture and execution. Even a woman who tried to cure a girl's malaria by a simple charm was condemned to death by the girl's father; a foolish aristocrat who killed a donkey as a cure for baldness was tortured and put to death. (Pl. 74)

It is a strange, contradictory, fascinating age. Pagans and Christians alike defend their attitudes with a variety of rational arguments, but irrationalism is not far below the surface.

CHAPTER X

SHAMANS AND SHAMS

THE FIGURE OF THE SHAMAN has become something of a cliché in recent years, and the term has been used loosely. The shaman in the strict sense is found in Central and Northern Asia, and shamanism in its strict sense is a technique of ecstasy. It is a magico-religious conception, and the shaman *pur sang* has special magical and spiritual powers, levitation and flight, ascent to the sky and descent to the underworld, the mastery of fire, and the power of communication with the spirit-world. In the home of the shamans the profession of shaman may be hereditary, it may arise from a supernatural call, or in some cases, regarded as inferior, it may come from appointment by the clan or an act of the individual will. In whatever manner the call comes, ecstatic experience is likely to be its test and seal, and it is followed by an initiation and a period of training, in which the accepted shamans and the spiritual powers are believed to share. This initiation and training is complex and varied. There is a strong sexual element, including a celestial marriage. There are dreams and visions. There are songs, chants and spells. There is medical knowledge, plant lore, animal lore, the study of rocks, ordeals, symbolical or actual ascents and descents.

It might seem at first that this North Asiatic institution would be confined to its own area. In fact we find similar or related ideas and practices over much of the world. Among the Teutons Wotan spends nine days and nights hanging on a tree to acquire understanding of runes; spirits in the shape of birds minister to him; he is metamorphosed into animals; he rides into the under-world on Sleipnir; he foreknows the future. In Indo-European myth the shamanistic traditions centre on Varuna, the Binder, the

Master of Magic. There is some reason to believe that Apollo may have come to the Greeks from an area in contact with the shamans, and in that blend of history and legend which forms so much of the early story of Greece we can trace various figures akin to shamans, Abaris, Musaeus, Aristeas and Hermotimus, Orpheus and Epimenides and Pythagoras. These are early. But in the melting-pot which was the Roman Empire ingredients poured in from all over the world and we shall find traditions highly reminiscent of those of the shaman, as well as quacks ready to play on the susceptibilities of men and women who were seeking for a shaman-figure to guide them.

One of the most interesting religious documents of the third century AD is the *Confessio* of Cyprian of Antioch. This may or may not be authentic history—the matter is highly controversial—but it is likely to preserve authentic ritual, and such ritual is notoriously conservative. Cyprian was in later life a Christian leader. But before his conversion to Christianity he had been consecrated to Apollo, an initiate of Mithras and Eleusis, and an attendant on Athene's sacred snake. He now went through another ceremony of pagan initiation. This took place on Mount Olympus; there were seven hierophants officiating, and it lasted for forty days. We do not know all that went on during those six weeks, and the meaning of the Greek is sometimes obscure. He was initiated into 'the sound of speech and narrative of noise', he saw imaged trees and plants seeming to operate by divine action; successions of seasons; winds (or spirits?) bringing changes; differences of days organized by opposite powers; packs of spiritual beings chanting, battling, plotting, practising deceit, causing confusion; a phalanx of every god and goddess. The mountain was the source of all winds (or spirits?), pouring out as from a royal court (or a festival of Zeus the King?), operating on earth among all peoples. He lays considerable stress on the fact that he ate only fruits, and that after sunset, and points out the importance of the spiritual as well as the scientific study of such things. We may suppose from this that he received instruction in music, in herbalism, in the cycle of birth and death in nature and man, in lucky and unlucky days, and in ritual spiritual combats. We cannot discern exactly into what he was being initiated. Comparison with other evidence, however, suggests that the initiation may have been not just initiation as a worshipper, but at least a partial training as a seer. It is an important reminder of the existence of such people, and the sort of discipline they must pass through.

Apollonius of Tyana is here relevant. He was a historical figure who spanned the first century AD, and died under Nerva. It is now almost impossible to disentangle fact from fiction in our records of him—Lucian regarded him as a fraud like Alexander—but we need not doubt that he played some part in the Pythagorean revival and had an exalted view of God. Eusebius quotes a doubtless authentic passage from a lost work *On Sacrifice*:

> In no other manner, I believe, can one exhibit a fitting respect for the divine being, and beyond any other men make sure of being singled out as an object of his favour and goodwill, than by refusing to offer any victim at all to God whom we termed First, who is One and separate from all, to whom we must recognize all the rest as subordinate; to Him we must not kindle fire or make promise to Him of any sensible object at all. For He needs nothing even from beings higher than ourselves. Nor is there any plant or animal which earth sends up or nourishes, to which some pollution is not incident. We should make use in relation to Him solely of the higher speech, I mean of that speech which does not issue from the lips; and from the noblest of beings we must ask for blessings by the noblest faculty we possess, and that faculty is intelligence, which needs no organ. On these principles then we ought not on any account to sacrifice victims to the mighty and supreme God.

We hear little of Apollonius during the second century AD, but in the early-third century, Julia Domna, an empress of real though eccentric culture, encouraged a member of her entourage named Philostratus to write a heroic life of Apollonius, no doubt to counterweigh the increasingly insistent propaganda of the

Christians. Philostratus professed to have discovered an old document by one Damis as his source, but such discoveries are the stock-in-trade of historical romances, and we can place no credence upon Damis. Philostratus did his work well. Already Alexander Severus was setting Apollonius alongside Orpheus, Alexander the Great, Abraham and Christ in his private *lararium*. By the end of the third century AD temples and shrines to Apollonius were scattered over Asia Minor, and under Diocletian a writer named Hierocles published a comparison of Apollonius and Christ to the latter's detriment. Nearly two centuries later Sidonius Apollinaris sent a copy of Philostratus' work to a friend at Toulouse and in his covering note said:

Throw aside your endless labours and steal a respite from the burdens and bustle of the Court, so that you may really study this long-expected volume as it deserves. When once absorbed in it you will wander with our Tyanean over Caucasus and Indus, to the Brahmins of India and to the naked philosophers of Nubia. It describes the life of very much such a man as you are, with due respect to your Catholic faith. Courted by sovereigns, but never courting them; eager for knowledge; aloof from money-getting; fasting at feasts; linen-clad among wearers of purple; rebuking luxury; self-contained; plain-spoken; shock-headed in the midst of perfumed nations; revered and admired for his simplicity by the satraps of tiara-ed kings, who themselves were reeking with myrrh and malobathrum and polished with pumice-stone; taking from the flocks nothing to eat or to wear; and notwithstanding all these peculiarities not distrusted but honoured wherever he went throughout the world, and although royal treasures were placed at his disposal accepting from them merely those gifts to his friends which it suited him better to bestow than to receive. In short, if we measure and weigh realities, no philosopher's biography equal to this has ever appeared in the times of our ancestors, so far as I know; and I am certain that in my time it finds a worthy reader in you.

In the pages of Philostratus Apollonius appears as a typical shaman. His birth was accompanied by miracles; Proteus appeared to his mother in a vision; she bore the child in a flowered meadow with swans dancing round her; at the moment of birth a thunderbolt made to fall to earth and then rose to the sky again. At the age of sixteen Apollonius adopted the life of a Pythagorean ascetic, becoming a vegetarian and teetotaller, wearing linen (to avoid animal fibres) and going without shoes, and wearing his hair and beard long. He maintained a Trappist silence for five years. Subsequently he travelled widely in Persia, India and Egypt. He was associated from early times with miracles of healing. He demonstrated his power over evil spirits, hobgoblins, vampires, satyrs, ghosts and the like. In one curious story a tame lion came up to him pleadingly, and he identified it as the reincarnation of Amasis, king of Egypt; in another he identified a boy who was bitten by a mad dog with Telephus of Mysia. His magical power appears in the accounts of his arrests. Before Tigellinus he made the writing disappear from the accuser's scroll. When imprisoned under Domitian and in fetters he withdrew his leg from the fetter by supernatural power and inserted it again. After his acquittal he vanished from the courtroom in the sight of all. Above all, he claimed foreknowledge of the future, and refused to go on board a ship which subsequently foundered and sank. Even after his death he appeared to a sceptic in a vision to convince him of the immortality of the soul.

The mood which swallowed this is seen in an amusing episode in Apuleius' novel. This tells of Diophanes the Chaldaean. His very name has a mystical aura; his title conveys the secret wisdom of the East, and an intimate knowledge of the stars. He has taken the trouble to create a picture and play on a mood before he appears. This was an age with an intense belief in favourable and unfavourable days; there are still people who will not journey on Friday the 13th. Diophanes obtained a reputation for showing people favourable and unfavourable days for enterprises. The man was a patent fraud: we may imagine a combination of shrewdness in economics and weather-lore joined to slick sales-talk and a readiness to help the predicted results where that should prove possible. He charged a merchant a hundred denarii for telling him the favourable day for sailing. He had just finished this profitable transaction when a friend saw him and greeted him, 'How did you get here?' 'I had a terrible journey—storms and hurricanes—shipwreck—I had to swim ashore—we lost all we had except for a few necessities—and were robbed of those by bandits.' He had forgotten the merchant, who was still within earshot, and who promptly grabbed back his money and made off. It does not matter whether Diophanes the Chaldaean was a real person or represents a real person. The point is that the story was plausible. There were these men, flaunting their mystique, and it was not easy to tell which were genuine and which were not.

Peregrinus is here of remarkable interest. He was a Cynic who had at one time been a Christian. Lucian depicts him during his Christian period: prophet, cult-leader, head of the synagogue, and everything—god, lawgiver, protector, the great man whom they still worship, crucified. So at least runs our text, and it is idle to emend it: Peregrinus claimed to be the Christ of the Second Coming. Later he left the Christians and became a typical Cynic, preaching mordantly and acting demonstratively. Somewhere he acquired the name of Proteus, perhaps with a jibe at his changes of faith, perhaps with a compliment to his slippery dialectic. He had a high reputation; Aulus Gellius speaks of him as a man of weight and firmness, *virum gravem et constantem*. He committed suicide dramatically in AD 169, and in the last scene gave evidence of his familiarity with Indian thought, gazing to the south (where Yama takes the dead) and invoking the spirits. His fame was such that in his birthplace at Parium his statue became an oracular shrine.

Peregrinus is only one example of a shamanistic figure who was at one time within the Christian Church. More important for his impact on Christianity was Montanus. He was a Phrygian by birth, and had been a priest of Cybele (or Apollo) before his conversion to the Christian faith. Prophetic utterances had played an important role in the first generation of Christians, when prophets ranked second only to apostles; indeed at Corinth their exuberance needed bringing under control. Further, the experience of the Holy Spirit was at that time a present reality. Then gradually the vision faded and the prophetic fires were banked, unless they flared out in an Ammia or a Quadratus. Montanus, whether he served Cybele or Apollo, was well acquainted with inspired utterance; he brought that knowledge and expectation into the Church. At Ardabau in Mysia he fell into a trance and began to prophesy; our sources dispute whether the year was AD 157 or 172. From this moment disciples began to come, women as well as men; indeed Priscilla and Maximilla left their husbands and entered positions of leadership; here again the Montanists were restoring something the Church had forgotten; one visionary even saw Christ in female form.

The movement became a sect; it was known as 'The New Prophecy'; prophecies were recorded and gathered into a third Testament. There are close parallels in some of the emergent African churches today. The sect was founded on the principle that the work of revelation was not complete, and Jesus had himself said so, and promised that the Spirit of truth would guide his followers into all truth. Montanus and his fellow-leaders offered themselves as the channels for the fulfilment of revelation. When the voice spoke through Montanus and said, 'I am the Lord God Almighty dwelling at this moment within a human being' or, 'I am no angel, no messenger, but the Lord Father-God now come,' Montanus was not claiming divinity for himself; he was in the strict sense acting as a medium. 'See, man is like a lyre and I play on him like a plectrum. Man may sleep, but I am awake. See, it is the Lord, who takes away the hearts of men and gives them new hearts.' The new prophets recaptured belief in the Parousia, the imminent arrival of the Heavenly City, which they expected at Pepuza in Phrygia. For the rest we find fasting, austerity, asceticism (especially over sex). Maximilla thought she belonged to the last generation of prophets. She was wrong. The Heavenly City did not visibly descend, but the movement spread to Rome, Africa, Spain, and despite persecution lingered on to the sixth century AD. Orthodoxy found the Holy Spirit too disturbing and unamenable to authority. But Wesley was to describe Montanus as 'one of the holiest men in the second century', and he left the Church one great legacy in heightening Tertullian's religious awareness.

Anthony is a strange figure, born in the middle of the third century AD and living on into the fourth, the subject of a piece of credulous adulation attributed to Athanasius and some fantastic pages from Jerome. He decided in his youth to abandon formal education, sell his possessions and retreat into the desert. He shut himself up first in a tomb and then in a fortress. He fasted all his life, and disciplined his body. We hear of him being tempted by demons, in the shape of women, wild animals, creeping things, monsters, and troops of soldiers, threatening and even scourging him, or offering him gold, power, light. We hear of a typical mystical experience by which he saw himself caught up in the spirit and ascending through the air to the frontier of earth and heaven. We hear of his miracles of healing, and of his telepathic knowledge, and mystical foresight. At one point he returned to Alexandria during a period of persecution; he encouraged the martyrs, but was not himself granted the martyr's crown; he was destined for the life of solitary contemplation, not of public action. We hear of him being guided by a friendly hippocentaur and a she-wolf to his fellow-hermit Paul; the raven who provided Paul with food conveniently produced double rations. We hear of him occasionally being persuaded out to preach the gospel of salvation or to refute heretics: his theme, 'Trust in the Lord and love him; keep away from dirty thoughts and carnal pleasure; be constant in prayer; keep a diary, honest and full, which might at any time be made public; live as though dying daily.' But before the public he felt like a fish out of water, and preferred to retire to his cell. He lived to a great age. The story is full of legendary accretions. Behind it stands a very real man, the type of the Christian shaman. Eliade has warned us against exaggerating the shamanistic elements at the expense of the culture-differences, but the parallels are there. None the less it was well for the Church that men like Pachomius and Basil in the East and Benedict in the West were to develop a more co-operative and constructive form of Christian monasticism.

But the most remarkable of all these figures is undoubtedly Alexander of Abonuteichos. He was not a Christian: indeed he was an anti-Christian. If we may believe Lucian he was undoubtedly a sham; yet he had an immense appeal. He was born in Paphlagonia about AD 105, and somehow came into the employment of a former disciple of the authentic Apollonius, who initiated him into the learning he himself had acquired. This is important in the light of the account in Cyprian. It is evident that there was a store of learning which was passed on from one shaman to the next, and preserved as a secret. On the death of his mentor he fell in with a rascal crudely nicknamed Cocconas; for a while they ran a profitable trade fleecing dupes. One such dupe was a wealthy Macedonian woman who took them to Pella. Here Alexander became familiar with a local breed of snake, harmless but impressive, and acquired one for a few coppers.

The two young scoundrels tired of Pella and decided that the most effective method of playing on gullibility was through an oracle, but fell out over where to try their hand. Cocconas went to Chalcedon where he lived the seedy life of an obscure oracle-monger, and died in experimenting with a less harmless snake. Alexander made for his home-town. Here, as coins show, there was already a snake-cult, and a prophecy that Asclepius would come to live in Abonuteichos, and the locals had already started to build him a temple. In these foundations Alexander concealed a blown goose-egg in which he had inserted a new-born snake. Next day in a state of assumed ecstasy he discovered the egg and produced the snake, Glycon, the very incarnation of Asclepius: so had they brought him to Rome centuries before. Alexander's fortune was made. He set himself up as the god's interpreter. In the most impressive form of consultation he sat in a darkened room with his giant snake from Pella on his lap. It carried a curious cloth mask, which could be manipulated by wires, to give it a human head; the snake with the human head now appears on coins. His second method of prophecy was that of incubation; this was commonly associated with Asclepius' healing cult, but in this case it was Alexander, not the patient or inquirer, who did the sleeping. The third method was to receive a question on a sealed scroll; he would take this into the temple to submit it to Glycon, where he was presumably adept with a hot knife: the answer was delivered and the question returned with an unbroken seal. (*Pl.* 71)

At some point Alexander went further and established an annual celebration of mysteries, no doubt with an expensive initiation-fee. It is difficult to reconstruct these mysteries from Lucian's attack on them. Epicureans and Christians tried to expose him: they were exorcized. It certainly appears that the original theophany of Glycon from the egg was annually re-enacted. There was also a holy marriage, *hieros gamos*, between Alexander and a girl named Rutilia who was genuinely in love with him, and who descended upon him from the sky in the guise of Selene. Alexander is now appearing as something more than man, though it is hard to discern exactly what role he is playing. His cry of 'Hail, Glycon' was echoed by his acolytes with 'Hail, Alexander' and he himself appeared in the light of torches baring a golden thigh (a gilded leather pad, but deceptive in artificial light), which may be part of a divine epiphany or may represent an identification with Pythagoras. It is however important to say that the coins show the snake and never Alexander, and that all the inscriptions except one speak only of Glycon. That exception is remarkable: a Syrian named Epitynchanus makes his offering to Jupiter, Juno, the male snake, the female snake, and Alexander. One suspects that the good man was muddled; but the evidence is clear: he made his offering to Alexander and Alexander did not disown it.

The reputation of the oracle was wide. Alexander took the trouble to have a good publicity service and a good intelligence service. Lucian tells us how he duped one Rutilianus; Rutilianus was no nonentity, but a man of consular rank who had served in a wide variety of high offices including that of proconsul of Asia. M. Sedatius Severianus, governor of Cappadocia, consulted Alexander, who induced him to march into Armenia, where he was disastrously defeated. Alexander caused some trouble to L. Lollianus Avitus, when he was governor of Bithynia; it was Rutilianus who protected him. In the plague of AD 167 Alexander was again involved in a public situation, and was selling apotropaic charms. Most astonishing of all, Marcus Aurelius listened to one of his oracles, which promised success on the Danube if he threw in two lions before crossing. This the emperor did; the Marcomanni killed the lions with clubs; and the Roman army was seriously defeated. Yet the oracle retained its reputation. Alexander died in about AD 175, but the evidence of coins, gems, inscriptions and reliefs shows that the cult survived to at least the middle of the following century, though possibly not much beyond. The whole story is a very curious one. Alexander was plainly a skilled operator who brought together the personal devotion to Asclepius, especially in an age of plague, the Pythagorean revival, the urge towards mystery-religions, the decay of Delphi, the yearning for an intermediary between the divine and human ('You will have all,' says Glycon, 'when I will it and my prophet Alexander asks it of me and prays on your behalf') and a personality which must have had some kind of charisma. (*Pl.* 71)

CHAPTER XI

PHILOSOPHERS AND THE GODS

THE HELLENISTIC AGE was an age which Gilbert Murray, follow-ing a hint from J. B. Bury, characterized by failure of nerve. The philosophies of that age trained men to live in a hostile world. They taught *autarkeia*, self-sufficiency, the quality which Aldous Huxley called non-attachment. Four schools of thought domi-nated the scene. Two were survivals from the age before Alex-ander. The Platonists went through a period when they were concerned with a sceptical theory of knowledge before re-emerg-ing as religious thinkers during the crisis of the Roman Empire. The Aristotelians had started under the tail of Plato, and remained close to the Platonists, though with their own particular scientific emphasis. The other two emerged to meet the needs of the new age, and Epicurus and Zeno spoke directly to those needs. What is so interesting is that philosophies designed for a Greece, and especially an Athens which had lost her grip, and whose citizens felt themselves the playthings of fortune, should have provided the staple fare for the thinking Roman from the last century of the Republic through the whole period of Empire.

EPICUREANISM

Epicurus stood apart from the other thinkers of his day; indeed one of the few regrettable traits in that admirable man is his scorn for his predecessors. The aim of life for him was pleasure and he accepted a physical basis for that pleasure. But pleasure was not crudely conceived: Epicurus indeed took a pessimistic atti-tude to the uncertainties of life, and in his hedonistic calculus it sometimes seems that pleasure consists in the avoidance of pain, and the aim of life becomes *ataraxia*, freedom from disturbance. Peace of mind is attained by the control of desire and the elimina-tion of fear: the main fears are fear of the gods and fear of death.

Hence the famous 'fourway cure': there is nothing to fear in god; there is nothing to feel in death; good can be readily attained; evil can be readily endured. So the Epicureans renounced worldly ambition and the pursuit of wealth and power and fame, though there were Roman Epicureans like Cassius, Hirtius and Pansa, who compromised as freely as Christians have compromised over Jesus' pacifism and indictment of the rich. The central tradition of Epicureanism was quietist, and centred upon the joy of friendship, though like a later Society of Friends they felt a 'concern' to proclaim to others 'the prescription of salvation': the words are from a remarkable inscription put up in the second century AD round the town-centre at Oenoanda in Asia Minor by a man named Diogenes. Further, one cause of fear lies in ignorance. The Epicureans therefore espoused a scientific world-view, accepting the general picture given by the Greek atomists. Nothing exists except atoms and void. Epicurus saved himself from a mechanistic determinism by attributing to the atoms a power of spontaneous swerve: it was an answer to the physical problem how, falling freely through a vacuum, they would ever collide to form a world. At the same time it led him to a denial of the immortality of the soul, since the atoms of the soul are simply dissolved at death; consequently, as Lucretius vigorously asserts, 'Death is nothing to us and matters not an iota'.

What of fear of the gods? The Epicureans believed in gods. They adduced three arguments: the appearance of gods in dreams and visions, which must, like everything else, have a physical origin; the consensus of mankind (a dangerous and delusive argument); and the curious principle of *isonomia* or balance, which suggests that there must be an equal number of immortal beings to balance the mortal. The gods are formed of atoms or they could not exist at all. But as they stand as the norm of bliss, they cannot be involved in atomic dissolution; they must therefore live in the interstices of the universe. They did not create the world and are utterly unconcerned with it; they neither reward nor punish; such busyness would denigrate their bliss. They live, remote and tranquil in the joys of philosophic conversation, like a society of Epicurean friends. But though they are not concerned with us, there are emanations from them which those rightly attuned can pick up to their benefit; it pays to be, in the title of a once famous book, in tune with the infinite; had Epicurus known radio-waves he would have used the analogy. Hence Epicurus can put himself under the protection of Asclepius. The Epicureans were ruthless critics of conventional religion, of the crimes of superstition, and what we might call 'the hell-fire school'. But they were not irreligious.

Epicureans were conservative, and the system of Epicurus remained unchanged in its broad outline. Unfortunately a conspiracy of silence, started by Augustus, has laid a pall over the Epicureans of the Empire, and we are liable to forget just how prominent they were. Thus Trajan's consort Plotina was an avowed Epicurean. We know of second-century AD Epicureans: Celsus (not the critic of Christianity), Antonius, Diogenianus, Zenobius, Lepidus and Timocrates of Heraclea; also perhaps the great doctor Soranus, and Diogenes of Oenoanda. Minucius Felix and Octavius appear both to have been Epicureans before their conversion; so perhaps was Arnobius in the following century. Lucian records the way in which Epicureans and Christians joined in the attempt to expose the fraudulent Alexander of Abonuteichos, while Stoics and Platonists swallowed his sales-talk. When Agrippa's Odeon in the agora at Athens was remodelled in the middle of the second century AD the new stair was decorated with pairs of seated statues of philosophers, one pair for each school, Stoic, Platonist, Aristotelian and Epicurean. Marcus Aurelius founded a chair of Epicurean philosophy. Epicurean expressions in epitaphs of the second and third centuries AD are frequent. Christian writers, Justin, Athenagoras, Irenaeus, Tertullian, Hippolytus, Clement, Origen are concerned to refute the Epicureans, and they were too busy changing the world to tilt at windmills; Origen's ablest pupil, Dionysius of Alexandria, wrote a detailed and important critical study. Aelian, writing as an orthodox pagan, is bitterly opposed to the Epicureans: he tells how an impious former temple-servant broke into the sacred place to show that he would remain unscathed, and died in agony. Even the Jewish rabbis of the Dispersion were fearful of the onset of the Epicureans. Rabbi Lazarus said, 'Be diligent to learn the Torah, as an instrument for answering the Epicureans,' and the tractate *Sanhedrin* denies them a place in the world to come. Their power of survival, in face of official discouragement, was certainly remarkable. In the fourth century AD the poet Claudian was at one time an Epicurean; in the fifth Augustine is still concerned to refute them, and in the West Hilary of Poitiers (who admittedly travelled in the East) and Claudius Mamertus show first-hand familiarity with the teachings. Epicureanism was decidedly a live religious option throughout the Empire; to the public it appeared as a rationalist rejection of religion, but to one who professed the creed it rejected superstition in favour of true religion. (*Pl.* 76)

STOICISM

The Stoics were pantheists. Jupiter, said Cato in the pages of Lucan, is everything you see and every movement you make; the totality of all things seen and unseen, said Seneca. He is called by many names: God, Zeus or Jupiter, Nature, the Universe, Omnipotence, Fire, Spirit or Breath, Aether, Logos (the Divine Reason or Word).

> *All are but parts of one stupendous whole,*
> *Whose body Nature is, and God the soul.*

They argued to the existence of God, as did the Epicureans, from the consensus of mankind. But they added other arguments: one from the search for the highest in a scale of being; one from the need for a principle to unify the universe; another from the order and constancy of nature implying an ordering mind; another in that piety, holiness and wisdom imply the existence of divinity as their object; yet another from divination. At this level Stoic treatises read very like Victorian handbooks of theology. But pantheism logically implies determinism, and the Stoics accepted the implications of this. God has determined all things, except our will; our actions are fixed, but not the way we fulfil them. It is as if we are thrown into a raging torrent; it makes no practical difference whether we swim with the current or against it, yet it does make a difference. We are cast for a role in the divine drama; our part is determined, but not the spirit in which we play it—and whether it is that of a top-line star or a walking-on extra, it is essential to the whole.

Stoicism preached acceptance, like Islam, whether of power or obscurity, beggary or wealth, and Seneca justified his millions on the ground that they happened to come his way, and he could use them better than the next man. Man's soul is a particle of the divine breath, a spark of the divine fire. Man has within himself a ruling principle, which Marcus Aurelius calls God within, King and Lawgiver, Director and Governor, Pilot. Furthermore the power of life is carried on by Generative Reason permeating the universe, and working within the soul. At death the soul survives the body, and apparently retains its individuality for a period, but is finally absorbed in the divine fire. Finally we may note that Stoic religious ethics contain much that is richly humane: cosmopolitanism and the unnaturalness of slavery for example. But the fact that for them virtue lay in a disposition of the soul and not in action combined with the general attitude of resignation to make them far less revolutionary than some of their professions might seem to imply, and led Macaulay to reserve for their practical indifference some of his most pungent pages. It is an unfortunate fact that though the Stoics penned moral sermons which are magnificent to read or hear, the Epicureans seem more attractive to meet.

EPICTETUS

An exception must be made for the outstanding Stoic of the second century AD, the exile and former slave Epictetus. Lame and poor, he settled at Nicopolis in Epirus, where he acquired a high reputation by his teaching. Tourists used to drop in while waiting for a ship; they could say that they had 'done' Epictetus. Some came to pick up catch-phrases to relay to their friends. Epictetus was scornful, and in his scorn produced a notable characterization of education: 'Sheep don't vomit up the grass they've eaten; they digest it and turn it into wool and milk.' Some came to learn, among them his diligent recorder, the future governor of Cappadocia, Flavius Arrianus. Epictetus' fame lasted beyond his death. He was the greatest philosophical influence on Marcus Aurelius. Sixty or seventy years after his death a man bought his old earthenware lamp for 3,000 drachmas.

Epictetus is more centrally religious than any of the other great Stoics. With the others one feels that their attention is fixed on the ethical teaching and religion is in the background. With Epictetus one feels that God is the centre of his thought, and his ethical teaching derives from this. For him the first lesson of philosophy is that there is a God, that he provides for the whole scheme of things, and that it is not possible to conceal from him our acts—no, nor our intentions and thoughts either. Atheists and deists come under Epictetus' censure, and he speaks severely of Epicurean theology and ethics without understanding either. Rather we should say, with Odysseus and Socrates, 'Without God's knowledge I cannot move.' Epictetus, above all the Roman Stoics, sees God as Providence. All things in the cosmos are a unity; things heavenly and things earthly are in sympathy. External nature is obviously a harmony, and we cannot refuse to our souls what we assert of our bodies. If man the finite can grasp so much, cannot God the infinite oversee all things? 'In truth, the whole scheme of things is badly managed if Zeus does not take care of his own citizens, so that they may be, like himself, happy.' It follows that we have all we really need. 'What does Zeus say? "Epictetus, had it been possible, I would have made your little body and your little property free [the diminutives are characteristic]. Since I was unable to do this, I have given you a little portion of myself."' Is he not to grumble at his lameness then, to take something which touches him closely? 'Must my leg be the object of blame? Slave! [a technical Stoic term opposed to the philosopher-king] do you, for one wretched leg, find fault with the cosmos? Will you not gladly surrender it for the whole?' All partial evil universal good. It is eloquent and moving, yet hardly convincing. For if the lameness of his leg is necessary to the well-being of the cosmos he may legitimately ask why; and if not, it does not really help to say, 'Where so much is right, why grumble at this?' because to theology a slight imperfection is as great a problem as a great imperfection (as the Stoics with their ethical paradoxes should have seen), and because it is his leg in a way in which it is not his cosmos.

Epictetus has the same sense of the closeness of God as Seneca. 'When you have shut your doors and made it dark inside, remember never to say that you are alone. You are not. God is within, and your guardian-spirit; they do not need light to see what you are about.' At the same time he is prepared to make compromises with popular belief which Seneca would not allow, a clear distinction between their social backgrounds. He accepts belief in intermediate spirits, daemons, which Seneca dismissed. He defines piety as having right opinions about the gods, an intellectualist view, but goes on to say that it is proper to pour libations and offer sacrifice according to the customs of our fathers.

The way for man is in fact a life founded at all points upon God. There is the practice of the presence of God. God has given every man his guardian-spirit, his daemon, in whose presence we constantly live. This is no god of gold and silver; we bear him within ourselves, and defile him with our impure thoughts and acts. There is the moral response to God. Epictetus tells us to clear away from our thoughts sadness, fear, desire, envy, avarice, intemperance and the like. But 'it is not possible to get rid of these things otherwise than by fixing your gaze on God alone, by setting your affections on him only, and being devoted to his commands'. This is a religious ethic. For man is to be the 'spectator and interpreter of God', even the son of God. Epictetus likes the military metaphor; we are, in Christopher Fry's phrase, 'man under the command of God'. We ought to swear an oath of allegiance to God within us parallel to that which the soldiers swear to the emperor. We are no Utopian community, but an army in battle-order. There is the praise of God, and this is the theme of Epictetus' most familiar and eloquent words:

If we had understanding, ought we to do anything else, jointly and severally, than to sing hymns, bless the Deity, and tell of his benefits? Ought we not, as we dig and plough and eat, to sing this hymn to God?—'Great is God, who has given us these tools to cultivate the earth; great is God, who has given us hands, the power of swallowing, a stomach, imperceptible growth and the power of breathing while we sleep.' This ought to be our song on every occasion. . . . What else can I do, a lame old man, but sing hymns to God? If I were a nightingale, I would behave like a nightingale; if a swan, like a swan. As it is, I am a rational being, and I ought to praise God: this is my job, and I perform it. I will not desert this post as long as I am allowed to keep it—and I charge you to join in the same song.

The note of detailed praise is very like that sounded by the Jews. Finally, at the last, death is return to God: 'Friends, wait for God. For the present stick to the place where he has set you. When he gives the signal and releases you from this service, go to him.'

MARCUS AURELIUS

It is strange that the two best-known second-century AD Stoics should be of such different social strata. In passing from Epictetus to Marcus Aurelius we pass (in Capes' words) from 'Stoicism in the cottage' to 'Stoicism on the throne'. Marcus was born for greatness, his father a Spaniard of consular family, his aunt married to Antoninus Pius, one of Hadrian's councillors and his eventual successor. Hadrian picked out the boy, solemn beyond his years, nominated him as an *eques* at the age of six, enlisted him among the priestly Salii contrary to regulations (since his father was dead) before he was eight. The Salii were priests of Mars; Marcus threw himself into his duties with solemn vigour, learning the complex dances and archaic liturgy, and becoming successively dance-leader, precentor and master of the order. In AD 136 Hadrian adopted L. Commodus as his heir and prospective successor, and Marcus was betrothed to the heir-apparent's daughter. When the heir died, the succession devolved on Antoninus Pius, and he in turn was induced to adopt Marcus, whose former engagement was cancelled so that he might marry Antoninus' daughter. The play with dynastic marriages recalls Augustus at his worst; the essential point is that Marcus was designated for the highest office at the time when the rule of the best man was becoming an accepted principle. He was just under forty when he reached the throne in AD 161, fifty-eight when he died at Vienna in AD 180. (*Pl.* 72)

The book on which his literary fame rests was written in lonely vigils during campaigns in the Danube territory. Popularly known as *The Meditations*, its true title is *The Emperor Marcus Antoninus: To Himself.* One strange fact is that it rests unrecorded in antiquity till *The Suda* in the eleventh century AD. It is a revealing document. Marcus, professed Stoic though he was, is revealed as an agnostic. He is certainly an agnostic with religious leanings and speaks freely of God, but the temper is agnostic: his doctrine of non-attachment takes him to non-attachment even to God. 'Atoms or gods?' he asks; or again says, 'The gods are either powerless or powerful.' He is attracted by providence but not committed. He adduces probable arguments for immortality but they remain probable only. He makes munificent sacrifices to the public gods, even delaying his departure against the Marcomanni to summon the priests, have the city solemnly purified and declare a seven-day *lectisternium*, a ceremonial banquet in which the gods themselves share—yet he has more than half a suspicion that these gods do not exist. F. W. H. Myers called him 'the saint and exemplar of Agnosticism'. Yet there is a positive side even to his doubts. 'As for the universe, either it is god and all goes well, or it is at random, some kind of molecules or atoms—don't you live at random!' 'If the gods have made decisions about me and all that must happen to me, they have decided for the best. . . . If they take no decisions about anything— a blasphemous thing to believe [like Epictetus, he is dead set against the Epicureans]—still I can take decisions about myself.'

With these reservations Marcus allows himself freely to use the Stoic religious language; but we do well to bear these reservations in mind. The truth is that Marcus was of an essentially religious disposition but doubtful mind. Seneca was a moralist, Epictetus a religious genius; Marcus Aurelius in the result is a moralist, but he speaks of morals in a mood of religious emotion. 'The poet has said [of Athens], "O lovely city of Cecrops." Shall you not say [of the universe], "O lovely city of Zeus"?' So he speaks of a higher and lower self. The true self is the guardian-spirit, the ruling principle, the commander and pilot, an emanation from God, a fragment of Zeus, an efflux of the Word that orders the whole, the god within, and in this spirit Marcus speaks freely of obedience to God. 'Live with the gods. That man lives with them who, all through life, lays bare his soul to heaven, well content with the dispensations of Providence and executing every wish of that godhead which Zeus has given man, to be his guardian and guide, a fragment of himself.' 'He that is thus exercised withdraws from the body and reflects that in a little while he must leave this world behind, and go out from among men. He dedicates himself completely to justice for what he achieves himself and to universal Nature for what comes to pass otherwise. What his neighbour will say or think about him or do against him, he never lets into his thoughts, finding contentment in these two things, doing with justice what he is doing, and acquiescing in his present lot. He drops every other business and care; his whole will is to walk in a straight line as he has been instructed, and in walking straight to follow God.' 'One order, one god, one being, one law.' The language is religious, the thought ethical.

It is hard to resist the conclusion that Marcus Aurelius has been overpraised. His mouth on his portraits is weak, and he was a weak man. His reign is ironical: the cosmopolitan engaged in war; the man to whom health was indifferent seeing his realm decimated by plague; the man to whom wealth was indifferent bankrupting the state; the man to whom family ties were nothing insisting on his worthless son Commodus succeeding him. Some of the most interesting—and pathetic—reflections relate to his position as emperor. 'Beware of playing Caesar, and being dyed in purple: it does happen. Keep yourself simple, pure, serious, devoted to justice, affectionate, steadfast in fulfilling your duties.' 'The very principle of the universe is a cataract which sweeps everything along . . . do not hope for Plato's state—but be content if it goes only a step forward.' 'I conceived the idea of a democratic state administered according to equality and free speech, and of a monarchy that honoured above all the freedom of the governed.' In second-century AD Rome—comment is superfluous. He takes office like one who is awaiting the signal for retreat; he knows the hollowness of earthly reputation; he sees that history does not change and that Croesus, Alexander, Hadrian and he were playing the same play with a different cast; he sees Alexander and his groom levelled in death, and values Alexander, Caesar and Pompey below Diogenes, Heraclitus and Socrates. 'The ruler's fate: good acts and unpopularity.' The line of great Stoics dies with Marcus, and it is not surprising, for he, fascinating study that he is, is not in any real sense a great Stoic. Festugière put it well: 'He is no longer the wise man of utter and inhuman detachment that the pure Stoic seems to us to be. He is, after all, a man like us, who needs consolation. . . .' (*Pl.* 77)

THE MIDDLE PLATONISTS

The great figure in the background of philosophical theism is Plato: the intellectual dualism of the Theory of Forms, the vision of divinity in *The Symposium*, the purging of false concepts of the gods in *The Republic*, the account of the creator-god in *Timaeus*, the insistence on theological orthodoxy in *The Laws* all left a permanent mark.

Of the Platonists with a religious bent we may briefly note Maximus of Tyre. He is a thinker without a scrap of originality, who was teaching at Rome in the reign of Commodus. He is an educationalist rather than a philosopher, and his philosophy does not extend far beyond Plato, though Aristotle at times peers through. Yet precisely because he is not an original thinker, he is representative of a wide range of educated opinion. For Maximus the central fact of religious experience is the gulf between God and the world. God is supreme, pure, remote, withdrawn, absolute. Maximus' vision of God recalls the Second Isaiah; he speaks of 'the Father and Creator of all, who is older than the sun, older than the heavens, stronger than time, stronger than the ages, stronger than the transient world. No lawgiver can name him, no tongue express him, no eye discern him.' Only Maximus, unlike the Hebrew prophet, clings to idols and images and anything that may call God to mind, as a lover cherishes a memento of his beloved. Between God and the world are the spirits, daemons, divine in power and knowledge, but sub-divine in feeling and passion; Maximus defends this belief in terms of the chain of being in the physical universe; he knows of good spirits only, not of evil. As to man, he is of mixed inheritance, a son of God, imprisoned in the flesh. Yet there is escape, through the toilsome upward path of moral virtue and through the glimpses of God afforded in visions on the way up. Only in death shall we know God fully; meantime we must not blaspheme by unworthy prayers. The only prayer which is answered is the prayer for goodness, peace and hope beyond the grave. Maximus' Platonic religion may be popular but it is not ignoble.

Numenius is a particularly interesting thinker. He ranks among the Platonists, but it is characteristic of the philosophy of the age, as of the general syncretism, that Plato is presented with a dash of Aristotle and a whole dose of Pythagoras. More, he came from Apamea in Syria at a time when Syria was a cosmopolitan centre with Jews, Arabs and Greeks already mingling, and contacts with Egypt, Mesopotamia, and through Mesopotamia with Persia and India. Perhaps his orientalism has been exaggerated; none the less, he shows a marked interest in Indian, Persian, Egyptian and Jewish thought and practice. For a Platonist to describe Plato as 'Moses speaking Greek' is, even without a context, a sufficient indication of an unusual breadth of sympathy.

Numenius held a doctrine of three gods. The supreme god is identified with the monad of Pythagoras, the Good of Plato and the divine Intellect of Aristotle; he is also called father and king, but a *roi fainéant*. Unmoved himself, like Aristotle's Unmoved Mover, he can yet be described as the primary artificer of the cosmos. He is the principle of being; he gives without being diminished. He is also the Platonic Form of the second god. The second god is Plato's divine artificer; he can also be described as Intellect, and is perhaps to be identified with Aristotle's Active Intellect. He participates in movement, as the supreme god does not; he is the farm-labourer where the supreme god is the farmer; he unifies matter. The third god is formed from the second by a process of fission, and we are told that the second and third gods are one; he is in fact the cosmos. But since we know that to Numenius matter was evil, we must think of the third god in terms of Plato's world-soul. But Numenius carried his dualism further; he believed in two distinct world-souls (the lower involved with matter), and in two distinct souls in the individual human. We must assume that Numenius believed in the downward journey of the soul from the heavenly realm, and the acquisition of a lower soul during the passage through the planetary spheres. Incarnation is thus an evil, the product of a fallen nature, and Numenius, with Pythagoras and Plato, believed in reincarnation as part of the cycle of guilt and punishment. Yet there is hope, through mystical contemplation. The soul can enjoy a vision of the Good; it can share with the Good, alone with the alone; the language is reminiscent of Plotinus and may have influenced him.

The most interesting of the Middle Platonists is Albinus, who has been persuasively identified as the author of a work called *Didaskalikos* or *The Teacher*, a well-presented elementary textbook of a modified Platonic philosophy. Like Numenius, Albinus admits the influence of Aristotle, especially in theology and ethics, but where Numenius appears a Pythagorean, Albinus presents Stoic views, though not uncritically, in logic and epistemology. After an introduction which exalts the contemplative life above the active, and a preliminary discussion of epistemology and logic, he turns to first principles and theological considerations. Albinus writes of three First Principles. The first is matter, in which his doctrine is based on Plato's in *Timaeus*, interpreted so that matter means space (Plato's 'receptacle'). The second is the Platonic Form. If we think of the Form in relation to God we may call it a process of thought; in relation to Man the primary object of intellect; in relation to matter a principle of measure; in relation to the sensible world a pattern; in its own right a principle of being. The view that the Forms are thoughts in the mind of God is doubtfully to be read back into Plato; it was however strongly supported by Aristotle's system. Thirdly, there is the transcendent God, final and efficient cause of the universe, and Albinus argues to a supreme God on the grounds that where there is a better there must be a best. But there are also intermediate spirits or daemons, who are responsible for dreams and oracles, and the universe itself, in a picture drawn from *Timaeus*, is described as eternal, animate and intelligent. The soul is immortal, and its residence in a human body is a fall and punishment. God is not responsible for the evil that afflicts men. But Albinus does not follow the majority of Platonists of this period in identifying evil with matter. Further, though the supreme God is withdrawn, the universe is the best of all possible worlds, and within it man is not left helpless. God holds in his hands the beginning, middle and end of all things, and the aim of the life of man is to leave the earthly world for the heavenly as speedily as possible; in short it is becoming like to God. The philosophy of Albinus is thus—and this he holds in common with other Platonists of the period—a religion.

CHRISTIAN PLATONISTS

If Numenius and Albinus blend Aristotle into a Platonic base, the next great Platonists, Clement and Origen, draw together Plato and Christ, as did Justin before them. Clement is a Christian; he believes in Christ as the ultimate revelation of God. But Christ had his forerunners, and philosophy was to the Greeks what the Torah was to the Jews. Clement in fact starts from the existence of a single transcendent god, the first cause of all things, who does not depend on his creation as it depends on him, and he finds in the pages of Plato the sort of god he believes in; he will have nothing to do with Stoic pantheism, or an identification of God with the world-soul. Apart from calling God one, there is little we can say of him; he is beyond oneness, beyond wholeness, which imply measurement and dimension. Even to call him one or being or good or father is to limit him, though from the coherence of all these names we may begin to glimpse his power. But the idea of God is part of our human inheritance. Clement thus accepts that the natural theology of Plato points in the same direction as the Bible, and finds no discrepancy between *Timaeus* and *Genesis*.

This causes an interesting point of tension. In the Jewish tradition creation is absolute; in Plato matter is taken as given. Clement speaks of creation out of nothing, but the Greek he uses is relative and ambiguous. To bridge the gap between God and the world Clement takes over from Plato the philosophy of the Logos, the divine Reason, the Word of God. It was a Stoic idea, but Clement explicitly equates the Logos with a Platonic Form in the mind of God. The Logos is thus for him the divine first principle of the universe, which we discern in the order and administration of the world, in those indications of providential government which are a commonplace of Greek thought from Socrates to the Stoics, and especially in human beauty, thought and action.

So far there is little which might not be found among the other Platonists. But Clement follows John in identifying the Logos with Jesus; 'he has now taken the long-sanctified name, the name worthy of his power, the Christ'. Even so Clement's thought is rather from the Logos to Jesus than from Jesus to the Logos; he is little concerned with Jesus' actual life, and the crucifixion is not central to his thought, as the incarnation is. As for the individual, Clement occasionally expresses himself in Platonic terms, as when he says that bodies are our framework in our period of discipline, or that the body blurs the soul's vision. But the incarnation of the Logos means too much to him to allow him to say that man's physical nature is evil, and he explicitly says, 'The soul is not good by nature, or the body by nature evil.' Hence the solid good sense of much of his ethics. Clement refuses to equate sex and sin; he honours the act of sex and preaches against its abuse. So too with wine; it is a gift of God to be enjoyed and not misused. In all, man, being immortal and built up in righteousness, is a noble hymn to God. 'If you are a ploughman, plough, but know God as you plough; if you enjoy seafaring, sail, but call on the heavenly pilot.'

Origen's intellect was a finer and more comprehensive instrument than Clement's; there have been few comparable intelligences in the whole story of mankind. Much of his work lay in biblical exegesis. But his thought was drenched in Greek philo-

débâcle to Antioch and Rome. In Rome he became the confidant of Gallienus, who invited him implausibly to found, in the region of Naples, Platonopolis, Plato's Republic come to life in the most disastrous period of Roman history: nothing came of it. Plotinus taught at Rome for a quarter of a century, a shy lecturer, and something of a saint, a pastor to his flock. He died in AD 270, perhaps of cancer of the throat, greeting a friend with the words, 'I was waiting for you, before the divine in me joins the divine in the universe.'

Plotinus' thought centres upon his vision of God, the One. Zeller called Plotinus' doctrine 'Dynamic Pantheism'. That it is not. The One is immeasurably beyond the world, and the materiality of the world faced Plotinus with a grave problem. He uses of the One Plato's language about the Form of the Good; it is 'beyond reality'. Plotinus' God is beyond personality—It rather than He. 'It is this to which all things are attached, and to which all existence aspires, having It as a first principle and needing It. It is without wants, sufficient to Itself, needing nothing, the measure and limit of all things, giving out of Itself mind, substance, soul and life, and—as far as concerns mind—activity.' It is beyond thought, beyond definition, beyond utterance, beyond comprehension, beyond reality. We may not predicate any attributes of It, for this would limit It; we may call It 'The Good' but not good. We may not predicate of It essence or being or life, not because It is less than these things but because It is greater. The One cannot be identical with the sum of individual things, for It is their source and principle, distinct from them and logically prior to them. If It were identical with them, they would be identical with one another, which is not so. 'Thus the One cannot be any existing thing, but is prior to all existents.' In this vision Plotinus is at one with our modern linguistic philosophers who, whether pro-religious or anti-religious, agree that it is nonsensical to apply to God the language appropriate to the world of sense-experience.

The higher produces the lower by a process of efflux, radiation or emanation: this is a kind of halfway house between theism and pantheism. It is important to realize that the process of emanation is an unconscious product of the Divine contemplation, not a deliberate creative act, and its results are naturally at all levels good. The first emanation is Mind or *Nous*, identified with the Divine Artificer of Plato's *Timaeus* and the ultimate Beauty of *The Symposium*. In *Nous* the Forms or Ideas alike of individuals and classes exist; in *Nous* therefore multiplicity comes in alongside the essential unity. The Forms of individuals are noteworthy; this is a notion not found in Plato. Plotinus, unusually among the great mystics, has a profound respect for individual personality. Socrates in the divine world must retain the individuality of Socrates on earth. It is also noteworthy that the Forms, being in the Divine Mind, themselves enjoy life and intelligence, and intermingle with one another. The Divine Mind is the highest level of the lower world.

From *Nous* proceeds Soul, the World-Soul of *Timaeus*, which serves as a link between the sensible and supra-sensible worlds. These three, the One, *Nous*, and Soul, may be formulated to some extent as a counter-blast to the Christian doctrine of the Trinity, *Nous* corresponding to the *Logos*, and Soul to the Holy Spirit, the Divine Energy. They are called *hypostases*. But there are two stages of Soul, the higher in contact with *Nous*, the lower with nature. The Forms in order to be materialized have to pass down through the two levels of Soul as 'generative thoughts', a term borrowed from the Stoics. Nature thus is Soul immanent. This is important, for it enables Plotinus to say that though matter is evil, the material universe is not. The visible, tangible universe stands midway between matter and the Ideal World. Plotinus is strong in his criticism of the Gnostics. The material world created problems for him, but he could not follow the Gnostic disparagement of creation and creator, their exaltation of the human soul and refusal to honour the order of the universe and glory of sun and stars. No good man will despise the world and all the beauty in it. To love God is to love the world that emanates from Him; to love the beauty of the world is to be led to love its cause and origin. Even matter, the principle of evil, proceeds ultimately from the One, though it is so far from the light that it is shading over into darkness. Plotinus here applies the Aristotelian concept of deprivation. Darkness is deprivation of light, evil is deprivation of good. There is no ultimate dualism, no eternal battle between good and evil, no devil defying God; evil is negatively not positively conceived. Matter, it should be clear, is nothing we experience. Plotinus explicitly says that it is incorporeal, and calls it non-Being, at most 'the image and phantasm of mass, a bare aspiration towards substantial existence'.

The highest life is the ascent of the soul to God. The impulse to this is called *Eros*, Love considered as aspiration, and Plotinus returns to the fullness of Plato's teaching. Love is 'an activity of the Soul desiring the Good'. Love of physical beauty, as with Plato, is the first step to a higher and purer love. The objects of earthly loves may be mortal and injurious, shadows which change and pass, but these are not the objects of our true love, the goal of our search, our real good. That, the true object of our love, lies beyond; it is possible to grasp it, live with it, and really possess it, since no envelope of flesh separates us from it. So the World-Soul has a love, which is its eyes, and which is born of the desire it has for the One. *Eros* is a spirit intermediate between God and man, a *daemon*. So it seems, but at one point Plotinus goes further, saying of God, 'He is worthy to be loved, and is Love as well, that is Love of Himself, inasmuch as He is beautiful only from Himself and in Himself.' This is an astonishing statement, and is perhaps a slogan rather than a philosophical assertion, 'God is *Eros*', countering the Christian 'God is *Agape*'. But it leads him into philosophical difficulties, for *Eros* is essentially an aspiration and can hardly be predicated of Him who is all in all, or put at the centre of the universe wherein He manifests Himself, and this is not really solved by making it an aspiration towards Himself.

There are stages in the soul's ladder of ascent. The first includes purification, *catharsis*, the freeing of soul from body, and the practice of the cardinal virtues. In the second the soul rises above sense-perception to *Nous* by means of contemplative virtue. A third and higher stage, beyond expression, leads to union with *Nous*. Finally there is the climax of the whole ascent in mystical and ecstatic union with the One. 'He will lapse again from the vision: but let him again awaken the virtue which is in him, again know himself made perfect in splendour; and he shall be again lightened of his burden, ascending through virtue to the Intelligence, and thence through wisdom to the Supreme. This is the life of gods, and of the godlike and happy among men, a quittance from things alien and earthly, a life beyond pleasure, a flight of the alone to the Alone.' 'This is the true end of the soul, to come into contact with this light, and to behold Him through it, not by the light of another thing, but to perceive that very thing itself through which it sees.' Alone, it must receive the Alone. Plotinus knew this at first-hand; his disciple Porphyry records that four times during their association Plotinus enjoyed the vision glorious. Plotinus himself says: 'Many times it has happened. Lifted out of the body into myself; becoming external to all other things and self-centred; beholding a marvellous beauty; then, more than ever assured of community with the loftiest order; enacting the noblest life; acquiring identity with the divine.'

CHAPTER XII

SYNCRETISM AND
CONFRONTATION

IN GENERAL ancient religions were accommodating. The Hellenes, invading Greece, had brought with them the sky-god typical of a nomadic people, Dyaus-Zeus, and, encountering, as they settled, the Earth-Mother in different localities, united the two. Hence the myths of Zeus' amours. When the Romans encountered Greek culture they had already taken over some of the Indo-European pantheon: Dyaus-piter had become Jupiter. Other identifications, as we have seen, were made, and the *numina* put on recognizable personalities and became involved in myth and legend. Thus Juno, the spirit of fertility in woman, took over the role of Hera as Jupiter's consort; Neptunus, a water-spirit, was an obvious candidate for Poseidon; Mercurius, a *numen* of trade, was identified with Hermes, and so became messenger of the gods; Saturnus, an agricultural *numen* of sowing, took the part of primeval Cronos; and the identification with Ares may have helped Mars to concentrate his function on war to the exclusion of agriculture. In the East, where the Great Mother went under various guises in different regions they were naturally identified. When the Greeks encountered Egyptian religion they saw in Osiris their own Dionysus, a god who was torn in pieces in a similar way. The process continued into more sophisticated times and was still operative as the Roman legions pushed into unfamiliar terrain. The Christian Arnobius taunted the pagans: 'You have three Jupiters, five Sun-gods, five Mercuries, five Minervas. . . .'

Roman Britain offers some excellent examples of the process. Thus at Bath the Celtic divinity Sulis presided over the spa. She was, it seems, originally a sun-goddess—the old Irish *suil* means 'eye' or 'sun'—and was worshipped on the hills around, where Little Solbury preserves the name. The hot springs do not seem to have been exploited before Roman times, but it was natural that she should take charge of them, as the dominant power of the region, and in this capacity she was identified with Minerva Medica. Another more obvious identification was of Maponus, the Celtic god of youth, with Apollo, as at Corbridge or Ribchester. Apollo has other aliases: at Nettleton was found an altar to Apollo Cunomaglus, dedicated by a local lady named Corotica; Cunomaglus was perhaps a divinity of the hunt, and Diana is depicted with a hound on another altar nearby. (Pl. 80)

The largest number of such identifications naturally pertain to Mars, since the soldiers would be likely to think of him first. Thus at Housesteads we find a shrine of Mars Thincsus with attendant goddesses the Alaisiagae; these three formed a familiar trinity in Germany. At Trier Mars appears as Mars Lenus, identified with the Rhenish god of healing; he in turn is identified at Caerwent with the Celtic Ocelus, and at Carlisle we have a dedication to Mars Ocelus. At Bewcastle, north of Hadrian's Wall, we have Mars Cocidius, perhaps the power of the River Coquet. In Hertfordshire Barkway produced dedications both to Mars Alator and Mars Toutates. Colchester offers a dedication by a Pict to Mars Medocius Campesium and the Victory of Alexander Pius Felix, our Augustus: Mars Medocius is otherwise unknown. Campesium may be an error for Campestrium 'of the Powers of the parade-ground'. Martlesham in Suffolk produced Mars Corotiacus. At Bowes we find Mars Condates; at Bakewell Mars Braciacae, who may be a god of malt and therefore beer or may perhaps represent a local place name. At Carvoran we have Mars Belaucairus; this is an identification with a god who appears severally as Belatucadrus, Balatucairus, Balaticaurus, Blatucairus, Blatucadrus, and Belatugagrus. At Birdoswald there is Mars Augustus. Nodens was perhaps an Irish deity who appears in legend as Nuada of the Silver Hand and has associations with hunting; he appears in Welsh as Lludd Llau Ereint; his temple at Lydney is one of the most interesting sites in Britain; here and at Lancaster there were dedications to Mars Nodens. At Custom

Scrubs in Gloucestershire there stood an altar to Mars Olludius; at West Coker in Somerset a shrine to Mars Rigisamus including a dedicatory plaque; in Lincolnshire there was a most unusual dedication by Q. Neratius Proxsimus of an arch to Mars Rigonemetis and the Numina Augustorum.

Other interesting identifications from Britain included Hercules Saegon (?) at Silchester, Mercury Andescociuoucus from Colchester, Silvanus Callirius (otherwise unparalleled) from Colchester, Silvanus Vinotonus at Bowes, Jupiter Tanarus from Chester; this last is presumably the Taranis or Taranucus of the Continent. An interesting fusion is found at Lancaster, where we have Ialonus Contrebis. Here neither is a familiar god from the Graeco-Roman pantheon. Ialonus is a Celtic god of the meadows, also attested from Nîmes; Contrebis is a local deity found in his own right, and apparently simply the god of those who live together. Another unusual fusion may be seen in the Ashmolean Museum in Oxford. It is a second-century AD bronze, found in Gloucestershire, and shows Horus wearing Roman dress; it was no doubt an import, but the blend of Egypt, Rome and Britain is revealing.

Finally we may notice the Celtic Mother-goddesses. This group of feminine divinities created some puzzlement. At Skinburness and Carlisle they were identified with the Parcae or Fates. More often they were simply sensed as alien intruders—the Deae Matres Ollototae, which seems to mean 'belonging to other peoples'. Occasionally this is more specific. As early as AD 100 at Winchester Antonius Lucretianus made a dedication to the Mothers, Italian, German, Gallic, British. A similar dedication at York casts the net wider, to the Mothers, African, Italian, Gallic. This was too impersonal for M. Rustius Massa: his dedication is 'to his own Mothers'.

Across the channel we see the same process. It dates back to the first exploration and contact. Caesar states that in Gaul Mercury was reckoned the greatest of the gods, and Apollo, Mars, Jupiter and Minerva were also found as objects of worship, but he did not speak from any intimate knowledge. Mercury was important, however; he appears in several hundred inscriptions from

Gaul, and Montmartre is his hill, not Mars'. His principal identification is with Lug, whose name is seen in Lugdunum, Lyons. A century later Lucan introduced into his poem Taranis, Teutates and Esus. The ancient annotations identified Taranis with Jupiter; Teutates became assimilated variously to Mercury and Mars, as did Esus. But dedications do not suggest that any of the three was really very important. Not all the divinities became assimilated. The Celts in Gaul had a group of nature-goddesses, Divona associated with water, Onuava with earth, Sirona with the sky, and Epona traditionally with horses, though from fertility aspects of her cult, and from her association with death, we may assume that she is in origin a corn-spirit; in general these retain their identity.

The three Mother-goddesses, the Matres or Matronae, who appear in the Rhineland under various titles, such as Alagabiae, Berhusiahenae, Hamavehae, are identified with or assimilated to the Parcae or Fates, or Iunones or spirits of femininity. We may add an assimilation to Cybele, leading to the popularity of the *taurobolium*. It is interesting to reflect on a further course of assimilation: the site of the Saintes Maries, three in number, on the Rhône delta was once sacred to the Iunones Augustae. Apollo finds various identifications, sometimes as the sun with Belenus, sometimes with gods of healing such as Grannus at Aix-la-Chapelle, or Moritasgus at Alesia. Identifications were casual and careless; thus the same deity may be identified with Mars or Mercury; witness Viducus and Vellaunus, as well as those mentioned above. This total process of the *interpretatio Romana* was two-way; the Romans might make their identification of local gods with their own, but in the process their own gods became Celtic; the *interpretatio Romana* was accompanied by an *interpretatio Celtica*. There is a curious example in a bronze in the Bibliothèque Nationale. This is a fourfold representation of Mercury, two of the heads being beardless in the Roman style, two bearded in the Celtic. Hercules again appears in Celtic representations seated cross-legged, rather like the Buddha.

North Africa is an exceptionally interesting area for the study of assimilation. Of the indigenous deities we know little, though from Cirta (the modern Constantine) we have references to two deities named Ifru and Bacax; the latter was a cave-god. Most of the surviving allusions do not name the gods; for example, one Roman governor gives thanks to 'the gods of the Mauri' for his victory over the fierce Bavares. In one instance we can see the process of assimilation at work in a dedication to Diana of the Mauri. We may reasonably assume that Silvanus, who appears in the countryside, represents a local god. Local divinities were even worshipped in classical times within the precincts of Jupiter, Juno and Minerva.

When the Phoenicians settled Carthage they brought their own gods; no doubt there was a process of assimilation with the local gods, but it is too remote to trace. Centuries established the Punic gods, and it is their assimilation to the Roman pantheon of which we have most evidence. Predominant was Ba'al, 'the Lord', who in Palestine is assimilated to Zeus-Jupiter, but in Africa is identified with Saturn, though Jupiter acquired some of the devotion which Ba'al formerly received. Ba'al was strong in Cirta and in the country districts; he was a fertility-power, and Saturnus, the *numen* of sowing, and the god of the *ancien régime*, was in fact a peculiarly apposite equivalent. The myth of Cronos-Saturn devouring his children may further have helped, for Ba'al was ruthless in his exaction of sacrifice.

Tanit, the Moon-goddess, who had already acquired many of the attributes of the Great Mother, was supreme at Carthage. Juno took over from Tanit, but Tanit herself survived as Caelestis. Caelestis is a title in its own right, though it becomes assimilated to Aphrodite-Venus, and at Sicca there was ritual prostitution in the cult. Her Great Mother associations remained in the games of Caelestis and Cybele, and the ritual washing of her statue recalls the washing of the Great Mother's image in the Almo. She remained as the moon, and the pitiable fanatic Elagabalus had the shapeless image which represented her brought to Rome for marriage to the Sun-betyl from Syria. In fact during the early third century AD she was popular in Rome, and was worshipped as 'the mighty protectress of the Tarpeian hill'. Other associations are with Diana, and more especially with Ceres. Ceres, in the singular or plural, was worshipped within Tanit's temple at Carthage, and is no doubt another of the goddess's guises. In Christian times her worship continued strong, even from professing Christians, another example of the power of the goddess to retain her hold.

Melkart of Tyre and Eshmun of Sidon were naturally found. Melkart for some reason not wholly clear was identified with Heracles-Hercules; he also appears in association with Jupiter and, in a temple dedicated by Septimius Severus, with Bacchus. Eshmun was identified with Asclepius-Aesculapius, and incubation was practised in his temples, a good example of syncretism in action. His cult was often linked with that of Caelestis; in the temple in the civil settlement at Lambaesis there are curious side-chapels, one of which is dedicated to Jupiter. These four Punic gods dominate our records, but Toutain has argued plausibly that Mercury has replaced a Punic god of traders.

An alternative to the absorption of a local god by the Roman deity was the establishment of a joint cult, such as Apollo and Sirona, or Sucellus and Nautosuelta, or Mercury and Rosmerta; Rosmerta is no doubt the unnamed goddess accompanying Mercury at Gloucester. The Seine boatmen in Tiberius' reign put up a truly remarkable four-sided monument in honour of Esus, Tarvos, Vulcan and Jupiter. Tarvos Trigaranos is the bull with three cranes, or three horns; he may be seen at Dorchester in unique association with the three-headed deity from Gaul, or at Autun. The Musée de Cluny has three of these square blocks. The others are less easy of reading. One shows a goddess with a torch, a god with a Phrygian cap, and an armed god with Gorgoneion and winged cap: we may say Venus, Vulcan and Mars or Mercury if we like. The other has a Hercules type, Castor, Pollux and Cernunnos. At the military station of Corbridge there is an altar with a dedication to Jupiter Dolichenus, Caelestis Brigantia, and Salus. Here absorption and co-ordination work side by side, since Brigantia is a regional goddess, the tutelary spirit of the Brigantes, but she is identified with Juno Caelestis, the Roman version of the Syrian Goddess, and so made into the god's consort, and Salus, the personification of the principle of healing, is brought into the triad. The dedicator, C. Julius Apol(l)inaris, may come from the East. Numerous inscriptions from other parts bring together the old Roman gods, local gods and gods from the East in this way. (*Pls.* 37, 78, 81–83)

When we turn to the East we find a good example of assimilation in Men Ascaenus. He was, as Strabo tells us, the chief god of Antioch-near-Pisidia. His temple, which stood 5,000 feet up, was approached by a Sacred Way; the precinct was actually 230 by 137 feet, and the walls 5½ feet thick. A stadium was associated with the precinct and there was a popular athletic festival. The god's symbol was the bull's head, which appeared above a crescent in a wreath; the bull's head is also to be seen on coins of about the year AD 200. The cult was immensely popular during the Empire, and a high proportion of those who made dedications were freedmen or from the poorer classes; inscriptions are in Greek, but the names are often Latin. The Romans did not like it—perhaps it was too closely associated with local nationalist sentiment—and tried to break it down, without success. The usual process of assimilation went on: the god was variously identified with Apollo, Dionysus and Asclepius. This suggests a healing-god with a strong element of enthusiastic personal religion. One broken inscription beginning Ouio . . . suggests that Men was identified with the Jewish Yahweh. In origin he was perhaps an Iranian Moon-god who did not fit readily into the Graeco-Roman pantheon, where the Moon was feminine.

A rather different example may be seen in an oracle of Apollo of Claros. The question asked was 'Who is IAO?' IAO are mystical letters representing the Jewish Yahweh, and not unnaturally playing an important part in magic. The oracle answers in hexameters, that he is Hades in winter, Zeus in spring, Helios in summer, Iao in autumn: all in all, beyond peradventure the supreme god. Here is the tendency, not merely of the sky-god and sun-god to draw together, but towards a wider unity of all religion. More simply, but in the same vein, an oracle from Rhodes declared the identity of Attis, Adonis and Dionysus. Elsewhere Attis is identified with the Sun; the literary evidence from the period when the Sun had been brought to dominance is confirmed by the statue from Ostia showing the god with rays emerging from his head. Other obvious identifications are of Sabazios with Dionysus-Liber, Astarte with Artemis-Diana, and Dea Caelestis with Aphrodite-Venus. The general claims of Sarapis and the Great Mother we have already noted.

Some of the gods went further. Isis made particularly extravagant claims: Juvenal's identification of her with Cybele is the smallest part of them, like Ovid's with Juno Lucina, Varro's with Terra, and Herodotus' with Demeter. She is described on inscriptions as 'having ten thousand names'. A Latin inscription calls her 'thou one who art all things'. In Apuleius there is a long list of her guises: she is the first of the heavenly beings, the single appearance of the gods and goddesses, the Mother of the gods, Minerva, Venus, Diana, Proserpina, Ceres, Juno, Bellona, Hecate, Nemesis; her true name, known in Ethiopia and in Egypt, is Queen Isis. The list is paralleled by a second-century AD papyrus from Oxyrhynchus: in various areas of Egypt she is Isis, or Hera, or Aphrodite, or Hestia, or Athene, or Praxidike, or Wisdom, or Good Fortune, or a host of other names or epithets; the papyrus goes on to list equivalences outside Egypt, in Arabia, Syria, Lycia, Cyprus and other islands, Asia, the Hellespont, Bithynia, Caria, India, Persia, and even Rome; the identities include Leto, Kore, Dictynnis, Themis, Helen and Hecate, Astarte, Atargatis, Hellas (!), Latina (!), name of the Sun, with numerous cult-adjectives.

Macrobius makes comprehensive claims for the Sun-god similar to those of Isis. If the Sun is the ruler of the other luminaries and sole sovereign of the wandering planets, then he must be responsible for all that goes on around us; the other gods are so many potencies of the Sun. So the Sun's healing power we call Apollo, his gift of speech Mercury. The Sun gives the gift of grain. Dionysus-Liber is to the hemisphere of night what Apollo is to the day. Mars is one with Liber; they bear common cult-titles and emblems. So with Aesculapius, Hercules, Salus, Sarapis, Adonis, Attis, Osiris and Horus, the signs of the zodiac, Nemesis, Pan and Saturn, and even Jupiter, who appears as the Sun among the stars. The interesting feature of this passage is not so much

Macrobius' own speculative syncretism, as the indication that there was a tendency of the gods to draw together in general. Other deities were also making comprehensive claims without the help of intellectuals. Fortuna might be Fortuna Panthea. She appears with Minerva's breastplate, Isis' lotus, or *sistrum*, Jupiter's thunderbolt or eagle, Bacchus' fawn-skin, Aesculapius' cock, Neptune's dolphin, Apollo's lyre, Vulcan's tongs, Mercury's staff, as well as her own rudder and cornucopiae. In the little bronze at Autun Mercury is shown bearing the whole pantheon on his back. Other inscriptions testify to Liber Pantheus and even Silvanus Pantheus.

In a polytheistic system no deity normally claims the exclusive adherence of a worshipper. Odysseus may be under the peculiar protection of Athene, but he acknowledges other gods. There is an interesting inscription from Smyrna. Apollonius Sparus, a former priest of Helios Apollo of Cisaulodda, dedicates to the god and the city the following items: the god on a marble base; a table; a slab of marble; a square incense-burner; a marble cult-image of Artemis; a cult-image of Men; a square multicoloured table for offerings; a marble table with the eagle of Zeus on it; a wooden shrine with cult-statues of Pluto Helios and Kore Selene; and eight iron weapons for decoration. The gods were accommodating to one another. Dea Caelestis might order an altar to Mercury, Aesculapius to Jupiter Dolichenus, Jupiter Dolichenus to holy Juno. At the civil settlement of Lambaesis in North Africa the temple of Aesculapius, god of healing, had two side-chapels attached, one of which was for Jupiter: he had his own temple elsewhere, but only as one of the Capitoline triad, Jupiter, Juno and Minerva. The Walbrook Mithraeum was amiably accommodating. In addition to the strictly Mithraic relics we can list as associated with the building: a headless statue of a Genius (paralleled from Dieburg and Stockstadt); a fine river-god (paralleled at Merida and S. Prisca); a head of Minerva (found occasionally on her own in Mithraea, more frequently with other Olympians); a magnificent Sarapis (again paralleled at Merida and S. Prisca: there may be an identification with Ahura-Mazda); a small statuette of Mercury (amply paralleled in the

Rhineland; the god was associated with the lowest grade of initiates, the Raven); and a Bacchic group. (*Pl.* 79)

Where the deities were accommodating the worshippers could hardly do less. A third-century AD inscription from Utrecht, to take one example out of many, honours Jupiter, the highest and most excellent god; the invincible Sun, Apollo, the Moon, Diana, Fortune, Mars, Victory and Peace. Another from Spain is even more comprehensive: it honours Juno, Minerva, the Sun, the Moon, the almighty god Fortune, Mercury, the Genius of Jupiter, the Genius of Mars, Aesculapius, Light, Sleep, Venus, Cupid, the two Castors, Ceres, Victory, the gods of passage—and the inscription breaks off. The emperor Alexander Severus is a particularly good example of the readiness to seek power wherever it may be found. In his private chapel, in the shrine of the Lares, he had a series of statues which included the deified emperors, revered spirits like Apollonius of Tyana, Christ, Abraham, Orpheus and all the others of that character. He also wanted to build a temple to Christ and enthrone him among the gods. It is interesting to compare V. S. Naipaul's West Indian, who had pictures of Joe Louis, Jesse Owens, Haile Selassie and Jesus Christ; the naïveté is the same, but the emperor's has an extra dimension. One mystery-initiation might well be deemed insufficient. Clea, for whom Plutarch wrote his work *On Isis and Osiris*, was an initiate alike of Isis and Dionysus; Tatian, before he ended up in Christianity, sampled a number of the mysteries. Inscriptions tell the same story: a single man might end up high in a number of cults:

PATER PATRUM DEI SOLIS INVICTI MITHRAE, HIEROFANTA HECATES, DEI LIBERI ARCHIBUCULUS, TAUROBOLIO CRIOBOLIOQUE IN AETERNUM RENATUS (*CIL* 6, 510).

In less elevated circles the muddle of thought is well seen in the Paris magical papyrus which Dieterich has shown to incorporate genuine Mithraic elements together with the fantastic sacred names consisting wholly of vowels, familiar in magical contexts.

The Jews remained exclusive. Their very being as a people

depended on racial and religious exclusiveness, and after the depopulation of the highlands round Jerusalem in a series of wars and revolts against the Romans they felt the need for survival more intensely. Hadrian actually tried to proscribe circumcision (though this was not directed exclusively against the Jews) but under his successor the ban lapsed. General tolerance ensued; Elagabalus was actually circumcised and began to abstain from pork; Alexander Severus was nicknamed the *archisynagogus*. The Jews clung to the symbols which had been associated with the Jerusalem temple; the temple was gone, but the symbols remained. The Menorah, or seven-branched candlestick, is ubiquitous. We see it appearing on an ornamental slab (now in the Louvre), whose other patterns are geometric; on a low relief from the second-century AD synagogue at Hamath; on a curious Corinthian-type capital from the courtyard of the slightly later synagogue at Capharnaum; on a superb piece of gilded glass found in the Jewish catacombs of Rome and datable to the fourth century AD; on innumerable lamps, jars and plaques from the later Empire. Other similar symbols are the Torah shrine; the *lulab* (palm-branch) and *ethrog* (citrus-fruit); the *shofar* (ram's horn trumpet); and the incense-shovel. Above all they clung to the Law, the Torah; the great compilations of interpretations of the Torah known as the Mishnah dates from about AD 200 and is the work of Rabbi Judah ha-Nasi, who was known as 'the Prince'. The relation of the Torah to the people of Yahweh is the subject of an exquisite parable:

It is as though a sovereign had an only daughter, and one of the kings comes and marries her, and then wants to return to his own country and to take his wife with him. Then the sovereign says to him: 'She whom I have given you is my only daughter; I cannot bear to be separated from her; yet I cannot say, "Do not take her," for she is your wife. So show me this kindness: wherever you go keep me a room so that I may stay with you, for I cannot bear to be separated from my daughter.' So the Holy One said to Israel: 'I gave you the Torah. I cannot separate myself from it; yet I cannot say to

you, "Do not take it." So wherever you travel make me a
home to live in.' For it is said: 'And let them make me a
sanctuary that I may live among them.' (*Exod.* 25, 8)

None the less it must not be supposed that the Jews were
isolated from all alien influence. Already long before the imperial
period Hecataeus of Abdera recorded that under the rule of the
nations the Jews greatly modified the traditions of their fore-
fathers. Local government on the Greek model affected their
political thought; the gymnasia helped to relax an unhealthy
physical repressiveness, some would say in favour of an unhealthy absence of restraint; the Greek language through the
stupendous achievement of the Septuagint helped subtly to
remould the categories of thought; Greek ideas drift through in
Ecclesiastes, Wisdom and especially the fourth book of *Maccabees*;
some attempt is made to reconcile the Platonic doctrine of the
immortality of the soul with the Jewish doctrine of the resurrection of the body. Similarly Goodenough has studied the way in
which pagan symbols come in alongside the more strictly Jewish
symbols just noted. Some of these, the bull, lion, tree and crown,
may be regarded as bridge-symbols: they were taken over from
pagan art but given obvious significance in a Judaic context.
Others, the rosettes and wheels, were not compromising. But
some are startlingly pagan: the Gorgon's mask seen at Chorazin
and on a Roman-Jewish amulet; the astral symbols, which suggest
a definite modification of religious thought; the fertility emblems,
birds, cupids and even centaurs. (*Pl.* 84)

The most interesting example of a blend is the worship of
Hypsistos in the Bosporus region. Hypsistos means 'Almighty'
or 'Most-Highest' and seems to be the title of a local supreme
god. But it is also a title of Yahweh in the Septuagint. The texts
extend from the second century BC to the third AD, and even in
the fourth century we hear of Hypsistarii in Cappadocia. The
original sectaries seem to have been Jews but to have included
proselytes known as 'adopted brothers'; yet they use the formula,
'under Zeus, Earth, Sun'. Where we have names a high proportion are non-Jewish; there were priests and therefore probably

sacrificial rituals; and in third-century AD texts we hear of 'The Society around Hypsistos and the priest—'. No orthodox Jew could so speak. We must suppose that in this cult liberal Jews and Gentiles attracted to Judaism came together, and in the process produced something new. We may well suppose that the 'synagogues of Satan', as the seer calls them, in Smyrna and Philadelphia, 'who say they are Jews but lie', practised some such cult. There were other examples of drawing together. An Egyptian might think of Yahweh as Osiris, a Roman as Jupiter. The accidental resemblance between Sabazios and Sabaoth led to another equation, and there is actually an inscription to Iuo Dionysus.

Two important studies by Saul Lieberman have now shown that during the period after the crushing of the Jewish revolt the Jewish scholars even of Palestine, let alone the Dispersion, were more open to pagan influence than has been generally allowed. The rabbis did not in fact ban the study of Greek Wisdom. There was an old ban on the *teaching* of Greek Wisdom to children; in AD 117 this was extended to the teaching of the Greek language, because of its association with the Roman imperialists. Still some of the rabbis knew Greek; they quote Homer (though it is possible that the quotations were commonplaces, as a man may quote Shakespeare without having read the plays: even that is significant of the permeation of the culture). For example, they apply to Asahel the description of the horses of Erichthonius, running over the ears of corn without breaking them; there is some evidence that they used Homer as a source for attacks on idolatry; it seems clear that many who were less stringent read Homer with enjoyment. Another interesting example relates to a story in Herodotus. Amasis had a golden basin for his guests; he melted it down and had it cast in the form of an idol, and used it as a parable of his own rise from lowness to glory. The story had a wide circulation, and wherever they got it from, rabbis knew it and used it. In the third century AD Rabbi Eleazar could quote a Greek proverb in Greek in the synagogue, and expect to be understood. Furthermore rabbinical methods of interpretation are closely parallel to those used by Alexandrian critics; the rabbinical tractate against idolatry

'*Abodah Zarah* (*Alien Worship*) shows first-hand knowledge and study of pagan rites and practices; and rabbinical science and natural history, although it is developed in a different spirit, is but part of the general scientific world-picture held by Graeco-Roman scholars.

Philo, the industrious Hellenistic Jew of the first century AD, is here important. He impresses by the catholicity of his sympathies and experiences. He discusses Greek education with intimate understanding. He is alert to current political problems. He appears to have studied medicine. He knows and quotes Homer and Euripides; he attends theatrical productions; he enjoys and is knowledgeable about music; he appreciates the sculpture of Pheidias; he has a close knowledge of athletics. His life-work accords with this breadth of vision. It was to reconcile Greek culture and Jewish faith. The bridge between the two was allegory. Philo did not compromise the essentials of his Judaism. He is a rigid monotheist, and his god is revealed in the Books of the Law. But Platonism enters in the tendency to a dualistic view of matter, finite and imperfect. Because of this Philo's god cannot intervene directly in the world of matter, and Philo, in common with most of his contemporaries, believes in intermediate beings, to the Jews angels, to the Greeks daemons. Supreme among these is the Logos. Whether Philo himself devised the use of this concept in a Jewish context, it is certainly a master-stroke. For here in one concept are fused the Jewish *memra*, the word of God ('God said Let there be light, and there was light'), the late Jewish Wisdom, as seen in *Proverbs, Job, Ecclesiasticus* and *Wisdom*, the Platonic doctrine of Forms, the Aristotelian doctrine of the Divine Intellect, and the Stoic Divine Reason; the ambiguity of meaning in Logos between word and reason made it an especially convenient term. Philo is no doubt exceptionally accommodating, but he is inescapably there, a humane man who moved through life from a pessimistic view of the world to a serene old age.

In general the Christians were reluctant to compromise; Gilbert Murray said once: 'Christianity, apart from its positive doctrines, had inherited from Judaism the noble courage of its disbeliefs.' Hence the martyrdoms; the one reference to the Christians in

68, 69 Heroes on sarcophagi. *Above*, the Labours of Hercules, through which he won divinity (p. 145): the Nemean Lion, Hydra of Lerna, Boar of Erymanthus, Hind of Ceryneia, and the Stymphalian Birds. *Below*, Achilles on Scyros. Disguised as a woman to evade the Trojan War he betrayed himself by snatching up arms at the sound of the war-trumpet (p. 147). Museo Borghese and Capitoline Museum, Rome.

70, 71 *Left*, a word-square from Cirencester, also giving a palindromic sentence ROTAS OPERA TENET AREPO SATOR, a Christian formula with an allusion to Ezekiel I, 15–21, and providing an anagram of two PATERNOSTERS crossing on the N, and tv as and os (p. 168). Corinium Museum. *Above*, the sacred snake of Abonuteich on a coin of Antoninus Pius (p. 187).

72, 73 Scenes of sacrifice. *Left*, Marc Aurelius prepares to sacrifice a bull befc the temple of Jupiter (p. 157). Mus dei Conservatori, Rome. *Above*, a *harus* consults the entrails (p. 154). Louvre.

74, 75 Magic. *Above*, a sorcerer's equipment from Pergamum, now in the Pergamum Museum, East Berlin. The bronze triangular table is covered with magical inscriptions, and bears on it figures of Hecate, with key, torch, snake and other emblems (p. 156). *Below*, Gnostic gemstones in the Metropolitan Museum of Art, New York. The figure on the left has a human body, cock's head and snakes for legs.

76, 77 *Left*, Epicurus, still revered
by his followers during the period
of the Empire. The face is strong
and ascetic (p. 192). *Above*, Marcu
Aurelius, on a contemporary
portrait medallion. A professing
Stoic, he was really more of an
agnostic, groomed for greatness
but full of uncertainty (p. 198).
The weakness of the features is in
marked contrast to those of
Epicurus. Both British Museum.

78–80 *Above*, a relief from Gloucester, showing Fortuna with the Celtic Rosmerta and Mercury (pp. 86, 216). *Left*, a head of Sarapis found in the Walbrook Mithraeum, London, and now in the Guildhall Museum. The god, a construct of a syncretistic age, is seen as a form of Jupiter (pp. 36, 219). *Below*, the Gorgon's head from the Temple of Sulis, deity of the hot springs of Bath, and identified with Minerva, is an excellent example of artistic and religious syncretism (p. 211).

81–83 A four-sided altar dedicated in Tiberius' reign by the Seine boatmen is a remarkable testament to religious syncretism. Volcanus belongs to the Graeco-Roman pantheon and has evidently become identified with one of the Celtic smith-gods. His hammer and forceps may be clearly seen. Esus was probably originally a tree-spirit, as the relief suggests. Tarvos Trigaranos is a curious being, a bull (bull-worship was widespread among the Celts), with three cranes perched on him. Possibly he was originally a bull with three horns, and there has been some confusion of language. The fourth side has a representation of Jupiter (pp. 69, 214, 216) Musée de Cluny, Paris.

84, 85 Two symbolic Roman-age mosaics. *Top, right*, symbols of Judaism, from an eastern synagogue. The seven-branched candelabrum or Menorah, with lions, palm-trees, birds and elephants enclosed in a vine (p. 222). *Right*, the vine as a Christian motif in the church of S. Costanza in Rome (p. 238).

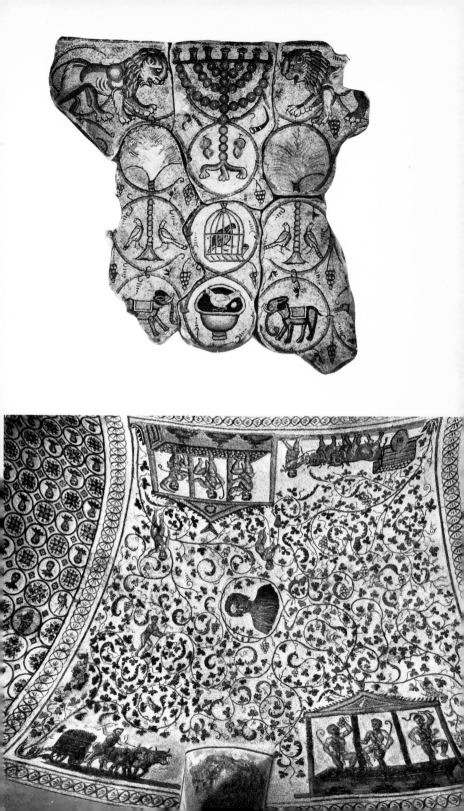

86, 87 Christian art in a Roman mould. *Left*, an early-fourth-century mosaic discovered under St Peter's, portraying Christ sweeping across the heavens in the sun-god's chariot. Note the vine in the background (pp. 56, 237). *Below*, a late-fourth-century ivory casket from Brescia with scenes from the life of Christ, who is depicted young and beardless. The fish, an old religious symbol, took on special significance for Christians, partly because it is a recurrent theme in our records of Christ, partly because the Greek word for fish ΙΧΘΥΣ is an acrostic of the Greek words for Jesus Christ God's Son, Saviour. The cock alludes to the story of Peter, and is a symbol of the need for repentance and for awakening to new life – the Day of the Lord is near. Christ is shown healing the woman with the issue of blood, expounding the scriptures, and saving the sheep from the wolf while the hireling shepherd runs away.

Marcus Aurelius is a half-contemptuous girding at their obstinacy.

The reasons behind the general suspicion directed against the Christians are relatively clear. They were involved in riot-situations with the Jews, whose loyalty to the Empire was already suspect. They were intolerant of other religions. Their founder had been executed by the Romans; they proclaimed a kingdom which was not Caesar's; they refused military service and civil office; they refused, too, to offer due worship to the Genius of the emperor. Their proclamation that the world would be consumed by fire led to accusations of arson; their celebration of the feast of the Lord's body and blood to accusations of cannibalism; the honour accorded to women (Prisca, Phoebe and Nympha in the first century, and martyrs like Perpetua and Blandina in the second, are good examples), the customary greeting with a kiss, the appellation 'Brother' and 'Sister', and the mixed meeting behind closed doors, combined to produce charges of sexual licence and incest. Because of the corruption of so much public life, they tended to withdraw, and were accused of anti-social tendencies, 'hatred of the human race'. They spread among the poorer classes, and were much more this-worldly than is sometimes believed; they were seeking the transformation of the world they knew; and their founder had spoken with some asperity of those with wealth and authority. They appeared in fact as immoral and dangerous revolutionaries.

The legal basis for the spasmodic persecutions is more controversial. It is however hard in the light of our present knowledge of Roman law to suppose that there was a general enactment forbidding the practice of the Christian religion. It seems rather that they were condemned under the general powers held by Roman government for the enforcement of public order, the powers of *coercitio*. Originally the Christians were arraigned for crimes allegedly practised by the sect. When innocence here was discovered, as by Pliny, the Christians still proved uncooperative; they would not offer the sacrifice which would fit them in as ordinary citizens. This laid them open to the charge, not of high treason, but of obstinacy, contumacy, and this charge, as can be amply substantiated, was regarded with great gravity.

Apart from popular and official opposition we know of two major works against Christianity written by pagan critics who had taken the trouble to get to know their opponents. The older was written by a Platonist named Celsus somewhere about AD 178, and entitled *The True Word*. The original is lost, but Origen, a fair-minded polemist, in answering it quotes at some length. To Celsus God is transcendent, a withdrawn god who exercises an indiscriminate care for the whole universe, in which men have a share as fish have a share, no less and no more. This care is exercised through subordinate gods, and worship of these enhances the honour paid to the power behind them. The gravamen of Celsus' charges against the Christians is that Christianity runs counter to all the traditions of the Graeco-Roman world; he argues in fact that Christianity is a corruption of the truths handed down in those traditions. Celsus is a religious conservative; for him 'new' and 'true' are mutually exclusive. But he does not dismiss the Christians unheard. On the contrary he recognizes that Jesus is central to them, and gives the gospels a thorough examination. He sees Jesus as a bastard, whose teaching was a garbled parody of Plato and other Greeks, whose miracles were so much Egyptian conjuring, whose life was ignominious, who was executed in a fate which he tried to avoid and could not, and who could not even control his thirst on the cross. Better an idol than a corpse!

When we try to analyse Celsus' underlying reasons for his attack on Christianity, three predominate. First, the scandal of particularity. Celsus regards Christians—and Jews—as insufferably parochial. He compares them to bats or ants or frogs or worms holding a parliamentary debate as if the world were centred on them. Second, the scandal of incarnation. Celsus takes a Platonic view which marks off the world of being, truth, intellectual knowledge from the world of becoming, opinion, sense-perception. It is absurd to think that God 'descended' from the world of perfection to the world of imperfection. Third, the lack of patriotic sentiment on the part of the Christians. The Christians are sentimental universalists; Celsus believes in Rome. The Christians are pacifists; to Celsus civilization can be safeguarded only by military power. The Christians will not pay homage to the emperor; in Celsus' thought everything on earth is granted to the emperor, and granted by him to others.

The other great intellectual critique of Christianity came from no less a person than Porphyry, the friend and biographer of Plotinus. It seems to have been written in Sicily, and to have extended to fifteen books; we can scarcely begin a systematic reconstruction from the fragments preserved in hostile citation. But we can discern certain broad lines along which Porphyry worked.

To begin with, the real gravamen of his charge against the Christians is that they were barbarians destroying the ancient traditions of the Graeco-Roman world and even of the Jews. Second, he applies a detailed and scholarly knowledge of the Bible and considerable critical acumen to show contradictions in the Christian case: thus, he demonstrates that *Daniel* is spurious, assails the genealogy of Jesus, lays bare contradictions in the gospel-narratives and the words of Jesus, pays particular attention to the story of the Gadarene swine, condemns Peter for the murder of Ananias and Sapphira, points to the conflict between Peter and Paul, lacerates Paul for the inconsistency of his thought. Third, Porphyry shows a certain bitter wit. It is clear in his treatment of the Gadarene swine. Pigs in a country which abominated them being drowned in a shallow lake? he asks. Or again he takes up 'With God all things are possible'. Can God bring it about that Homer was not a poet? Can he make $2 + 2 = 100$? Can he sin? Or again he argues that the Christians are inconsistent in saying that a god cannot occupy the material body of a statue, but can occupy the material body of a Jesus. Fourth, the great stumbling-block of Christianity was for him the Incarnation, as Augustine said and saw, and what he regarded as the consequent parochialism of the Christians. Finally, there is the positive side of his critique, which gives it depth and stability. For Porphyry does believe in God, a god of majesty who has his subordinates; whether we call them gods or angels hardly matters. He does believe in revelation; he believes in self-discipline; and he believes in a god who saves and offers man life beyond death.

Christians were divided over pagan culture. A study, of major importance, by H. Richard Niebuhr, has identified five answers found in the history of the Church to the relation between Christ and what we may call secular culture. The first is *opposition*: the demands of Christ are totally opposed to those of the world and incompatible with them; Tertullian is one of the great exponents of this view. The second is *agreement*: Christ confirms the best in all that has gone before, and leads civilization to its proper goal; the Christian Platonists exemplify this well. The third Niebuhr calls *synthetic*; it is close to but not identical with the second, for Christ, while seen as fulfilling cultural aspirations, is not contained within them; Niebuhr's example is Thomas Aquinas. The fourth is *polarity* and *tension*: the authority of society and the authority of Christ are both valid in their different ways; so Luther. The fifth is *conversionist*, and sees Christ as seeking to convert man in his culture and society; so Augustine. Plainly between Tertullian ('What has Jerusalem to do with Athens?') and Origen justifying the words of Christ on the grounds that they are found in the Greek philosophers, there is a chasm.

In fact much of the influence was unconscious and inevitable. Judaism had already absorbed attitudes from the Graeco-Roman world. How much might permeate through to a rabbi like Jesus is uncertain. In any case the assured conclusions of Form-criticism warn us to exercise extreme caution in trying to pass back beyond the environment in which the material of the gospels was first preserved. There the Graeco-Roman element is inescapable, and it is a theological error of the first water to seek to eliminate it. The letters of Paul, our earliest Christian documents, were written in Greek, by a man who, while claiming to be a Pharisee of the Pharisees, could quote Aratus or Menander. The gospels were written in Greek, though we may discern Aramaic underneath; Luke indeed was a cultured Greek doctor who moved at ease in the Greek-speaking world; John (whoever he was), like Philo, found the Logos a fruitful concept, and identified Jesus with the Logos in a human body. When the Christians needed intellectual arguments to set alongside moral and spiritual witness, they found them, as we have seen, in Plato and to a lesser extent the Stoics; and Justin, Clement and Origen started building a Christian philosophy.

In the Latin-speaking West progress was slower; the educated Roman, despite the examples of Lucretius and Cicero, tended to go to Greek to express the things of the intellect or spirit: witness Marcus Aurelius composing his diaries of Thoughts in Greek. What is of special interest is the writing of the Latin Bible, as it seems, in North Africa at some point in the second century AD. Of special interest because it is an early example of African Latinity, which through Fronto, Minucius Felix, Tertullian, Apuleius, Cyprian, Arnobius, Lactantius and eventually Augustine, long led the world of Latin letters. All except Fronto and Apuleius were Christians; all the Christians were converts. Latin meant, even for Fronto, Cicero, and Cicero was an intellectual as well as a stylistic influence. In Lactantius, known as 'the Christian Cicero', we can see the broad Platonism and rich *humanitas* which characterized the older man.

Jewish tradition eschewed the representation of the human figure in art. Here then Christians were inevitably directed to Graeco-Roman models, and in so doing absorbed something of the pagan originals. So Isis and Horus became the type of Madonna and child, Orpheus of Christ. There is a particularly good example recently rediscovered in the excavations under St Peter's; it is a mosaic of Christ as the Sun-god, radiate, cloak flying in the wind as he drives his two-horse chariot across the sky; in the background is the sprawling vine. The exact date is controversial, but a period after the middle of the third century is unlikely to be far out. The vine itself is an ambiguous emblem, meaningfully adapted from Dionysiac worship to the Christian expressions found in *The Gospel according to John*; it may be seen in the catacombs from an early stage. The concept of the Sun of Righteousness is found in Malachi. What is remarkable about this mosaic is that, so far as we can see, Christ was usually portrayed as beardless at this period. This strongly bearded figure thus represents an assimilation to the Sun-god; it should be remembered that this is the time of that god's greatest power.

Another interesting example merits examination just because

it is appreciably later. This is the mausoleum of S. Costanza, from the middle of the fourth century AD. It is adorned with a remarkable series of mosaics of considerable beauty and considerable technical skill. The large majority of the motifs are taken over from pagan art. It has been argued, not very plausibly, that they are purely decorative; since so much is overtly Christian, the rest becomes Christianized. Thus above the sarcophagus was a golden chi-rho against a background of stars, and in the two apses are representations of Christ which must, despite some scepticism, be dated with the rest of the building. The great mosaics of the colonnade thus fit into an integral scheme. We see birds, fruits and flowers, typical pagan emblems, here expressing the joys of paradise; we see the vine-scroll which Christ shares with Dionysus, and putti harvesting the grapes; much as Cupids engage in miscellaneous activities at Pompeii, here putti share in the great harvest which the Day of the Lord brings; we see Cupid and Psyche, and recall the allegorical interpretation of *The Song of Songs*; we see dolphins, and remember that the fish was one of the most ancient Christian symbols.

Another example, far less fine, but telling none the less, is the remarkable fourth-century AD mosaic discovered in 1963 at Hinton St Mary in Dorset. In the centre is a bust of a male, beardless, fair-haired, and with commanding gaze: behind the head is a chi-rho symbol: in the field two pomegranates. It is hard not to think that this is a head of Jesus. If so the other decorations on the pavement take on a new meaning from their context. The great tree below the central medallion becomes the Tree of Life; the four corner figures, akin to the winds elsewhere, but here with pomegranates and rosettes (both symbols of life beyond the grave), are perhaps the four evangelists with the life they offer; the hunting-scenes take up the symbolism of the sarcophagi and represent the theme of conflict and triumph; and Bellerophon killing the Chimaera (found also in the Christian villa at Lullingstone) represents Christ's victory over the power of evil.

Festivals offer another example of dangerous adaptation. The early Christians did not celebrate the birthday of Jesus; it was unrecorded. In Egypt and the East generally it became tied in with a New Year festival on 6 January. But 25 December was the winter solstice in the Julian calendar and the nativity of the Sun; in the rituals of Syria and Egypt the worshippers cried, 'The Virgin has brought forth! the light is waxing,' and the Egyptians represented the returning Sun by a new-born babe. Further Mithras, who tended to be identified with the Sun, had his birthday on 25 December. By about the year 300 in the West the Christians had adopted 25 December for the birth of Christ. A Syrian writer offers the explanation:

> The reason why the fathers transferred the celebration of 6 January to 25 December was this. It was the custom of the heathen to celebrate on the same 25 December the Sun's birthday, and to kindle lights in token of festivity. In these solemnities and festivities the Christians also took part. So, when the doctors of the Church perceived that the Christians had a leaning to this festival, they took counsel and resolved that the true Nativity should be celebrated on that day and the festival of Epiphany on 6 January. And so, along with this custom, the practice has prevailed of kindling fires till 6 January.

But Augustine has to exhort Christians to celebrate Christmas not for the Sun but for him who made it, and Leo the Great still rebukes the 'pestilent' belief that Christmas is for the Sun not for Christ.

What is true of Christmas is true of other festivals; Easter in the East took over from an Attis festival; the Parilia in April gave way before St George; the Midsummer Water-Festival was usurped by John the Baptist; the November Festival of the Dead became All Souls; and as late as the fifth century Pope Gelasius in abolishing the Lupercalia substituted a Christian festival. A study of the way Christian saints have taken over from pagan gods is a major task in itself. Mary has taken over not merely the iconography of Isis but her title *Stella Maris*, 'Star of the Sea'; the title Theotokos 'Mother of god' comes from Cybele. Elias occupied many a throne of Zeus. Bridget, a sturdily historical figure, adopted some of the attributes of Briganda or

Brigantia. In Greece St Dionysius was accredited with the invention of wine. At Joppa and Lydda George, a Christian martyr,
became blurred with Perseus the dragon-killer, and with an older
tradition of Zeus and the sea-monster; that Zeus had the title
Georgos or Farmer helped the process.

The confrontation is poignantly seen at Autun. The first evidence of Christianity there is legendary, but there is no reason to
doubt it. Its *mise-en-scène* belongs to the late-second century.
Symphorianus, a young Christian, made a demonstrative protest
against a procession in honour of Cybele, and was condemned
to death; as he was being carried off to execution his mother
shouted encouragement to him from the city-walls. It was
precisely this Christian exclusiveness which offended. To the
third century AD belongs a more positive memorial in the inscription of Pectorios: it is written in Greek, and, though it is defective,
a reasonable reconstruction is possible:

> *Divine race of the heavenly Fish, preserve a holy*
> *   heart, taking among mortals an immortal spring*
> *of god-sent waters, friend, refresh your soul*
> *   with the eternal waters of wisdom's rich giving.*
> *Receive the honey-sweet food of the Saviour of saints,*
> *   eat eagerly holding the Fish in your grasp.*
> *Let me be filled with the Fish, I yearn for it, my Master, my Saviour.*
> *   May my mother sleep well, I implore you, Light of the dead.*
> *Father Aschandios, dear to my heart,*
> *with my sweet mother and my brothers,*
> *   in the peace of the Fish remember your Pectorios.*

There is some play on the Latin meaning of *pectus* 'heart'. It is
a moving expression of faith.

From much the same time there is an exciting memorial, now
in the Bordeaux museum. One face bears the inscription: 'To the
divine dead and to the memory of Domitia, a citizen of Trevera
who died aged 20 years. Leo set this up for his dearest wife.'
Another face reads: 'Here lies without spirit (or breath: *exanimen*)
the body of Domitia, a citizen of Trevera who died on 28
January when Postumus was consul.' The interpretation of the

double inscription is controversial. The opening formula of the first part and the preoccupation with the age mark it as pagan; Leo was no doubt a pagan, and honoured her memory in the way he understood. But in the second part the phrase *exanimen corpus*, the indifference to age, and the precision of the birth-date to new life strongly suggest a Christian origin. Leo must have permitted and perhaps encouraged this second inscription; equally the Christians were prepared to put their inscription alongside his. We have seen something very similar in West Africa in a double memorial to a Christian from a pagan family. We have the impression of a husband and wife living in deep love and tolerance of one another's religion: more important, of two tolerant religious communities. But by the end of the fourth century the Christians were on the offensive again, and Martin was spreading the gospel by destroying non-Christian places of worship.

A confrontation of especial bitterness was the encounter with Asclepius. Harnack in particular has stressed Jesus in his aspect as the Divine Healer; the healing miracles of the gospels were carried on in the early Church 'in the name of Jesus Christ', and the Christians maintained a constant and careful ministry towards the sick. A head-on collision with the votaries of Asclepius was inevitable. To them Christ was a rival to Asclepius, to the Christians Asclepius appeared as a demon leading man away from the truth, and in the course of their offensive they fasten upon the legend that Asclepius was suckled by a bitch, upon his mortality, and upon the association with the snake. The clearest evidence of the counter-attack lies rather later, when Julian in his reassertion of paganism sets up Asclepius as a heroic figure of nobler birth than Jesus, wider ministry, profounder grace, 'setting upright souls which are out of tune and bodies which are sick'; Julian showed his practical support by his own consultations in illness, and by his insistence on the restoration of the temple at Tarsus. He failed of course, though at Ascalon the cult continued into the sixth century AD. Once the battle was won the Christians were prepared to admit an element of syncretism. St Sebastian took on the work of Apollo as averter of plague, and the arrows of his martyrdom were the symbol of pestilence. Asclepius helped, with the Dioscuri, to form the image of SS. Cosmas and Damian, doctors and martyrs of the year 303, whose cult included the characteristically Asclepian practice of incubation.

Yet Christians might also compromise. Ausonius is an interesting case in point, although he is somewhat later than the date on which we are concentrating. That he was a Christian we cannot doubt. His father, a doctor, was loyal to the Hippocratic oath, but in other respects was firmly Christian; his aunt took a Christian vow of celibacy. Ausonius himself was a loyal celebrant of Easter, his morning prayer is the work of a sincere and devout spirit. Yet, in the correspondence with Paulinus of Nola we see a great difference of temperament. How we interpret it depends on our presuppositions. Paulinus is an enthusiast, a fanatic perhaps, firm in his faith, Ausonius is cooler, more worldly, more compromising. Paulinus' gaze is set on the city of God, Ausonius wants to work out his faith in the city of men. Hence Ausonius does not in his poems reject polytheistic expressions; he has a deep affection for pagan mythology. He is really a pantheist, and was able to honour Bacchus Pantheos in his villa. Etienne, a sympathetic critic, wrote of him: 'He had a sense of the geographical relativism of human beliefs; the names of divinities are of small importance since they bear witness to the fact that God is everywhere.' Ausonius would no more have cursed the name of Jesus than did Polycarp, but he did not see why he should curse the name of Bacchus either.

So we are left with the dilemma. The highest creed of paganism was expressed by Maximus of Madaura to Augustine: 'We adore the sole divinity under different names; we render homage to the total divinity under its parts; we invoke through subordinate gods the father of gods and men, whom all men in ways at once different and similar invoke.' To Jews and Christians this was blasphemy. They banged their heads against the wall of tolerance which tried to encircle them; it hurt, but the wall broke. Christianity won, but it had changed in the winning. For one thing the refusal of Christians to betray their master, itself wholly commendable, led to an unloving intolerance of other people which was not at all commendable. For another the rejection of compromise was, as we have seen, not as absolute as might at first sight appear. For a third the very achievement of power brought with it spiritual peril. The uneasy question remained. When Jesus said, 'No man comes to the Father but by me,' did he mean that only the professed Christian could find God, or that all those who come to God are led by the Divine Logos, whether they know it or not? The question still remains.

BIBLIOGRAPHY AND REFERENCES

ABBREVIATIONS

AJA	*American Journal of Archaeology*
Arch. Ael.	*Archeologia Aeliana*
Arch. Jahrb.	*Archäologisches Jahrbuch*
Ath. Mitt.	*Athenische Mitteilungen*
BCH	*Bulletin de Correspondence Hellénique*
Bücheler	F. Bücheler, *Carmina Latina Epigraphica*
Bull. J. Ryl. Lib.	*Bulletin of the John Rylands Library*
Cat. Cod. Ast. Gr.	*Catalogus Codicum Astrologorum Graecorum*
CIA	*Corpus Inscriptionum Atticarum*
CIG	*Corpus Inscriptionum Graecarum*
CIL	*Corpus Inscriptionum Latinarum*
CQ	*Classical Quarterly*
CR	*Classical Review*
Dessau	H. Dessau, *Inscriptiones Latinae Selectae*
Eph. Arch.	*Ephemeris Archaeologice*
ERE	*Encyclopedia of Religion and Ethics*
E.T.	English Translation
Forsch. in Eph.	*Forschungen in Ephesos*
GRBS	*Greek, Roman and Byzantine Studies*
HTR	*Harvard Theological Review*
IG	*Inscriptiones Graecae*
IG Rom.	*Inscriptiones Graecae Urbis Romae*
IGRR	*Inscriptiones Graecae ad res Romanas pertinentes*
IN	Th. Mommsen, *Inscriptiones Regni Neapolitani latinae*
I. Perg.	*Die Inschriften von Pergamon*
JHS	*Journal of Hellenic Studies*
JRS	*Journal of Roman Studies*
JTS	*Journal of Theological Studies*
Kaibel	G. Kaibel, *Epigrammata Graeca ex lapidibus conlecta*
MAMA	*Monumenta Asiae Minoris Antiqua*
Mon. Ant.	*Monumenti Antichi*
N. Jahrb. f. d. Kl. Alt.	*Neue Jahrbucher für des Klassische Altertum*
OCD	*Oxford Classical Dictionary*
OGIS	W. Dittenberger, *Orientis Graeci Inscriptiones Selectae*
PBA	*Proceedings of British Academy*

PBSR	Papers of the British School at Rome
P. Giess	Giessen Papyri
P. Oxy.	Oxyrhynchus Papyri
P. Tebt.	Tebtunis Papyri
Preisigke	F. Preisigke, Sammelbuch griechischer Urkunder aus Aegypten
PW	Pauly-Wissowa, Real-Encyclopädie
REA	Revue des Etudes Antiques
Rev. Num.	Revue numismatique
Rh. M.	Rheinisches Museum für Philologie
RIB	R. G. Collingwood and R. P. Wright, Roman Inscriptions of Britain
Röm. Mitt.	Römische Mitteilungen
Rostovtzeff, SEHRE	M. Rostovtzeff, Social and Economic History of the Roman Empire
SEG	Supplementum Epigraphicum Graecum
SIG	W. Dittenberger, Sylloge Inscriptionum Graecarum
SMSR	Studie materiali di storia delle religioni
TAPA	Transactions of the American Philological Association
Vermaseren, CIMRM	M. J. Vermaseren, Corpus Inscriptionum et monumentorum religionis Mithriacae
YCS	Yale Classical Studies

Ael. Arist.	Aelius Aristides	Cod. Theod.	Codex Theodosianus
Aesch.	Aeschylus	D.C.	Dio Cassius
Amm. Marc.	Ammianus Marcellinus	Dem.	Demosthenes
		D.H.	Dionysius of Halicarnassus
Anth. Lat.	Anthologia Latina		
Anth. Pal.	Anthologia Palatina	D.L.	Diogenes Laertius
Ap. Rhod.	Apollonius Rhodius	D.S.	Diodorus Siculus
Apul.	Apuleius	Epict.	Epictetus
Ar.	Aristophanes	Epiphan.	Epiphanius
Arist.	Aristotle	Eur.	Euripides
Arnob.	Arnobius	Eus.	Eusebius
Ath.	Athanasius	Firm. Mat.	Firmicus Maternus
Athenag.	Athenagoras	Hdn.	Herodian
Aug.	Augustine	Hdt.	Herodotus
Aus.	Ausonius	Hes.	Hesiod
Calp.	Calpurnius Siculus	Hipp.	Hippolytus
CH	Corpus Hermeticum	Hom.	Homer
Cic.	Cicero	Hor.	Horace
Cl. Al.	Clement of Alexandria	Iambl.	Iamblichus
		Ign.	Ignatius

Iren.	Irenaeus	Plat.	Plato
Jer.	Jerome	Plut.	Plutarch
Jul.	Julian	Polyb.	Polybius
Juv.	Juvenal	Prud.	Prudentius
Lact.	Lactantius	Quint.	Quintilian
Lib.	Libanius	Rufin.	Rufinus
Liv.	Livy	Sen.	Seneca
Luc.	Lucan	Serv.	Servius
Lucr.	Lucretius	SHA	Scriptores Historiae
Lyd.	Johannes Lydus		Augustae
M.A.	Marcus Aurelius	Sid. Ap.	Sidonius Apollinaris
Macrob.	Macrobius	Simpl.	Simplicius
Mart.	Martial	Soph.	Sophocles
Mart. Cap.	Martianus Capella	Sozom.	Sozomen
Mart. Pol.	Martyrdom of Poly-	Stat.	Statius
	carp	Strab.	Strabo
Men.	Menander	Suet.	Suetonius
Min. F.	Minucius Felix	Tac.	Tacitus
Or. Sib.	Oracula Sibyllina	Tat.	Tatian
Orig.	Origen	Tert.	Tertullian
Ov.	Ovid	Tib.	Tibullus
Pan. Lat.	Panegyrici Latini	V. App.	Appendix Vergiliana
Paus.	Pausanias	Val. Max.	Valerius Maximus
Petr.	Petronius	Verg.	Vergil
Phil.	Philostratus	Xen. Eph.	Xenophon of Eph-
Philop.	Philoponus		esus
Pind.	Pindar	Zos.	Zosimus

GENERAL

Alföldi, A. *A Festival of Isis in Rome under the Christian Emperors of the IVth Century* (Budapest 1937)

Altheim, F. *A History of Roman Religion*, E.T. (London 1938)

Axtel, H. L. *The Deification of Abstract Ideas in Roman Literature and Inscriptions* (Chicago 1907)

Baumgarten, F., Poland, F., and Wagner, R. *Die hellenistische-römische Kultur* (Leipzig 1913)

Bayet, J. *Histoire politique et psychologique de la religion romaine* (Paris 1957)

Beaujeu, J. *La religion romaine à l'apogée de l'Empire*, Vol. 1 (Paris 1955)

Boissier, G. *La religion romaine d'Auguste aux Antonins*, 2 Vols (Paris 1909⁷)

Cambridge Ancient History, Vol. 12 (Cambridge 1939)

Caster, M. *Lucien et la pensée religieuse de son temps* (Paris 1937)

Cook, A. B. *Zeus*, 3 Vols (Cambridge 1914–40)

Dill, S. *Roman Society from Nero to Marcus Aurelius* (London 1920²)

✓Dodds, E. R. *Pagan and Christian in an Age of Anxiety* (Cambridge 1965)

Eliade, M. *Patterns in Comparative Religion*, E.T. (Cleveland and New York 1963)

Farnell, L. R. *Cults of the Greek States*, 5 Vols (Oxford 1896–1909)

Fowler, W. W. *The Religious Experience of the Roman People* (London 1911)

Friedländer, L. *Darstellungen aus der Sittengeschichte Roms in der Zeit von August bis zum Ausgang der Antonine* (Leipzig 1881⁵)

Glover, T. R. *The Conflict of Religions in the Early Roman Empire* (London 1920⁹)

Grant, F. C. *Hellenistic Religions: The Age of Syncretism* (New York 1953)

✓Grant, M. *The Climax of Rome* (London 1968)

Grupp, G. *Kulturgeschichte des römischen Kaiserzeit*, 2 Vols (München 1903–04)

Kahrstedt, U. *Kulturgeschichte der römischen Kaiserzeit* (Bern 1958²)

Latte, K. *Die Religion der Römer und der Synkretismus der Kaiserzeit* (Tübingen 1927)

Latte, K. *Römische Religionsgeschichte* (München 1960)

Mattingly, H. and Sydenham, E. A. *The Roman Imperial Coinage*, 9 Vols (London 1923–51)

Momigliano, A. (ed.) *The Conflict between Paganism and Christianity in the Fourth Century* (Oxford 1963)

Nestle, W. *Griechische Religiosität*, 3 Vols (Berlin 1930–33)

Nilsson, M. P. *Geschichte der griechischen Religion*, 2 Vols (München 1940–49)

✓Nock, A. D. *Conversion* (Oxford 1933)

✓Ogilvie, R. M. *The Romans and their Gods* (London 1969)

Platner, S. B. and Ashby, T. *A Topographical Dictionary of Ancient Rome* (London 1929)

Réville, J. *La religion à Rome sous les Sévères* (Paris 1886)

Roscher, W. H. *Ausführliches Lexikon der Griechischen und römischen Mythologie*, 6 Vols. (Leipzig 1884–1937)

Toutain, J. *Les cultes païens dans l'empire romain* (Paris 1911)

Turchi, N. *La Religione di Roma antica* (Bologna 1939)

Weber, M. *The Sociology of Religion*, E.T. (Boston 1963)

Wendland, P. *Die Hellenistisch-römische Kultur in ihren Beziehungen zu Judentum und Christentum* (Tübingen 1912²)

Wissowa, G. *Religion und Kultus der Römer* (München 1912²)

CHAPTER I

THE GREAT MOTHER

Altheim, F. *Terra Mater* (Giessen 1931)

Baudissin, W. W. F. von. *Adonis und Esmun* (Leipzig 1911)

Carcopino, J. *Aspects mystiques de la Rome païenne* (Paris 1942)

Dieterich, A. *Mutter Erde* (Berlin 1925³)

Fishwick, D. 'The *Cannophori* and the March Festival of Magna Mater', *TAPA* 97 (1966), 193–202

Frazer, J. G. *Adonis, Attis, Osiris* (London 1907)

Glueck, N. *Deities and Dolphins* (New York 1965)

Graillot, H. *Le culte de Cybèle, Mère des Dieux* (Paris 1912)

Hepding, H. *Attis, seine Mythen und sein Kult* (Giessen 1903)

James, E. O. *The Cult of the Mother-Goddess* (London 1959)

Lambrechts, P. 'Les fêtes "phrygiennes" de Cybèle et d'Attis', *Bull. Inst. Belg. Rom.* 27 (1952), 141ff.

Lambrechts, P. 'Attis à Rome' in *Mélanges Smets* (Bruxelles 1952)

Liungman, W. *Traditionswanderungen: Euphrat-Rhein*, 2 Vols (Helsinki 1931)

Neumann, E. *The Great Mother* (New York 1963²)

Pestalozza, U. *Pagine di religione mediterranea* (Milano 1942)

Radet, G. *Cybebe* (Bordeaux 1909)

Robert, P. C. 'Mythe de Cybèle et d'Attis', *Rev. Num.* 3 (1885), 34ff

Showerman, G. 'Was Attis at Rome under the Republic?' *TAPA* 31 (1900), 46ff

Showerman, G. 'The Great Mother of the Gods', *Bull. U. Wisconsin Philology and Lit.* 1, 3 (1901), 221–333

Vermaseren, M. J. *The Legend of Attis in Greek and Roman Art* (Leiden 1966)

Weinstock, S. 'Tellus', *Glotta* 22 (1933–34), 140–62

PAGE 14 Aphrodite: *Hom. Hymn* 4, 68ff

15 Plutarch: *Def. Or.* 17

15 Celts: McCulloch, J. A. *The Religion of the Ancient Celts* (Edinburgh 1911); Strab. 4, 4, 6; *RIB* 1331

16 Atargatis: Glueck

16 Ephesus: Miltner, F. *Ephesos* (Wien 1958)

16 Ma: Strab. 12, 535; Tib. 1, 6, 43–50, Hor. *Sat.* 2, 3, 223; Mart. 12, 57, 11; Juv. 4, 124

16 Bellona: Liv. 8, 9, 6; 10, 19; Ov. *Fast.* 6, 201; *CIL* 6, 490; 9, 314b

17 Khirbet-Tannur: Glueck

17 Hatra goddess with lions: Glueck, N. *Deities and Dolphins*, 335 and Pl. 10 A and B; Ingholt, H. *Parthian Sculptures from Hatra* (1954), 33 and Pl. VII, 2

17 Dura: Rostovtzeff, M. I. and others *Dura: the Excavations at Dura-Europos* (New Haven 1929–52)

17 Petra Turkomaniyeh tomb inscription: Kennedy, A. B. W. *Petra* (1925), 25, 49 and n. 76

19 Derceto: Lucian *Syr. D.* 14

19 Caesarea: Artemis Ephesia unpublished but see Halliday, W. R. in *Ann. of Arch. and Anthr.* 19 (1932), 23–27

19 Spain: *CIL* 2, 178–79; supp. 5260; 5521

19 Ascalon: D.S. 2, 4

19 Hierapolis (Syr.): Lucian *Syr. D.* 44–48

20 Dervish-priests: Apul. *Met.* 8, 27

20 Gaia: Hes. *Theog.* 126ff

21 Ephesus: original exploration in Wood, J. T. *Discoveries at Ephesus* (1877) and further investigations in the British Museum's reports, *Ephesus*, in several volumes

21 Magnesia: Strab. 14, 1, 40; *SIG* 679

22 Perge: Mansel, A. M. and Akarca, A. *Excavations and Researches at Perge* (Ankara 1949)

22 Aphrodite: Lucian *Syr. D.* 71–73

22 Paphos: *IGRR* 3, 967; Cl. Al. *Protr.* 1, 13; Arnob. *Adv. Gent.* 5, 9; Firm. Mat. *Err. Prof. Rel.* 10, Amm. Marc. 14, 8, 14

22 Corinth: American School of Classical Studies *Corinth*, 15 Vols (Harvard 1929–53)

23 Pergamum: Robinson, D. M. in *Art and Archaeology* 9 (1920), 157ff; Hansen, E. V. *The Attalids of Pergamon* (New York 1947)

23 Hierapolis (Phryg.): Johnson, S. E. in *Bibl. Arch.* 13 (1950), 1ff

23 Smyrna: Cadoux, C. J. *Ancient Smyrna* (Oxford 1938)

23 Isis: Xen. *Ephes.* 3, 11–12; 4, 3; 5, 4; 5, 13; Paus. 1, 41, 4; 2, 2, 3; 2, 4, 7; 2, 13, 7; 2, 32, 6; 2, 34, 1; 2, 34, 10; 3, 22, 13; 4, 32, 6; 7, 26, 7; 10, 32, 13 (Tithorea); *CIL* 2, 33, 981, 2416, 3386–87, 3730, 4080, 4491; 3, 4809–10; 5, 10, 484, 517, 779, 1869, 2109, 2796–97, 3229–32, 8222–29 etc.

26 The Parabiago patera: Strong, D. E. *Greek and Roman Silver Plate* (1966), 198; Levi, A. *Opera d'Arte*, Fasc. 5 *passim*

26 *Hilaria* (Festival of Joy): *SHA Alex. Sev.* 37, 6; *Aurel.* 1; Macrob. *Sat.* 1, 21, 10

26 Kostrubonko: Ralston, W. R. S. *Songs of the Russian People* (London 1872²), 221

27 Eunuchs: Onians, R. B. *The Origins of European Thought* (Cambridge 1951)

27 Rome: Introduction of Cybele: Liv. 29, 10–14; Ov. *Fast.* 4, 178ff; Arnob. *Adv. Nat.* 7, 49; Varro *Ling. Lat.* 6, 15

28 Cato: Cic. *Sen.* 13, 45

28 Genucius: Val. Max. 7, 7, 6

28 Claudian reform: Lyd. *Mens.* 4, 41; *Fasti Philocali*

28 Capitoline relief: Darembeg-Saglio, s.v. Gallus, p. 1457 (reproduction). For another relief showing an *archigallus* from Isola Sacra see Meiggs, R. *Roman Ostia* (Oxford 1960), 359, 362f and Pl. XXXI a and b

28 Processions etc.: Lucr. 2,600ff; D.H. 2, 19; Ov. *Fast.* 4, 337ff; Cic. *Leg.* 2, 16, 40

29 *Lavatio* (Ceremony of Washing): Lucan 1, 599ff; Hdn. 1, 10, 5; Prud. *Peristeph.* 10, 154ff

29 taurobolium: Prud. Peristeph. 10, 1006ff; Riese Anth. Lat. 1, 1, 4, 57ff;
    CIL 2, 5260; 6, 497–505; 512; 1779; 9, 1540; 3014; 10, 1596; 4726;
    6075; 12, 1; 1567; 1569; 1744; 1782; 4321–22, 4325; 13, 573, 1751–54;
    14, 39; 2790 etc.; I. Perg. 2, 554; Duthoy, R. The Taurobolium (Leiden
    1969) reached me too late to use

29 Cult under empire: CIL 6, 494; 497–99; 511; 2183; 2257; 13, 1751;
    14, 34; 35, 385

29 Greece: Paus. 3, 22, 4; 7, 17, 9; 7, 20, 3; 9, 25, 3; CIA 3, 172–73

30 Mauretania: CIL 8, 9401

30 Carthage: Aug. Civ. Dei 2, 4

30 Gaul: Showerman, 295

30 Italy: Showerman, 296

30 Britain: Harris, E. and J. R. The Oriental Cults in Roman Britain (Leiden
    1965). Castration clamp from the Thames with busts of Attis and Cybele
    in relief: Proc. Royal Soc. Medicine 19 (1929), 95ff. Stone statuette of Attis
    from Bevis Marks (British Museum Guide, 55) and bronze statuette of
    Attis from the Thames (Smith, 47). Discussion in Lewis, M. J. T. Temples
    in Roman Britain (1966), 117

30 Cybele: For the textile: Friedländer, P. Documents of Dying Paganism
    (Berkeley 1945) but contrast Nilsson, M. P. Greek Popular Religion (New
    York 1940), 51. There are other interpretations

30 Attis: Chadwick, H. in JTS 3 (1952), 90–92

31 Revival of AD 394: Riese Anth. Lat. 1, 1, 4

31 Gnosticism: Bossuet, W. Hauptprobleme der Gnosis (Göttingen 1907)

CHAPTER II

THE SKY-FATHER

Cook, A. B. Zeus, 3 Vols (Cambridge 1914–40)

Cumont, F. 'Iupiter Summus Exsuperantissimus', Archiv f. Religionswiss. 9
(1906), 323

Dumézil, G. Jupiter, Mars, Quirinus (Paris 1941)

Foucart, G. 'Sky and Sky-gods' in Hastings, J. ERE 11, 580

Kan, A. H. Jupiter Dolichenus (Leiden 1943)

Koch, C. Der römische Jupiter (Frankfurt 1937)

Merlat, P. Jupiter Dolichenus (Paris 1960)

PAGE 32 Yahweh: Exod. 19, 16; Job 37, 5; Ps. 7, 13; Gen. 9, 13

32 Ahura-Mazda: Nyberg, H. S. Die Religionen des alten Iran (Leipzig 1928);
    Pettazoni, R. La Religione di Zarathustra (Bologna 1920); Yasna 30, 5

33 Antioch: Downey, G. A History of Antioch in Syria (Princeton 1961)

33   Samaria: Crowfoot, J. W. and others *Samaria-Sebaste*, 3 Vols (London 1938–57)

33   Jupiter: Macrob. *Sat.* 1, 15, 14; D.H. 2, 34; Dessau 2996–3095, 3927; Dumézil.

34   Solarization: Pettazzoni, R. *Dio* (Rome 1922), 1, 367

34   Heliopolitanus: *CIL* 3, 3462, 3908, 3955; suppl. 7280, 11138–39; 6, 470–73; 4287; 7, 752; 12, 404, 3072; 14, 24; Dessau 4283–96; Macrob. *Sat.* 1, 23, 10

34   Dolichenus: Dessau 4314–16; 4296–97

34   Philo of Byblus: Eus. *Prep. Ev.* 1, 10, 7

35   Baalbek: Wiegand, Th. *Baalbek*, Vols 1 and 2 (1921) and Wiegand, E. 'Baalbek und Rom' in *Arch. Jahrb.* (1914)

35   Jupiter Dolichenus: Esquiline: Merlat, *Répértoire des inscriptions . . . de Jup. Dol.*, 212–17 (with full bibliography), Nos 223 and 224; Aventine: Merlat *Répértoire*, Nos 176–222, pp. 155–211; Nash, E. *Pictorial Dictionary of Ancient Rome* (1961), Vol. 1, 521ff; Corbridge: *Arch. Ael.* 3, 7 (1911), Pl. 2 and *Arch. Journal* 48 (1942), Pl. 2; Cirencester: Corinium Museum, Cirencester, No. C 105; Toynbee, J. M. C. *Art in Roman Britain* (1963²), No. 34, p. 140, Pl. 38; Antonine Wall: Nat. Mus. Antiquities of Scotland *Proc. Scot. Soc. Ant.* 66 (1931–32), 268–76; Toynbee, J. M. C. *Art in Britain under the Romans* (1964), 168

36   Lily: Cook 1, 621ff

36   Sarapis: Min. F. 22, 2; Ael. Arist. 8, 56; D.L. 5, 5, 76 cf. *IG* 14, 1034; Jul. *Or.* 135 D; Rufin. 2, 24; Bauer, A. and Strzygowski, J. *Eine alexandrinische Weltchronik* (Wien 1905) Pl. VI

36   York Serapeion: Royal Commission on Historical Monuments *Eburacum*, 53 and 119; Mithras head from Walbrook Mithraeum: Toynbee *Art in Britain under the Romans*, 97–98; *JRS* 45 (1955), 1378, Pl. 45, Fig. 1; Toynbee *Art in Roman Britain*, 143–44, No. 38, Pl. 43

37   Laodicea: Johnson, S. E. in *Bibl. Arch.* 13 (1950) 1ff

37   Tarsus: Goldman, Hetty *Tarsus* (Princeton 1950)

38   Tralles: *CIG* 2, 2296

38   Tyre: Eus. *Prep. Ev.* 9, 34, 18; Malalas 2, 30

39   Dio: *Or.* 12; Quint. 12, 10, 9

40   Stoics: Tert. *Apol.* 21; Sen. *Quaest. Nat.* 2, 45; Epict. *Diss.* 1, 1; 1, 12; 3, 24 etc.; Plut. *Def. Or.* 29; M.A. 4, 23; 5, 8; 5, 27; 11, 8

40   Trajan: Plin. *Pan.* 80, 4; 88, 4; *Anth. Pal.* 6, 332

40   Beneventum arch: Pietrangeli, C. *L'Arco di Traiano a Benevento* (Documentario Athenaeum Fotografico 1943), 40–61, Pl. 20, 21; Curtius, C. *Arches*, 47–54; Strong, E. *Art in Ancient Rome*, Vol. 2, 81–83; Hassell, F. J. *Der Trajansbogen in Benevent* (1966); Lepper, F. A. *JRS* (1969), 250ff

41   Coin of Jupiter with prow and reed: Mattingly, Vol. 4, 198

41   Commodus coin: IOVI IVVENI, Mattingly, Vol. 4, 735 and 738

42 Maximus and Balbinus: *SHA* 3

43 Diocletian: *Pan. Lat.* 10(2), 11, 6 cf. 10(2), 4, 1; Jullian, C. *Histoire de la Gaule*, 8 Vols (Paris 1920–26), 7, 50

45 Prima Porta cuirass: Alföldi, A. 'Zum Panzerschmuch der Augustusstatue von Prima Porta' in *Röm. Mitt.* 57 (1937), 48ff; Gagé, J. *Apollon Romain*, 598 and Pl. VIII

CHAPTER III

THE SUN-GOD

Cumont, F. *La théologie solaire du paganisme romain* (Paris 1909)

Dölger, F. J. *Sol Salutis* (Münster 1925²)

Gagé, J. *Apollon Romain* (Paris 1955)

Grant, M. *The Climax of Rome* (London 1968)

Schmidt, P. 'Sol Invictus. Betrachtungen zu spätrömischer Religion und Politik', *Eranos Jahrb.* 10 (1944), 169–252

PAGE 44 Helios: Ar. *Pax* 404; Plat. *Crat.* 397d; Pind. *fr.* 44; *Isth.* 5, 1 etc.

45 Utopia: Ferguson, J. 'The Children of Heaven and Children of the Sun', *Nigeria and the Classics* 7 (1964), 12ff

45 Numa: Jul. *Or.* 4, 155 D

45 Sol Indiges: Paulus 23; Varro *Ling. Lat.* 5, 52; Quint. 1, 7, 12; Fowler, W. W. *The Roman Festivals* (London 1899)

46 Nero: D. C. 62, 6, 2; 63, 5–6; [Sen.] *Apoc.* 4, 1, 5, 25; Calp. *Ecl.* 4, 5, 87 cf. 159; Holleaux, M. in *Et. d'épig. et d'hist. gr.* 1 (1938), 165

46 Beneventum: Tac. *Hist.* 3, 24

47 Mithras: See Chapter VII notes; *SHA Comm.* 9; Jer. *Ep. ad Laet.* 57; Sozom. 5, 7. Vermaseren regards the snake as beneficent

48 York: *RIB* 641

48 S. Prisca: Duchesne-Guillemin, J. in *Numen* 2 (1955), 190–95

48 Commodus: Gnecchi, F. *I Medaglioni Romani* (Milan 1912), Vol. 2 Pl. 78; D.C. 72, 34; *CIL* 14, 66

49 Domitian: Stat. *Silv.* 4, 1

49 Hadrian: P. *Giess.* 3; *SHA* 13, 3; 19–12; Kornemann, E. in *Klio* 7 (1907), 178ff

50 Ephesus relief: earlier this was thought to depict Marcus Aurelius, but J. M. C. Toynbee has now shown that in all probability the emperor depicted was Trajan; see *The Art of the Romans* (1965), 65f

50 Antoninus Pius: Gnecchi, F. *I Medaglioni Romani* (Milan 1912), Vol. 2 Pl. 50; Malalas 11, 280; Fronto *ad Marc. Caes.* 2, 1

51 Philostratus: *Vit. Ap.* 1, 16; 2, 24; 2, 26; 2, 32; 3, 15; 5, 25; 6, 10; 6, 11; 7, 10

51 Septizonium: Platner and Ashby *Topographical Dictionary of Ancient Rome* s.v.; Nash, E. *Pictorial Dictionary of Ancient Rome*, s.v.; Strong, E. *Art in Ancient Rome*, Vol. 2, 140; Dombart, Th. *Das Palatinische Septizonium* (1922)

51 Caracalla: D.C. 78, 10, 3; Brendel *Die Antike* (1936), 275

52 Elagabalus: Hdn. 5, 6, 6; *SHA*; D.C. 79, 31, 1; *CAH* 12, 50ff

53 Gallienus: *SHA* 18

54 Aurelian: *SHA* 1; 4; 5; 25; 28; 31; 35; 39; 48; Zos. 1, 61; Dessau 1203, 1210–11; 1217, 1243, 1259 *et al.*

54 Palmyra: Starcky, J. *Palmyre* (1952) with a full bibliography pp. 128–30; Rostovtzeff, M. *Caravan Cities* (1932); Richmond, I. A., *JRS* (1963), 43ff

54 Odenathus: *Or. Sib.* 14

55 Constantius: Eus. *Vit. Cons.* 1, 17. Gold medal: Sutherland and Carson *Roman Imperial Coinage* (1967), 143, 144, 167

55 Constantine: *Pan. Lat.* 6 (7), 21, 4. See especially Dölger, J. *Sol Salutis* (1925²); Alföldi, A. *The Conversion of Constantine and Pagan Rome* (Oxford 1948). For another view Karayannopulos, J. 'Konstantin der Grosse und der Kaiserkult', *Historia* 5 (1956), 341ff. The literature is immense. See Baynes, N. H. in *PBA* 15 (1929), 303–11; Bruun, P. M. in *Arctos* 2 (1958), 15–37; 3 (1962), 5–35; Jones, A. H. M. in *J. Eccl. H.* 5 (1954), 196–200; Seeck, O. *Geschichte des Untergangs der Antike Welt*, 6 Vols (Berlin 1897–1920); Schwartz, E. *Kaiser Constantin und die Christliche Kirche* (Leipzig 1913); Batiffol, P. *La Paix Constantinienne et le Catholicisme* (Paris 1914); Kraft, H. *Kaiser Konstantins religiose Entwicklung* (Tübingen 1955); Piganiol A. *L'empéreur Constantin* (Paris 1932)

56 Arch of Constantine: Strong, E. *Art in Ancient Rome*, Vol. 2, 179–81; Nash, E. *Pictorial Dictionary of Ancient Rome*, Vol. 1, 104ff (with full bibliography)

CHAPTER IV

THE DIVINE FUNCTIONARIES

Duval, P. M. *Les dieux de la Gaule* (Paris 1957)
Fowler, W. W. *The Religious Experience of the Roman People* (London 1911)
Guthrie, W. K. C. *The Greeks and their Gods* (London 1950)
Latte, K. *Römische Religiongeschichte* (München 1960)
Seltman, C. T. *The Twelve Olympians* (London 1952)
Wissowa, G. *Religion und Kultus der Römer* (München 1912²)

254 BIBLIOGRAPHY AND REFERENCES

PAGE 65 Zielinski, Th.: *The Religion of Ancient Greece* (Oxford 1926), 15

65 Springs: Dessau 3868–69, 3895

65 Trees: Plin. *Nat. Hist.* 12, 3; 15, 77; 15, 137; Suet. *Aug.* 92; *Galb.* 1; *Vesp.* 5; Aug. *Civ. Dei* 6, 10

65 Pan: Herbig, R. *Pan* (Frankfurt 1949)

66 Mountains: Cook, A. B. *Zeus*; Phil. *Vit. Ap.* 2, 5; Poeninus: cf. *ILS* 4850

66 Groves: Verg. *Aen.* 8, 352; 597; Ov. *Am.* 3, 1, 1; 3, 13, 7; *Fast.* 3, 295–96; Luc. 3, 399

66 Clitumnus: Plin. *Ep.* 8, 8 tr. G. Highet

67 Landscapes: Hanfmann, G. M. A. *Roman Art* (London 1964), Pls XXIX–XXXII; Nilsson, M. P. *Greek Piety* (Oxford 1948), 9; Strab. 8, 343. I have borrowed some sentences from my forthcoming *From Ilissus to Niger*. Paris on Mount Ida: *Mon. Ant.* (1898), 403; Helbig, W. *Wandgemälde der vom Vesuv verschutteten Städte Campaniens*, No. 1279; shepherd and ram: Helbig, No. 1564; Boscotrecase island with gods: Blankenhagen, P. von, and Alexander, C. *The Paintings from Boscotrecase* (1962); Schedfold, K. *Vergessenes Pompeji*, 59, 61ff and Pl. 8; Polyphemus and Galatea: also in Blankenhagen and Alexander; House of Livia: Nash, E. *Pictorial Dictionary of Ancient Rome*, Vol. 1 (s.v. Domus Augusti), 310–15, with full bibliography

68 Numina: Varro apud Nonus 108, 22; 532, 27 etc.; Aul. Gell. 16, 16; Tert. *Nat.* 2, 11; Arnob. 3, 115; 4, 131; 7, 227; Serv. ad *Georg.* 1, 21; Mart. Cap. 2, 149; Aug. *Civ. Dei* 4, 8, 11, 21, 24, 34; 6, 9

69 Arval Brethren: Henzen, W. *Acta Fratrum Arvalium* (Berlin 1874)

69 Celts: MacCulloch, J. A. *The Religion of the Ancient Celts* (Edinburgh 1911) and refs.; *The Celtic and Scandinavian Religions* (London 1949); Powell, T. G. E. *The Celts*; Duval; Adamnan *Vit. Col.* 2, 10; Jocelyn *Vit. Kent.* 32; Gildas 2, 4

70 Samian citizenship decree: *IG* 2², 1; Meiggs and Lewis, *Greek Historical Inscriptions to the end of the fifth century BC* (1969), 283–87

71 Mars: for another view v. Bailey, C. *Ovid Fasti III*, pp. 33ff

71 Quirinus: Serv. ad *Aen.* 6, 860

71 Lyons, Apollo and Mercury inn: *CIL* 13, 2031 and Wuillemier, P. *Lyon, Metropole des Gaules* (1953), 53

72 Abstractions: Lact. *Inst. Div.* 1, 20: Charlesworth, M. P. in *PBA* 23 (1937), 105–33; Nock, A. D. in *HTR* 23 (1930), 107ff

72 Antoninus Pius: *SHA* 8

73 Hadrian: *SHA* 22, 10; Aymard, J. *Essai sur les chasses romaines* (Paris 1951), 523 ff.

73 Roman gods in Asia Minor: Magie, D. *Roman Rule in Asia Minor* (1950)

74 Temples in Rome: Platner-Ashby *Topographical Dictionary of Ancient Rome* (1929); Nash, E. *Pictorial Dictionary of Ancient Rome* (1961)

74 Vespasian: Dessau 252

75 Secular Games: Hülsen, Chr. in *Rh.M.* 81 (1932), 366
75 Dura-Europos: Rostovtzeff, M. *The Excavations of Dura-Europos*, 5th *Season* (1931–32), 295
76 Alexander Severus: *SHA* 22, 5

CHAPTER V

TYCHE

Allègre, F. *Etude sur la déesse grecque Tyché* (Lyon 1892)
Cioffari, V. *Fortune and Fate from Democritus to St Thomas Aquinas* (New York 1935)
Cook, A. B. *Zeus*, 3 Vols (Cambridge 1940)
Dohrn, T. *Die Tyche von Antiochia* (Berlin 1960)
Harrison, Jane E. *Themis* (London 1911²)
Patch, H. R. 'The Tradition of the Goddess Fortune', *Smith Coll. Studies in M.L.* 3, 131–235
Wissowa, G. *Religion und Kultus der Römer* (München 1912²)

E 77 Homer: *Hymn* 2, 420
77 Hesiod: *Theog.* 360
77 Archilochus: *fr.* 8
77 Pindar: *Olymp.* 12, 1; *fr.* 20; 21
77 Aeschylus: *Ag.* 663
77 Sophocles: *Ant.* 327; 1158
78 Plato: *Laws* 10, 889c; see now Zimmermann, A. *Tyche bei Platon* (Bonn 1966)
78 Aristotle: *Phys.* B 197a8ff; *Met.* E 1025a14; Simpl. 337, 15; Philop. 270, 4; Balme, D. M. in *CQ* 33 (1939), 129–38
78 Epicurus: D. L. 10, 134, cf. Lucr. 5, 77; 5, 107; Men. *fr.* 594
78 Democritus: Eus. 14, 27, 5
78 Fortuna: Latte, K. in *Archiv f. Religionswiss.* 24 (1926), 247; Platner–Ashby
78 Seneca: *Prov. passim*, cf. 5, 4
78 Lucan: Ferguson, J. in *Durham U.J.* N. S. 8 (1957), 116ff
78 Vergil: *Aen.* 8, 334
78 Sallustius: *De Dis et Mundo* 9; Murray, G. *The Five Stages of Greek Religion* (Oxford 1925), 217ff
79 Pliny: *Nat. Hist.* 2, 22
79 Plutarch: *Fort.*; *Fort. Rom.*; *Fort. Alex. passim*, cf. 316c
80 Herskovits, M.: *The Myth of the Negro Past* (Boston 1941), 62
80 Achilles Tatius: 5, 17
80 Apuleius: 7, 16, 1; 7, 17, 1; 7, 25, 3; 8, 24, 1; 9, 1, 5; 11, 15, 14
81 Isis: Peek, W. *Der Isishymnos von Andros* (Berlin 1930) 124
81 Dieterich, A.: *Eine Mithrasliturgie* (Leipzig 1923²)

81   Epitaphs: Kaibel 149, 208, 244, 248, 257, 334, 418, 440, 489, 492, 519, 526, 538, 640, 664; *IG* 3, 2, 1416; 12, 5, 303, 1017; 14, 2052; *I. Perg.* 581; *CIL* 8, 1445; *Rh. M.* 34 (1879), 215a; *Ath. Mitt.* 56 (1931), 129; Bücheler 1498

82   Lebadeia: Paus. 9, 39

82   Athenian Zeus Philios relief: Poulsen, F. *Catalogue of Ancient Sculpture in the Ny Carlsberg Glyptotek* (1951), No. 362, pp. 176–78 (with bibliography)

82   Elis: Paus. 6, 25, 4

82   Thebes: Paus. 9, 16, 2

82   Melos: *JHS* 18 (1898), 60

82   Antioch: Jul. *Mis.* 346B; Lib. *Or.* 30, 51; Paus. 6, 27; Downey, G. *A History of Antioch in Syria* (Princeton 1961)

83   Commagene: *OGIS* 383; Cook 1, 742ff

84   Mylasa: *CIG* 2693e

84   Simplicius: *Ausc.* 11, 74b

84   The Tyche of Antioch: Paus. 6, 2, 6; Bieber, M. *The Sculpture of the Hellenistic Age* (1955), 40 and Pl. 102

84   Athens: *SIG³*, 856

84   Thera: *SIG³*, 852

84   Selgae: *IGRR* 3, 382

84   Trapezopolis: *CIG* 3953d

84   Thasos: *SIG³*, 1155

84   Smyrna: Paus. 4, 30, 6; *SIG³*, 911 cf. 2, 755

84   Edessa: Cook 2, 1, 429

85   Pacuvius: *Chryses*

85   Juvenal: 14, 315

85   Fortune: Latte, K. *Römische Religionsgeschichte* (1960), 175ff

86   Domitan's temple of Fortune Redux: Platner and Ashby *Topographical Dictionary of Ancient Rome*, 218 (with bibliography)

86   Fortuna, Bearded: Tert. *Nat.* 2, 11; Aug. *Civ. Dei* 4, 9

87   Palladas: *Anth. Pal.* 9, 180–83; 10, 80; 10, 87; Bowra, C. M. in *CQ* N.S. 10 (1960), 118ff

87   Macrobius: *Sat.* 1, 19, 17

87   Constantinople: Zos. 2, 31; Alföldi, A. in *JRS* 37 (1947), 10–16

CHAPTER VI

THE SACRED FIGURE OF THE EMPEROR

Abaecherli, A. L. 'The Institution of the Imperial Cult in the Western Provinces of the Roman Empire', *SMSR* 11 (1935), 173–87

Beurlier, E. *Le culte impérial, son histoire et son organization* (Paris 1891)

Buechner, W. *De neocoria* (Gissae 1888)

Cerfaux, L. and Tondriau, J. *Le culte des souverains dans la civilisation gréco-romaine* (Paris 1957)

Charlesworth, M. P. 'Some Observations on Ruler Cult', *HTR* 28 (1935), 8ff

Eitrem, S. 'Religious Calendar concerning the Imperial Cult', *Papyri Osloenses* 3 (1936), n. 77

Etienne, R. *Le culte impérial dans la péninsule ibérique d'Auguste à Dioclétien* (Paris 1958)

Fink, R. O., Huey, A. S., Snyder, W. F. 'Feriale Duranum', *YCS* 7 (1946)

√Fishwick, D. 'The Imperial Cult in Roman Britain', *Phoenix* 15 (1961), 159–73, 213–20

Fishwick, D. 'The Institution of the Provincial Cult in Africa Proconsularis', *Hermes* 92 (1964), 342–63

Goodenough, E. R. 'The Political Philosophy of the Hellenistic Kingship', *YCS* 1 (1928), 55–102

√Hammond, M. *The Antonine Monarchy* (1959), ch. VI

Kornemann, E. 'Geschichte der antiken Herrscher kulte', *Klio* 1 (1901), 51–146

Krascheninnikoff, M. 'Ueber die Einfuhrung des provinzialen Kaisercultus in römischer Westen', *Philologus* 53 (1894), 147–89

Latte, K. *Römische Religionsgeschichte* (München 1960)

Lohmeyer, E. *Christuskult und Kaiserkult* (Tübingen 1919)

Magie, D. *Roman Rule in Asia Minor*, 2 Vols (Princeton 1950)

Mattingly, H. 'The Consecration of Faustina the Elder and her daughter', *HTR* 41 (1948), 147–51

Nock, A. D. 'A Diis Electra', *HTR* 23 (1930), 266–68

Nock, A. D. 'Notes on Ruler Cult', *JHS* 48 (1928), 21ff

Nock, A. D. 'Roman army and religious year', *HTR* 45 (1952), 187ff

Oliver, J. H. 'The Diui of the Hadrianic Period', *HTR* 42 (1949), 35ff

Pettazoni, R. *La Regalita Sacra* (Leiden 1959)

Pleket, H. W. 'An Aspect of Emperor Cult: Imperial Mysteries', *HTR* 58 (1965), 331ff

Raubitschek, A. E. 'Hadrian as the son of Zeus Eleutherios', *AJA* 49 (1945), 128–33

Scott, K. *The Imperial Cult under the Flavians* (Stuttgart–Berlin 1936)

Stein, A. 'Zur sozialen Stellung der provinzialen Oberpriester' in *Epitymbion H. Swoboda dargebracht* (Reichenberg 1927)

Strong, Eugénie *Apotheosis and After-Life* (London 1915)

Sweet, L. M. *Roman Emperor Worship* (Boston 1919)

Taylor, L. R. *The Divinity of the Roman Emperor* (Middletown 1931)

89　Pompey: *BCH* 8 (1884), 148; 34 (1910), 401; *IG Rom.* 4, 40; Plut. *Pomp.* 2, 4; Luc. 8, 679

89　Demetrius: Plut. *Dem.* 11; Ath. 6, 253c; D.S. 20, 100

89 Jesus: *Lk.* 22, 25; *Jn.* 4, 42; 20, 28
89 Marcellus: Cic. 2 *Verr.* 2, 51
89 Flamininus: Plut. *Flam.* 16
90 Isauricus: *Forsch. in Eph.* 3, 148
90 Aquilius: *IG Rom.* 4, 297
90 Verres: Cic. 2 *Verr.* 2, 54, 114, 154; 4, 24
90 Cicero: *Att.* 5, 21, 7; *Ad Quint. Frat.* 1, 1, 20
90 Prusias: Polyb. 30, 16; Liv. 45, 44
90 Marius: Plut. *Mar.* 27, 5
90 Gratidianus: Cic. *Off.* 3, 80
90 Caesar: D.C. 43, 14, 6; 43, 42, 3; 43, 44, 1; 43, 45, 3; 44, 4, 4; 44, 6, 4
90 Antony: D.C. 50, 5, 3; Plut. *Ant.* 78; *IG Rom.* 1, 1054
90 Augustus: Suet. 94; D.C. 51, 19, 7; 54, 35, 2; 55, 1; 56, 36; Liv. *Epit.* 134;
    Hor. *Od.* 3, 3, 9ff; Cic. *Som. Scip.* 3, 1; *PBSR* 15, 3
92 Geta: *SHA* 2
92 Julia Domna: *IN* 1090, 1091; *CIG* 2815, 3642, 3956
92 Severus Alexander and Julia Mamaea as Jupiter and Juno: Merlat *Répértoire*,
    329
92 Carnuntum statue: Swoboda, E. *Carnuntum* (1953), 108 and Pl. 14f
    Chesters: Toynbee, J. M. C. *Art in Britain under the Romans* (1964), 96.
    and Pl. XXIII
94 Commodus: *SHA* 5–9
94 Pilate's shrine to Tiberius: *L'Année épigraphique* (1963), no. 104
95 Imperial cult in Narbonensis: Herzog-Hauser, G. *PW*, Suppl. 4, 837; but
    see Hammond, M. *The Antonine Monarchy* (1959), 222
95 Pertinax: D.C. 74, 4–5
96 Trajan: *P. Giess.* 3; Ephesus relief: see note to p. 50
96 Apotheosis of Sabina (relief in the Palazzo dei Conservatori): Reinach
    Répértoire des reliefs, Vol. 1, 375, No. 2 (with bibliography)
96 Herodian: 4, 2
98 Aurelian: Nock in *HTR* 23 (1930); Mommsen, Th. *Römisches Staatsrecht*
    (Leipzig 1887–88) 2, 706n.2

CHAPTER VII

PERSONAL RELIGION

Angus, S. *The Mystery Religions and Christianity* (New York 1925)
Anrich, G. *Das antike Mysterienwesen in seinem Einfluss auf das Christentum*
    (Göttingen 1894)
Campbell, J. (ed.) *The Mysteries* (London 1955)
Carcopino, J. *Aspects mystiques de la Rome païenne* (Paris 1941⁵)

Cumont, F. *Oriental Religions in Roman Paganism* (Chicago 1911)
de Jong, K. H. E. *Das antike Mysterienwesen* (Leiden 1919²)
Festugière, A. J. *Personal Religion among the Greeks* (Berkeley 1954)
Glassé, J. *The Mysteries and Christianity* (Edinburgh 1921)
Loisy, A. *Les Mystères païens et le Mystère chrétien* (Paris 1921²)
Reitzenstein, R. *Die hellenistischen Mysterienreligionen* (Leipzig 1927³)
Rostovtzeff, M. I. *Mystic Italy* (New York 1928)
Sabbatucci, D. *Saggio sul misticismo greco* (1965)
Turchi, N. *Le Religioni misteriche del mondo antico* (Milano 1948)
Willoughby, H. R. *Pagan Regeneration* (Chicago 1929)

Eleusis

Brillant, M. *Les Mystères d'Eleusis* (Paris 1920)
Foucart, P. *Les Mystères d'Eleusis* (Paris 1914)
Jung, C. G. and Kerenyi, K. *Introduction to a Science of Mythology*, E.T. (London 1951)
Magnien, V. *Les Mystères d'Eleusis* (Paris 1950)
Mylonas, G. E. *Eleusis and the Eleusinian Mysteries* (Princeton 1961)
Noack, F. *Eleusis, die Baugeschichte Entwicklung des Heiligtumes* (Leipzig 1927)

GE 99 Augustus: Suet. 93
   100 Marcus Aurelius: *Eph. Arch.* 5 (1885) 150
   100 Nero: Suet. 34
   100 Apollonius: Phil. 4, 18
   100 Proclamation: Orig. *C. Cels.* 3, 59; Libanius *Or. Cor.* 4, 356R
   100 Initiate: *Eph. Arch.* 3 (1883) 81
   100 Baptism: Tert. *Bapt.* 5
   100 Drama: Cl. Al. *Protr.* 4, 27; Lact. *Epit. Div. Inst.* 23
   100 Marriage: Asterius *Encomium* 113B; Lucian *Alex.* 38–39; Foucart pp. 475ff
   100 *Epopteia*: Plut. *Prof. in virt.* 10; Hipp. *Phil.* 5, 1, 8; Tert. *Nat.* 1, 12; *Eph. Arch.* (1883) 79
   100 Communion: Cl. Al. *Protr.* 2, 21
   101 Gallienus: Alföldi, A. in *Z. f. Numismatik* 28 (1928), 197–212
   101 Promise: *Hom. Hymn* 2, 480
   101 Cicero: *Verr.* 5, 72, 187; *Nat. D.* 1, 42, 119; *Leg.* 2, 14, 36
   101 Jesus: *Jn.* 12, 24

Dionysus

Blinkenberg, C. *Archaeologische Studien* (Copenhagen 1904)
Guthrie, W. K. C. *Orpheus and Greek Religion* (London 1952²)
Jeanmaire, H. *Dionysos* (Paris 1951)
Kern, O. *Orphicorum Fragmenta* (Berlin 1937)
Lagrange, M. J. *Les Mystères: l'Orphisme* (Paris 1937)

Linforth, I. M. *The Arts of Orpheus* (Berkeley 1941)
Macchioro, V. *Zagreus* (Florence 1920)
Quandt, G. *Orphei Hymni* (Berlin 1953)
Vogliano, A. and Cumont, F. 'The Bacchic Inscription in the Metropolitan Museum', *AJA* 37 (1933), 215–70

PAGE 101 Plutarch: *Is. et Os.* 69; *Mul. Virt.* 13; *Prim. Frig.* 18; *Symp.* 5, 3, 1
101 Macrobius: *Sat.* 1, 18, 10
102 Bacchanalia in Italy: Liv. 39, 8
102 Villa of the Mysteries: Mudie Cooke, P. B. in *JRS* 3 (1913), 157–74; Maiuri, A. *Roman Painting* (Geneva 1953); Dem. *Cor.* 259; *Fals. Leg.* 199; Eur. *Bacch.* 677ff; Zuntz, G. *PBA* (1963), 177ff
104 Diodorus: 4, 3
104 Pliny: *Nat. Hist.* 16, 12
104 Firmicus Maternus: *Err. Prof. Rel.* 6, 5
104 Nonnus: *Dionysiaca*
104 Prudentius: see note to p. 29

Cybele

See Chapter I bibliography and notes.

Isis

Bleeker, C. J. 'Isis as Saviour Goddess' in Brandon, S. G. F. (ed.) *The Saviour God* (Manchester 1963), 1–16
Brandon, S. G. F. 'Ritual Technique of Salvation' in *ibid.* 17–36
Burel, J. *Isis et Isiaques sous l'Empire romain* (Paris 1911)
de Jong, K. H. E. *De Apuleio isiacorum mysteriorum teste* (Leiden 1900)
Erman, A. *Die Religion der Aegypter* (Berlin 1934)
Festugière, A. J. *Personal Religion Among the Greeks* (Berkeley 1954)
Frankfort, H. *Ancient Egyptian Religions* (New York 1948)
Frazer, J. G. *Adonis, Attis, Osiris* (London 1907)
Griffiths, J. Gwyn *The Conflict of Horus and Seth* (Liverpool 1910)
Lafaye, G. *Histoire du culte des divinités d'Alexandrie en dehors de l'Egypte* (Paris 1884)
Merkelbach, R. *Isisfeste in griechisch-römischer Zeit* (Meisenheim 1963)
Morenz, S. 'Das Werden zu Osiris' *Staatliche Museen zu Berlin: Forschunger und Berichte*, 1 (1957), 52–70
Moret, A. *Mystères égyptiens* (Paris 1913)
Nock, A. D. *Conversion* (Oxford 1930)
Reichel, C. *De Isidis apud Romanorum cultu* (Berlin 1849)
Roeder, G. *Die ägyptische Religion in Text und Bild*, 4 Vols (Zürich-Stuttgart 1959–61)
Sander-Hansen *Der Begriff des Todes bei den Aegyptern* (Copenhagen 1942)

Tran Tam Tinh, V. *Le Culte d'Isis à Pompéi* (Paris 1964)
Witt, R. E. *Isis in the Graeco-Roman World* (London 1970)
Wittmann, W. *Das Isisbuch des Apuleius* (Stuttgart 1938)

GE 106 Plutarch: *De Iside et Osiride*
106 Tacitus: *Hist.* 4, 83–84
107 Rhind papyrus: Peet, T. E. *The Rhind Mathmatical Papyrus* (1923)
107 Painted shroud with Anubis and Osiris: Parlasca, K. *Mumienporträts und Verwandte Denkmäler* (1966), 170, Pl. 61 (2)
107 Apuleius: *Met.* 11
108 Juvenal: 6, 526
108 Pausanias: 10, 32

Corpus Hermeticum

Creed, J. M. 'The Hermetic Writings', *JTS* 15 (1914), 513–38
Festugière, A. J. *L'Hermétisme* (Lund 1948)
Festugière, A. J. *La Révélation d'Hermes Trismégiste*, 4 Vols (Paris 1944–54)
Kroll, W. 'Hermes Trismegistos', *PW* 8, 791–823
Nock, A. D. and Festugière, A. J. *Corpus hermeticum*, 4 Vols (Paris 1945–54)
Reitzenstein, R. *Poimandres* (Leipzig 1904)
Scott, W. *Hermetica*, 4 Vols (Oxford 1924–26)
Zielinski, Th. 'Hermes und die Hermetik', *Archiv f. Religionswiss.* 8 (1905), 221–72; 9 (1906), 25–60
For other references see Lact. *Inst. Div.* 1, 6; 2, 15; 4, 6–9; 4, 13; 4, 27; 7, 4; 7, 9; 7,13; 7,18; *De Ira Dei* 11; Arnob. *Adv. Nat.* 2, 13; *CH* 1, 28; 10, 25; 12, 12

Asclepius

Edelstein, E. J. and L. *Asclepius*, 2 Vols (Baltimore 1945)
Festugière, A. J. *Personal Religion among the Greeks* (Berkeley 1954)
Harnack, A. *Medicinisches aus der ältesten Kirchengeschichte* (Leipzig 1892)
Wilamowitz-Moellendoerff, U. von 'Der Rhetor Aristeides', *Sitz. Berl. Akad.* phil-hist. 30 (1925), 333ff

For other references see *CIA* 3, 171a; Cl. Al. *Protr.* 2, 30, 1; *Strom.* 5, 1, 13; Euseb. *Vit. Cons.* 3, 56; Galen *San. Tuend.* 1, 8, 19–21; Ignat. *Eph.* 7; Jul. *C. Gal.* 200 A. B., cf. 235C; Lact. *Inst. Div.* 1, 15, 26; 2, 7, 13; 2, 16, 11; 4, 27, 12; M. A. 5, 8, 1; Tert. *Ad Nat.* 2, 14; Zonaras *Epit.* 13, 12 C–D

GE 110 Herodas: 4
110 Asclepius and Hygieia statue: Lippold *Die Sculpturen des Vaticanischen Museums*, Vol. 3 (2), 553, No. 19 (231)
110 Apuleius: *Apol.* 55; *Flor.* 18
110 Aelius Aristides: *Or.* 26, 105; 47–55

Mithras

Cumont, F. *The Mysteries of Mithra* (Chicago 1910)
Dieterich, A. *Eine Mithrasliturgie* (Leipzig 1910)
Duchesne-Guillemin, J. 'Ahriman et le Dieu Suprême', *Numen* 2 (1955), 190–95
Gasquet, A. L. *Le culte et les mystères de Mithra* (Paris 1899)
Geden, A. S. *Select Passages Illustrating Mithraism* (London 1925)
Harris, E. and J. R. *The Oriental Cults in Roman Britain* (Leiden 1965)
Laeuchli, S. *Mithraism in Ostia* (Northwestern University 1967)
Vermaseren, M. J. *Mithras, the Secret God*, E.T. (London 1963)
Vermaseren, M. J. *Corpus inscriptionum et monumentorum religionis Mithriacae*, 2 Vols (The Hague 1956)

PAGE 112 Ostia Mithraeum mosaic: Becatti, G. 'I Mosaici' in *Scavi di Ostia* (1961), 32, No. 56, Pl. CVI
112 *taurobolium*: *CIMRM* 420; 514; 523; 524. 206 Kamenius, a Father in Mithraic cult, is *tauroboliatus* in the Mother's cult; 515, 520, 522 are all dedications to the Mother
121 magical papyrus: Dieterich
122 Julian: *Or.* 7; Eunapius *fr.* 26

Cabeira

Cole, Susan 'The Cult of the Great Gods at Samothrace'. Unpublished
Fraser, P. M. *Samothrace: The Inscriptions on Stone* (New York 1960)
Hemberg, B. *Die Kabiren* (Uppsala 1950)
Kerenyi, C. 'The Mysteries of the Kabeiroi' in Campbell, J. *The Mysteries* (London 1955)
Kern, O. 'Kabeiros und Kabeiroi' in *PW*
Lehmann, K. *Samothrace: The Inscriptions on Ceramics* (New York 1960)
Lehmann, K. *Samothrace: A Guide to the Excavations and the Museum* (New York 1955)
Lehmann, K. 'The Mystery Cult of Samothrace', *Archaeology* 7 (1954), 91–95
Lewis, N. *Samothrace: The Ancient Literary Sources* (New York 1958)
Sabbatucci, D. *Saggio sul misticismo greco* (1965)
Wolters, P. H. A. and Bruns, Gerda *Das Kabiren heiligtum bei Theben* (Berlin 1940)
I am heavily indebted to Mrs Cole's remarkable paper.
See also: Schol. ad Ap. Rhod. 1, 917; Hdt. 2, 51–52; Plut. *Mor.* 217c–d

Judaism

Bousset, W. and Gressmann, H. *Die Religion des Judentums* (Tübingen 1926³)
Epstein, I. *Judaism* (London 1959)

Goodenough, E. R. *An Introduction to Philo Judaeus* (New Haven 1940)

Juster, J. *Les Juifs dans l'empire romain*, 2 Vols (Paris 1914)

Liebermann, S. *Greek in Jewish Palestine* (New York 1942)

Liebermann, S. *Hellenism in Jewish Palestine* (New York 1950)

Moore, G. F. *Judaism in the First Centuries of the Christian Era*, 3 Vols (Cambridge, Mass. 1927–30)

Nock, A. D. *Conversion* (Oxford 1933)

Strack, H. L. *Introduction to the Talmud and Midrash* (Philadelphia 1931)

Wolfson, H. A. *Philo*, 2 Vols (Cambridge, Mass. 1947)

GE 124 Numenius: his philosophy in Armstrong, A. H. *The Architecture of the Intelligible Universe in the Philosophy of Plotinus* (1940)

Christianity

Bigg, C. *The Church's Task under the Roman Empire* (Oxford 1905)

Bigg, C. *Origins of Christianity* (Oxford 1909)

Bigg, C. *The Christian Platonists of Alexandria* (Oxford 1913²)

Carrington, P. *The Early Christian Church*, 2 Vols (Cambridge 1957)

Cochrane, C. N. *Christianity and Classical Culture* (Oxford 1940)

Dodd, C. H. *The Apostolic Preaching and its Development* (London 1937)

Duchesne, L. *Early History of the Christian Church*, 3 Vols (London 1909–24)

Grant, R. M. *Second Century Christianity: a Collection of Fragments* (London 1946)

Harnack, A. *The Mission and Expansion of Christianity in the First Three Centuries*, E.T. (New York 1908)

Hatch, E. *The Influence of Greek Ideas and Usages upon the Christian Church* (London 1890)

Lietzmann, H. *History of the Early Church*, E.T. (London 1937)

Manson, T. W. *The Teaching of Jesus* (Cambridge 1931)

Nock, A. D. 'Early Gentile Christianity and its Hellenistic Background' in Rawlinson, A. E. J. *Essays on the Trinity and the Incarnation* (London 1928)

Nock, A. D. *Conversion* (Oxford 1933)

Oakeshott, W. *The Mosaics of Rome* (London 1967)

Origen *Contra Celsum* ed. Chadwick, H. (Cambridge 1953)

Pruemm, K. *Der Christliche Glaube und die altheidnische Welt*, 2 Vols (Leipzig 1935)

Ramsay, W. M. *The Church in the Roman Empire before AD 170* (New York 1913¹⁰)

Sherwin-White, A. N. 'The early persecutions and Roman Law again', *JTS* 3 (1952), 199–213

Wendland, P. *Die hellenistisch-römische Kultur in ihren Beziehungen zu Judentum und Christentum* (Tübingen 1912²)

See also *Acts* 2, 22–24; *Mt.* 5–7; *Rom.* 12–13; *Gal.* 5, 16–24; *Mart. Pol.* 3, 7–11;

Luc. *Peregr.* 12; Orig. *C. Cels.* 3, 55, 59; 8, 65; M. A. 11, 3; Justin *Apol.* 2, 12; Tert. *Apol.* 50; *Scap.* 5

Gnosticism

Bianchi, U. *Il dualismo religioso* (Rome 1958)

Bianchi, U. 'Le problème des origines du gnosticisme et l'histoire des religions', *Numen* 12 (1965) 161–78

Bianchi, U. *Le Origini dello Gnosticismo* (Leiden 1967)

Böhlig, A. and Labib, P. *Die koptisch-gnostische Schrift ohne Titel des Codex II von Nag Hammadi im Koptischen Museum zu Alt-Kairo* (Berlin 1962)

Böhlig, A. and Labib, P. *Koptisch-gnostiche Apokalypsen aus Codex V von Nag Hammadi in Koptischen Museum zu Alt-Kairo* (Halle 1963)

Bousset, W. *Hauptprobleme der Gnosis* (Göttingen 1907)

Bultmann, R. *Das Urchristentum in Rahmen der antiken Religionen* (Zürich, 1963)

Burkitt, F. C. *The Church and Gnosis* (Cambridge 1932)

Casey, R. P. 'The Study of Gnosticism', *JTS* 36 (1935), 45–60

Cross, F. L. *The Jung Codex* (New York 1955)

Doresse, J. *Les livres secrets des Gnostiques d'Egypte* (Paris 1958)

Doresse, J. *L'Evangile selon Thomas, ou les paroles secrètes de Jesus* (Paris 1959)

Faye, E. de *Gnostiques et Gnosticisme* (Paris 1925²)

Grant, R. M. *Gnosticism* (New York 1961)

Grant, R. M. *Gnosticism and Early Christianity* (New York 1959)

Guillaumont, A. and others *Evangelium nach Thomas* (Leiden 1959)

Jonas, H. *Gnosis und spätantiker Geist*, 2 Vols (Gottingen 1934–54)

Jonas, H. *The Gnostic Religion* (Boston 1958)

Krause, M. and Labib, P. *Gnostische und hermetische Schriften aus Codex II und VI* (Wiesbaden 1967)

Liesegang, H. *Die Gnosis* (Stuttgart 1955)

Malinine, M., Puech, H-Ch., Quispel, G. *Evangelium Veritatis* (Zürich 1961)

Pétrement, S. *Le dualisme chez Platon, les gnostiques et les manichéens* (Paris 1947)

Quispel, G. *Gnosis als Weltreligion* (Zürich 1951)

Sagnat, F. M. M. *La Gnose Valentinienne et le témoignage de saint Irénée* (Paris 1947)

Schoeps, H. J. *Urgemeinde, Judenchristentum, Gnosis* (Tübingen 1956)

Scholem, G. *Jewish Gnosticism, Merkabah Mysticism, and Talmudic Tradition* (New York 1960)

Till, W. C. *Die gnostischen Schriften des koptischen Papyrus Berolinensis 8502* (Berlin 1955)

Till, W. C. *Das Evangelium nach Philippos* (Berlin 1963)

Volker, W. *Quellen zur Geschichte der Christlichen Gnosis* (Tübingen 1932)

Wendland, P. *Die hellenistisch-römische Kultur in ihren Beziehungen zu Judentum und Christentum* (Tübingen 1912²)

Wilson, R. McL. *The Gospel of Philip* (London 1962)

Wilson, R. McL. *The Gnostic Problem* (London 1958)
The Nag-Hammadi papyri have added immeasurably to our knowledge: some
of the principal publications relating to them are listed above. Before this our
principal sources of information were: Irenaeus, Hippolytus, Epiphanius,
Pseudo-Clement, Tertullian and Plotinus.

CHAPTER VIII

BEYOND DEATH

Budde, L. and Nicholls, R. *A Catalogue of the Greek and Roman Sculpture in the
  Fitzwilliam Museum Cambridge* (Cambridge 1964)

Cumont, F. *Recherches sur le symbolisme funéraire des Romains* (Paris 1942)

Cumont, F. *After-Life in Roman Paganism* (New Haven 1922)

Hanfmann, G. M. A. *The Season Sarcophagus at Dumbarton Oaks*, 2 Vols
  (Cambridge, Mass. 1951)

Lattimore, R. *Themes in Greek and Latin Epitaphs* (Urbana 1948)

Lehmann-Hartleben, K. and Olsen, E. C. *Dionysiac Sarcophagi in Baltimore*
  (Baltimore 1952)

Nock, A. D. 'Cremation and Burial in the Roman Empire', *HTR* 25 (1932),
  321–59

Pesce, G. *Sarcophagi Romani di Sardegna* (Roma 1957)

Redlich, R. *Die Amazonen sarkophage des 2. und 3. Jahrhunderts n. Chr.*

Reinach, S. *Répertoire de reliefs grecs et romains*, 3 Vols (Paris 1909–12)

Richmond, I. A. *Archaeology and the After-life in Pagan and Christian Imagery*
  (London 1957)

Robert, R. *Die Antiken Sarkophag-Reliefs* (Berlin 1890–1919)

Strong, Eugénie *Apotheosis and After-Life* (London 1915)

Toynbee, J. M. C. *The Hadrianic School* (Cambridge 1934)

Toynbee, J. M. C. *Death and Burial in the Roman World* (London 1970)

Turcan, R. *Les Sarcophages Romains à Représentations Dionysiaques* (Paris 1966)

Wegner, M. *Die Musensarkophage* (Berlin 1966)

Wilpert, G. *I sarcofagi cristiani antichi* (Roma 1929)

PAGE 132 Fame: Cic. *Tusc. Disp.* 1, 15, 33; *Arch.* 11, 26; *Par. Stoic.* 2, 18; *Val. Max.*
    8, 14, 3; Epicurus: D.L. 10, 16; Plin. *Nat. Hist.* 35, 5; Sen. *Ep.* 79, 17;
    Tac. *Agr.* 46. See interestingly Hands, A. R. *Charities and Social Aid in
    Greece and Rome* (London 1968) 49–61

132 Tacitus: *Agr.* 46

133 Punishment: Cic. *Tusc. Disp.* 1, 6, 10; 1, 21, 48; *Nat. D.* 2, 2, 5; Ov.
    Met. 15, 152; Sen. *Ep.* 24, 18; Juv. 2, 149

134 Afterlife in tomb: Petr. 71; *CIL* 1, 1108; Bücheler 434; 1555; Dessau 8090, 8154, 8204; Richmond p. 19; Tert. *Test. An.* 4; Aug. *Mor. Eccl.* 34

135 Lollius: Dessau 6746

135 Chain of Life: *CIL* 6, 18385, 29609, 35887; 8, 9473; 9, 3184

135 Philosophical: *CIL* 13, 8371, cf. 3, 6384

135 Pleasures: Bücheler 187, 243–44, 1500; Rostovtzeff *SEHRE*, Pl. VII

136 Troubles: Bücheler 507, 573, 1247, 1274, 1498

136 Sleep: Dessau 8024

136 Annihilation: Bücheler 1495; Dessau 8162

136 Horsley: *RIB* 133

136 Bath: *RIB* 164

136 Ribchester: *RIB* 594

137 Isis: *CIL* 12, 734

138 St. Médard-d'Eyrans: Etienne, R. 'Les sarcophages de Saint-Médard d'Eyrans', *REA* 55 (1953), 361–78

142 Igel: Strong p. 222

142 Muses: Cumont 253ff

142 Seasons: Min. F. *Oct.* 34; Tert. *Apol.* 48, 7; *Anth. Lat.* 1, 439

143 Prometheus: Kerenyi, K. *Prometheus* (New York 1963)

144 Carnuntum: Dessau 9093

149 Nicopolis: Preisigke 2134

CHAPTER IX

THE MENACE OF THE FUTURE

Abt, A. *Apologie des Apuleius* (Giessen 1908)

Audollent, A. *Defixionum Tabellae* (Paris 1904)

Barb, A. A. 'The Survival of Magic Arts' in Momigliano, A. (ed.) *The Conflict between Paganism and Christianity in the Fourth Century* (Oxford 1963), 100–25

Bonner, C. *Studies in Magical Amulets, Chiefly Graeco-Egyptian* (Ann Arbor 1950)

Bouché-Leclerq, A. *Histoire de la Divination dans l'Antiquité*, 4 Vols (Paris 1879–82)

Butler, H. E. and Owen, A. S. *Apulei Apologia* (Oxford 1914)

Cramer, F. H. *Astrology in Roman Law and Politics* (Philadelphia 1954)

Cumont, F. *The Oriental Religions in Roman Paganism*, E.T. (Chicago 1911)

Delatte, A. *Herbarius* (Liège–Paris 1938²)

Halliday, W. R. *Greek Divination* (London 1913)

Harris, E. and J. R. *The Oriental Cults in Roman Britain* (Leiden 1965)

Hubert, H. 'Magia' in Daremberg-Saglio

Hubert, H. and Mauss, M. *Sacrifice: its Nature and Function*, E.T. (Chicago 1964)

James, E. O. *Origins of Sacrifice* (London 1933)

Lang, A. *Magic and Religion* (London 1901)

Lowe, J. E. *Magic in Greek and Roman Literature* (Oxford 1929)

Money-Kyrle, R. *The Meaning of Sacrifice* (London 1930)

Mooney, J. J. *Old Roman Magic*

Neugebauer, O. and Van Hoesen, H. B. *Greek Horoscopes* (Philadelphia 1959)

Parke, H. W. and Wormell, D. E. W. *History of the Delphic Oracle*, 2 Vols (London 1956)

Parke, H. W. *Greek Oracles* (London 1967)

Preisendanz, K. *Papyri Graecae Magicae* (Leipzig 1928)

Smith, K. F. 'Magic (Greek and Roman)' in Hastings, J. *ERE*

Tavenner, E. *Studies in Magic from Latin Literature* (New York 1916)

Thorndike, L. *A History of Magic and Experimental Science*, Vol. 1 (New York 1923)

Yerkes, R. K. *Sacrifice in Greek and Roman Religions and Early Judaism* (New York 1952)

GE 150 Delphi: Plut. *Mor.* 408Bff; 413Dff; Strab. 9, 420; Juv. 6, 555; Parke and Wormell; Bowra, C. M. in *Hermes* 87 (1959), 426

151 Apollo of Claros: Buresch, K. *ΑΠΟΛΛΩΝ ΚΛΑΡΙΟΣ* (Leipzig 1889); Picard, Ch. *Ephèse et Claros* (Paris 1922); Robert, L. *Les Fouilles de Claros* (Limoges 1954); Xen. Eph. 1, 6; *CIL* 3, 2880; 7, 633; Tac. *Ann.* 2, 54; Eus. *Prep. Ev.* 5, 22–23

152 Oxyrhynchus: *P. Oxy.* 1477 cf. 1148–49

152 Julianus and Alexander: see Chapter X

153 Astrology: Plin. *Nat. Hist.* 2, 29, 95; *SHA Hadr.* 2; 16; *Cat. Cod. Astr. Gr.* 2,223; 3,100; 5, 2, 34, 123; Firm. Mat. *Math.* 3 prooem.; Boll, F. in *N. Jahrb. f. d. kl. Alt.* 21 (1908), 103–26; Dieterich, K. *Eine Mithrasliturgie* (Leipzig 1910); *Gal.* 4, 3; *Rom.* 8, 38; Tat. *Or. ad Graec.* 4, 9–12; Eus. *Prep. Ev.* 3, 6; Aug. *Civ. Dei* 1, 1; *Ep.* 246 etc. In general Cumont, F. *Oriental Religions* (his *Astrology and Religion* is far less useful); Angus, S. *Rel. Quests.*

154 Paris: Delatte 100

155 The bronze liver from Piacenza: Pallottino, M. *Etruscologia* (1963⁵), Pl. XXVIII

155 Omens: *SHA A.P.* 9; *Comm.* 16; *Al. Sev.* 60; *Duo Max.* 30 etc.; Suet. *Aug.* 90–92; Amm. Marc. 21, 14

156 Pergamum: Wünsch, R. *Antikes Zaubergerät aus Pergamon* (Berlin 1905); Agrell, S. *Die pergamenische Zauberscheibe und das Tarockspiel* (Lund 1936)

156 Sacrifice: Hom. *Il.* 9, 497ff; Plat. *Euthyphr.* 14c; Iambl. *Myst.* 5, 9. Hubert-Mauss is standard, Yerkes rather disappointing

158 Weber: *Soc. of Rel.* 26

158 Betony: Delatte 102

158 Jesus: Preisendanz 4, 3019

158 Apuleius: Abt; Butler

159 Witchcraft: Hor. *Epod.* 5; *Sat.* 1, 8; Verg. *Ecl.* 8; *Aen.* 4, 504ff; Tib. 1, 2, 4; Ov. *Am.* 1, 8; *Fast.* 2, 571; *Met.* 7, 191; Sen. *Med.* 670; Luc. 6, 507; Plin. *Nat. Hist.* 18, 8; 28, 6–7, 23; Apul. *Met.* 1, 8; 2, 5; 3, 16, 9, 29; *Apol.*

164 Flamen Dialis: Plut. *Quaest. Rom.* 109–12; Aul. Gell. 10, 15

164 Herbs: Delatte; Plin. *Nat. Hist.* 24, 2, 106; 27, 106

164 Vervain: Ohrt, F. in *Folklore Fellowship Communications* (Helsinki), 82 (1929), 17–18

165 Galen: *Simpl.* 10, 19

165 Caracalla: *SHA* 5, 7

165 Impetigo: Plin. *Nat. Hist.* 27, 75

166 Toothache: Plin. *Nat. Hist.* 28, 23

166 Curses: *RIB* 154, 306, 323; Audollent

167 Caernarvon: Bonner; Harris; *Quarterly Rev.* (1828), 488; Wheeler, R. E. M. *Segontium and the Roman Occupation of Wales* (London 1923)

167 Silchester: Harris

167 York: Harris

167 Jerome: *Ep.* 75, 3, 1

168 Kok Kouk Koul: *P. Tebt.* 275

168 Wordsquare: Last, H.M. in *JTS* 3 (1952), 92–97

168 Numbers: Verg. *Ecl.* 8, 76; Serv. ad loc.

168 *Revelation*: 13, 18

177 Constantine: *Cod. Theod.* 9, 16, 1–3

177 Constantius II: *Cod. Theod.* 9, 16, 4–6; Amm. Marc. 19, 12, 13

177 Valentinian and Valens: *Cod. Theod.* 9, 16, 7–9; Amm. Marc. 29, 1, 5ff; 29, 2, 26f; 30, 5, 11

177 Divination: Bouché-Leclerq; Halliday; good art. by Pease, A. S. in *OCD* with bibliography; Aug. *Conf.* 4, 3; 8, 12, 19; D.C. 78, 8; Plut. *Pyth. Or.* 25; *SHA Al. Sev.* 14 etc.

CHAPTER X

SHAMANS AND SHAMS

Caster, M. *Lucien et la Pensée Religieuse de Son Temps* (Paris 1937)

Dodds, E. R. *The Greeks and the Irrational* (Berkeley 1957)

Eliade, M. *Shamanism*, E.T. (New York 1964)

Halliday, W. R. *Greek Divination* (London 1913)

GE 180 Cyprian: *Acta Sanctorum* September Vol. 7, 205

181 Apollonius: Phil. *Vit. Ap.*; Luc. *Alex.* 5; Eus. *Prep. Ev.* 4, 13; Sid. Ap. *Ep.* 8, 3; Amm. Marc. 23, 7; Eells, C. P. *Life and Times of Apollonius of Tyana* (Stanford 1923); Halliday, W. R. *Folklore Studies*; Birth: Phil. 1, 4–5; Pythagorean 1, 7–8; silence 1, 14; travels 1, 18 etc.; healing 1, 9 etc.; evil spirits 2, 4; 4, 20; 4, 25; 5, 42; 6, 27; reincarnations 5, 42; 6, 43; magic 4, 44; 7, 38; 8, 5; foreknowledge 1, 32; 3, 42; 5, 18; immortality 8, 31

183 Diophanes: Apul. *Met.* 2, 13–14

184 Peregrinus: Lucian *Peregrinus*, cf. *Drapetai*; Aul. Gell. 12, 11 cf. 8, 3; Athenag. *Leg. de Chr.* 26

184 Montanus: Bonwetsch, G. N. *Texte zur Geschichte des Montanismus* (Bonn 1914); Calder, W. M. in *Bull. J. Ryl. Lib.* 7 (1923), 309; Labriolle, P. de *La crise montaniste* (Paris 1913); *Les sources de l'histoire du Montanisme* (Fribourg 1913)

186 Anthony: Ath. *Vit. Ant*; Jer. *Vit. Pauli*.

187 Alexander: Lucian *Alexander*; Caster, M. *Etudes sur Alexandre ou le Faux Prophète de Lucien* (with bibliography); Nock, A. D. in *CQ* 22 (1928), 160ff; Cumont, F. in *Mem. Couronnes Acad. Roy. Belge* 40 (1887); Sutton, D. 'Alexander of Abunoteichos' (unpublished). I have borrowed some of Mr Sutton's phrasing.

CHAPTER XI

PHILOSOPHERS AND THE GODS

Epicureanism

Chilton, C. W. *Diogenis Oenoandis Fragmenta* (Leipzig 1967)

Dal Pane, F. 'Se Arnobio sia stato un epicureo: Lucrezio e gli apologeti cristiani Minucio Felice, Tertulliano, Cipriano, Lattanzio' *Riv. di stor. antica* 10 (1906), 400–35; 11 (1907), 222–36

De Witt, N. W. *Epicurus and his Philosophy* (Minneapolis 1954)

Festugière, A. J. *Epicure et ses dieux* (Paris 1946)

Freymuth, G. *Zur Lehre von den Götterbildern in der epikureische philosophie* (Berlin 1953)

Klussmann, E. 'Arnobius und Lukrez oder ein durchgang durch den Epikuraismus zum Christentum', *Philologus* 26 (1867), 362–67

Schmidt, W. 'Götter und Menschen in der Theologie Epikurs', *Rh. M.* 94 (1951), 97ff

Simpson, Adelaide D. 'Epicureans, Christians, Atheists in the Second Century', *TAPA* 72 (1941), 372ff

Usener, H. *Epicurea* (Leipzig 1887)
See also: Dittenberger *SIG*[3] 834; Eus. *Prep. Ev.* 4, 3; 6, 8; Simpl. ad Arist. *Phys.* 489, 21D; Luc. *Alex.* 25, 43, 57; Aelian *Prov. fr.* 10H; *Pirke Aboth* 2, 18; *Sanhedrin* 11, 1

The Stoics and Epictetus

Arnold, E. V. *Roman Stoicism* (Cambridge 1911)
Bonhöffer, A. *Epictet und die Stoa* (Stuttgart 1890)
Glover, T. R. *The Conflict of Religions in the Early Roman Empire* (London 1920[9])
Pohlenz, M. *Die Stoa*, 2 Vols (Göttingen 1959[2])
See also: Luc. 9, 580; Sen. *Quaest. Nat.* 1 Prol. 13; Pope *Essay On Man*; Cic. *Nat. D.* 2 *passim*; M.A. 3, 5; 4, 12; 5, 10; 5, 27; 7, 64; 12, 1; Epict. *Ench.* 46, 2; *Diss.* 1, 1, 6, 9, 12, 14, 16; 2, 16; 3, 13, 22

Marcus Aurelius

Birley, A. *Marcus Aurelius* (London 1966)
Farquharson, A. S. L. *The Meditations of the Emperor Marcus Aurelius*, 2 Vols (Oxford 1944)
Festugière, A. J. *Personal Religion among the Greeks* (Berkeley 1954)
See also: M.A. 1, 14; 3, 5; 4, 3, 23, 27, 43; 5, 27; 6, 10, 24, 30, 44; 7, 9, 36; 8, 3, 17; 9, 28–9, 40; 10, 6, 27

Maximus

See also: 4, 7; 8, 10; 11, 2; 11, 7; 14, 7–8; 15, 3–4; 17, 8–11

Numenius

Armstrong, A. H. *The Architecture of the Intelligible Universe in the Philosophy of Plotinus* (Cambridge 1940), 7–9
Beutler, R. E. *PW* Suppl. 7 (1940), 664–78
Dodds, E. R. in *Les Sources de Plotin* (Fondation Hardt–Genève 1960) 1–61
Festugière, A. J. *Le Révélation d'Hermes Trismégiste* (Paris 1944–54), 3, 42–47; 4, 123–42
Guthrie, K. S. *Numenius of Apamea: The Father of Neo-Platonism* (Grantwood, N.J. 1913)
Leemans, E. A. *Studie over den Wijsgeer Numenius van Apamea* (Bruxelles 1937)
Puech, H-Ch. in *Mélanges Bidez* (Bruxelles 1934), 745–78

Albinus

Witt, R. E. *Albinus and the History of Middle Platonism* (Cambridge 1937)

Clement

Chadwick, H. *Early Christian Thought and the Classical Tradition* (Oxford 1966)

Faye, E. de *Clément d'Alexandrie* (Paris 1898)

Glover, T. R. *The Conflict of Religions in the Early Roman Empire* (London 1920[9])

Pohlenz, M. 'Klemens von Alexandreia und sein hellinisches Christentum', *Nachr. der Akad. d. Wiss. in Göttingen Phil.-hist.* (1943), 3

Tollinton, R. B. *Clement of Alexandria*, 2 Vols (London 1914)

Völker, W. *Der wahre Gnostiker nach Clemens Alexandrinus* (Berlin 1952)

See also: *Paed.* 1, 67–8, 71; 2, 19–34; 3, 99–100; *Protr.* 6, 68, 100, 116–17; *QD* 33; *Strom.* 1, 28, 94; 3, 12–21, 63, 82, 91, 103; 4, 12, 164; 5, 16, 22, 81–2, 87, 92, 94, 133; 7, 6–9, 70

Origen

Bardy, G. 'Origène et l'Aristotélisme', *Mélanges Glotz* (Paris 1932), 1, 75ff

Chadwick, H. *Early Christian Thought and the Classical Tradition* (Oxford 1966)

Crouzel, H. *Origène et la philosophie* (Paris 1962)

Daniélou, J. *Origène* (Paris 1948)

Faye, E. de *Origène: sa vie, son oeuvre, sa pensée*, 3 Vols (Paris 1923–28)

Hanson, R. P. C. *Allegory and Event* (London 1959)

Koch, H. *Pronoia und Paideusis* (Berlin-Leipzig 1932)

Lubac, H. de *Histoire et Esprit* (Paris 1950)

See also: *Prin.* 1, 1, 7; 1, 2, 10; 1, 3, 1; 1, 7, 4; 3, 3, 5; 3, 6, 1–3; 4, 2, 4; 4, 4, 7; 4, 34; *CC* 1, 4; 2, 5; 2, 11; 3, 40; 3, 69; 3, 81; 4, 83; 6, 43; 6, 63; 7, 66; *Hom. in Gen.* 1, 13; 13, 4; *Hom. in Lev.* 7, 2; *Hom. in Cant.* 1, 7; *Comm. in Ioh.* 1, 17, 104–05; 2, 3, 20; 6, 13, 74; 13, 25; Eus. *Hist. Eccl.* 6, 19; Epiphan. *Pan.* 64, 72, 9

Plotinus

Armstrong, A. H. in *The Cambridge History of Later Greek and Early Medieval Philosophy* (Cambridge 1967)

Armstrong, A. H. *The Architecture of the Intelligible Universe in Plotinus* (Cambridge 1940)

Armstrong, A. H. '"Emanation" in Plotinus', *Mind* 46 (1937), 61–66

Bréhier, E. *La Philosophie de Plotin* (Paris 1928)

Fondation Hardt *Les Sources de Plotin* (Genève 1960)

Harder, R. *Plotins Schriften*, 5 Vols (Hamburg 1956–60)

Henry, P. *Plotin et l'Occident* (Louvain 1934)

Henry, P. and Schwyzer, H. R. *Plotini Opera*, 2 Vols (Paris-Bruxelles 1951–59)

Inge, W. R. *The Philosophy of Plotinus*, 2 Vols (London 1929[3])

Rist, J. M. *Plotinus, the Road to Reality* (Cambridge 1967)

Schwyzer, H. R. 'Plotinos', *PW* 21, 472–74

See also: *Enn.* 1, 8, 2; 2, 9; 3, 5, 3–4; 3, 6, 7; 3, 8, 8; 4, 8, 1; 6, 8, 15; 6, 9, 9; 6, 9, 11 (this last translated by E. R. Dodds)

CHAPTER XII

SYNCRETISM AND CONFRONTATION

Barnes, T. D. 'Legislation against the Christians', *JRS* 58 (1968), 32ff

Causse, A. *Le conflict du christianisme primitif et de la civilisation* (Paris 1920)

Charles-Picard, G. *Les religions de l'Afrique antique* (Paris 1954)

Frend, W. H. C. *Martyrdom and Persecution in the Early Church* (Oxford 1965)

Guterman, S. L. *Religious Toleration and Persecution in Ancient Rome* (London 1951)

Labriolle, P. de *La réaction païenne* (Paris 1934)

Leglay, M. *Saturne Africain* (Paris 1966)

Niebuhr, H. R. *Christ and Culture* (London 1952)

Reitzenstein, R. and Schaeder, H. H. *Studien zum antiken Synkretismus aus Iran und Griechenland* (Leipzig 1926)

Sherwin-White, A. N. 'The Early Persecutions and Roman Law Again', *JTS* 3 (1952), 199–213

Usener, H. *Religionsgeschichtliche Untersuchungen* (Bonn 1911)

PAGE 211 Mercurius: Andesociuoucus: *RIB* 193; Vellaunus: *CIL* 12, 2373 cf. *RIB* 309; Viducus: Espérandieu, E. *Inscr. Lat. de la Gaule Narb.* (Paris 1929) 1614 cf. *CIL* 13, 576. See also Toutain.

211 Arnobius: 4, 148

212 Apollo: Maponus: *RIB* 583; Clarios: Buresche, K. *ΑΠΟΛΛΩΝ ΚΛΑΡΙΟΣ* (Leipzig 1889), cf. Macrob. *Sat.* 1, 18–19

212 Mars: Medocius: *RIB* 191; Corotiacus: *RIB* 213; Alator: *RIB* 218, 1055; Toutates: *RIB* 219; *CIL* 3, 5320; 6, 31182; Lucan 1, 445; Lact. *Inst. Div.* 1, 21; Braciaca: *RIB* 278; Lenus: *RIB* 309; Ocelus: *RIB* 310,949; Cocidius: *RIB* 602, 993; Nodens: *RIB* 305, 616–17; Condates: *RIB* 731; Thincsus: *RIB* 1593; Augustus: *RIB* 1900, cf. *CIL* 8, 895; 2635; Belaucairus: *RIB* 1784; cf. 772–77, 1775ff, 1976; Rigonemetis: *JRS* 52 (1962): 192

213 Hercules: *RIB* 67

213 Silvanus: Callirius: *RIB* 194; Vinotonus: *RIB* 732–23

213 Jupiter: *RIB* 452; *CIL* 3, 2804; 8, 2611–12; Lucan 1, 446; Dolichenus: *CIL* 6, 367

213 Ialonus Contrebis: *RIB* 600

213 Matres: Ollolotae, *RIB* 574, cf. 1030–32; Parcae 881, 951; see also 88, 653–54

214 Divona: Aus. 19, 157

214 Onuava: *CIL* 13, 581

214 Sirona: *CIL* 13, 582; Duval, P. M. *Les dieux de la Gaule* (Paris 1957)

214 Epona: Magnen, R. and Thévenot, E. *Epona* (Bordeaux 1953); Duval, P. M. *Les dieux de la Gaule* (Paris 1957)

214 Roman Gods adopted by Celts: Thevenot, E. *Divinités et Sanctuaires de la Gaule, passim*; four-headed Mercury: Babelon et Blanchet, *Catalogue des bronzes antiques de la Bibliothèque Nationale*, No. 362, pp. 158–59

215 Mauri: *Eph. Epig.* 7, 165

215 Caelestis: Val. Max. 2, 6; Aug. *Civ. Dei* 2, 4; Merlat, P. *Jupiter Dolichenus* (Paris 1960)

216 Joint cults: e.g. *CIL* 6, 504; 8, 4578; 9195; 12, 3070, 4316

216 Rosmerta: Dessau 4609

216 Seine boatmen: Dessau 4613d

217 Men Ascaenus: Anderson, J. G. C. in *JRS* 3 (1913), 267–300

217 Attis: Macrob. *Sat.* 1, 21, 9; Jul. 5, 168D; Arnob. 5, 42

217 Sun: Macrob. *Sat.* 1, 17–23

218 Dea Caelestis: *CIL* 8, 8433

218 Isis: Apul. *Met.* 11; Juv. 6, 526; Varro 5, 57; Hdt. 2, 42, 59, 144; Ov. *Am.* 2, 13, 11; Dessau 4362, 4376; *P. Oxy.* 1380; Dessau 4362 (*una quae*); Plut. *Is.* 53; *CIL* 10, 3800

218 Aesculapius: *CIL* 3, 1614

219 Bronze Mercury with Pantheon from Autun: illustrated in Thevenot, E. *Divinités et Sanctuaires de la Gaule*, 91

219 Cisaulodda: *SEG* 996

219 Mithras: See Harris, E. and J. R. *The Oriental Cults in Roman Britain*; Vermaseren, *CIMRM*

220 Utrecht: Dessau 3094

220 Spain: *CIL* 2, 2407

220 Alexander Severus: *SHA* 29, 2; 43, 6; Richmond, I. A. in Gordon, D. J. *Fritz Saxl 1890–1948* (London 1957)

220 Clea: Plut. *Is.* 35

220 Tatian: *Or. ad Graec.* 29

221 Judaism: *Koheleth Rabba* 9, 11; *Bereshith Rabba* 8, 8; *Shemoth Rabba* 15, 17; 33; *TP Rosh Hashanal* 3, 57a; Hom. *Il.* 20, 337; Hdt. 2, 172; *Rev.* 2, 9; 3, 9; Goodenough, E. R. *Jewish Symbols in the Graeco-Roman Period*, 12 Vols (New York 1953–64); Leon, H. J. *Jews of Ancient Rome* (Philadelphia 1960); Smallwood, E. M. in *Latomus* 18 (1959), 334ff

222 Hypsistos: Cumont, F. *Hypsistos*; Nock, A. D. *Conversion*; Roberts, C. H., Skeat, T. C., Nock, A. D. in *HTR* 29 (1936), 39ff. A different view: Kraabel, A. T. in *GRBS* 10 (1969), 81ff

223 Yahweh: Osiris: Lyd. *Mens.* 4, 53; Jupiter: Aug. *Cons. Ev.* 1, 30; Sabazius: Val. Max. 1, 3, 2; Dionysus: *JHS* 31 (1911), 196

223 Jewish scholars: see the two books by Lieberman quoted in notes to Chapter VII, s.v. Judaism

224 Philo: Education: *Ebr.* 49; *Cong. Erud.* 15; *Somn.* 1, 205; Politics: *Jos.* 32ff, 54ff; Medicine: *QDSI* 65; *Sacr. Ab.* 123; Theatre: *Ebr.* 49; Music: *Post. Cain.* 105; *Cherub.* 110; Pheidias: *Ebr.* 89; Athletics: *Agr.* 111ff;

Cherub. 81ff; Logos: *Somn.* 2, 37; *Op. Mund.* 5, 20; *L.A.* 3, 73; *Sacr.* 28; Wolfson, H. *Philo* (Cambridge 1947); Goodenough, E. R. *By Light, Light* (New Haven 1935); Bréhier, E. *Les Idées Philosophiques et Religieuses de P. d'Alexandrie* (Paris 1925)

224 Murray: *Five Stages of Greek Religion* (Oxford 1925), 232

233 Marcus Aurelius: 11, 3

233 Persecutions: Sherwin-White, A. N. in *JTS* 3 (1952), 199–213; Frend

234 Celsus: Orig. *CC* 1, 12, 14, 28, 69; 2, 23–4, 37; 4, 14, 23, 73ff, 99; 5, 25–33; 6, 16–9, 42, 47, 62ff; 7, 42, 45; 8, 31, 66–75. Andresen, C. *Logos u. Nomos* (Berlin 1955); Bader, R. *Der Ἀληθὴς Λόγος des C.* (Stuttgart–Berlin 1940); Miura-Strange, A. C. *C.u.O.* (Giessen 1926); Rougier, L. *Celse* (Paris 1925)

235 Porphyry: Macarius *Apocriticus*; Harnack, A. *Texte und Untersuchungen* 37, 4; Hulen, A. B. *Porphyry's Work against the Christians* (Scottdale 1933)

236 Niebuhr, H. R.: *Christ and Culture* (1952)

237 S. Peter's: *Malachi* 4, 2; Toynbee, J. M. C. and Ward Perkins, J. *The Shrine of St Peter and the Vatican Excavations* (London 1956), 72ff

238 S. Costanza: *Rev.* 14, 17ff; Oakeshott, W. *The Mosaics of Rome* (London 1967)

238 Hinton St Mary: Toynbee, J. M. C. *The Christian Roman Mosaic H. St. M. Dorset* (Dorchester 1964); Lullingstone: Toynbee, J. M. C. *Art in Britain under the Romans*, 264; Iren. *Haer*, 3, 11, 8

239 Syrian: Ephraem, cf. Epiphan. *Pan.* 51, 22

240 Autun: Grivot, D. *Autun* (Lyon 1968), 4, 17

240 Domitia: *CIL* 13, 633

240 Etienne, R. *Bordeaux Antique* (Bordeaux 1962); Jullian, C. *Ausone et Bordeaux* (Bordeaux 1893); Martino, P. *Ausone et les commencements du Christianisme en Gaule* (Alger 1906)

242 Ausonius: see the works, esp. *Opusc.* 4, 3; *Ep.* 23–25; *Epig.* 30–31

242 Maximus of Madaura: Aug. *Ep.* 16

CHRONOLOGICAL TABLE

A GUIDE TO SOME OF THE CHIEF AUTHORS AND EVENTS MENTIONED IN THE TEXT

DATE	ROMAN EMPERORS	HISTORICAL EVENTS	AUTHORS ETC.	RELIGIOUS EVENTS	
BC 800			? Homer: epic poet		800 BC
700			? Hesiod: poet		700
600				? Zoroaster	600
500		480–479 Greeks defeat Persians 431–404 War between Sparta and Athens	Aeschylus, Sophocles, Euripides: tragic dramatists Socrates: philosopher	Pythagoras	500
400		336–323 Alexander the Great	Democritus: philosopher Plato: philosopher Aristotle: philosopher	c. 300 Ptolemy establishes cults of Alexander and of Sarapis	400
300		304–c. 282 Ptolemy I rules in Egypt 218–202 War between Rome and Carthage	Zeno, Epicurus: philosophers Cleanthes: philosopher Herodas: writer of mimes	296 Temple of Bellona vowed at Rome 204 Introduction of Great Mother to Rome	300
200				191 Temple of Mother on Palatine 186 Suppression of Bacchic mysteries	200

CHRONOLOGICAL TABLE (continued)

100

CHRISTIAN ERA

ROMAN EMPERORS	HISTORICAL EVENTS	AUTHORS ETC.	RELIGIOUS EVENTS
	49–45 Civil War 44 Assassination of Julius Caesar	Lucretius, Catullus: poets Cicero: orator and philosopher Diodorus Siculus: historian	
Augustus 31 BC–AD 14	31 Augustus defeats Antony at Actium	Vergil, Horace, Tibullus: poets	2 Temple dedicated to Mars Ultor at Rome

CHRISTIAN ERA

ROMAN EMPERORS	HISTORICAL EVENTS	AUTHORS ETC.	RELIGIOUS EVENTS
Augustus 31 BC–AD 14 Tiberius AD 14–37 Caligula 37–41		Ovid: poet. Livy: historian Strabo: geographer Philo: Jewish philosopher	14 Sept. 17th Augustus decreed a god 33 Possible date of crucifixion of Jesus 37 Temple consecrated to the divine Augustus
Claudius 41–54		Calpurnius Siculus, Lucan: poets	38 Jewish pagan riots in Alexandria
Nero 54–68	64 Fire in Rome	Seneca: philosopher Petronius: novelist	64 Persecution of Christians 66–70 Jewish War with Rome: fall of Jerusalem
Galba, Otho, Vitellius Vespasian 69–79 Titus 79–81 Domitian 81–96 Nerva 96–98	79 Destruction of Pompeii	Quintilian: educationalist Elder Pliny: encyclopedist Statius: poet	71 Rebuilding of Capitoline temple Mithraists recorded at Carnuntum 97 Dio of Prusa at Olympic Games Death of Apollonius of Tyana

AD 100

ROMAN EMPERORS	HISTORICAL EVENTS	AUTHORS ETC.	RELIGIOUS EVENTS
Trajan 98–117		Dio of Prusa: orator Younger Pliny: letter-writer Epictetus: philosopher	105 Taurobolium recorded at Pergamum
Hadrian 117–38		Tacitus: historian Plutarch: man of letters Juvenal: satirist	114 Taurobolium at Puteoli 115 Arch at Beneventum 143–44 Aelius Aristides journeys to Rome
Antoninus Pius 138–61		Fronto: orator Pausanias: geographer Albinus: philosopher	155 Martyrdom of Polycarp c. 165 Martyrdom of Justin
Marcus Aurelius 161–80	165–66 Plague	Marcus Aurelius: philosopher Vettius Valens: astrologer Lucian: man of letters, satirist	169 Peregrinus commits suicide 175 Death of Alexander of Abonuteichos c. 178 Celsus 'The True Word'
Commodus 180–92			

100

CHRISTIAN ERA

100 AD

		novelist	
Geta, Caracalla Elagabalus 218–22 Severus Alexander 222–35		Herodian: historian Origen: biblical scholar	250 Decius' persecution o, Christians begins
Numerous brief-lived emperors Gallienus 253–68 Claudius Gothicus 268–70 Aurelian 270–75 Brief-lived emperors	260 Major Persian victory	Plotinus: philosopher	270 Death of Plotinus 274 Temple to Sun-God at Rome
300 Diocletian 284–305 Numerous emperors Constantine 306–37 Constantine II, Constantius, Constans Julian 361–63 Jovian 363–64 Valentinian I 364–75 in W. Valens 364–78 in E. Valentinian II 375–92 in W. Theodosius 379–95 in E.	286 Division of Empire 330 Constantinople becomes capital	Arnobius: Christian writer Porphyry: pagan philosopher Lactantius, Eusebius: Christian writers Sallustius: pagan writer Servius: commentator on Vergil. Ausonius: poet	**300** 303 Persecution of Christians 312 Constantine's vision 321 Sunday proclaimed day of rest 361–63 Attempt to restore paganism c. 385 Destruction of Temple of Sarapis at Alexandria c. 390 Valentinian bans pagan sacrifice
400 Honorius 395–423 in W. Arcadius 395–408 in E.	410 Fall of Rome	Prudentius: Christian poet Macrobius: pagan writer Jerome, Augustine: Christian writers Nonnus: epic poet	**400** 440–61 Leo I pope

INDEX

SOURCES OF ILLUSTRATIONS

The author and publishers are grateful to the many official bodies and individuals listed below, who have supplied illustrations. Plates not listed are from originals in the archives of Thames and Hudson.

Metropolitan Museum of Art, New York, 1, 2, 35, 62, 64, 75; John Webb (Brompton Studio) from coins and medallions in the Department of Coins and Medals, British Museum, 3, 4, 7, 10–12, 15–22, 24, 25, 31, 32, 43, 44, 71, 77; Mansell-Alinari, 5, 9, 14, 29, 41, 51, 53, 54, 55, 57, 68, 69, 72, 85; Maurice Chuzeville, 6, 26, 36, 73; Bonn, Landesmuseum, 8; London Museum, 23; Archive Fotografico delle Antichità e Belle Arte, Rome, 27; John Freeman, 30; Giraudon, 33, 37, 67; A.C.L., Brussels, 34; Berne, Historical Museum, 39; Vatican Museums, 40, 49, 65, 86; Bibliothèque Nationale, Paris, 42; Edwin Snell, 45; D.A.I., Rome, 46; Trustees of the British Museum, 47, 52, 76; Fototeca Unione, Rome, 48; Max Hirmer, 50, 87; R. Bessier, Fribourg, 56; Walters Art Gallery, Baltimore, 61; Sansaini, Rome, 63; Soprintendenza alle Antichità, Naples, 66; Corinium Museum, 70; Gloucester City Museums, 78; West Advertising, 80; Guildhall Museum, London, 79; Department of Antiquities, Israel, 84.